Follow Me!

Follow Me!

A History of Israel's Military Elite

SAMUEL M. KATZ

ARMS AND
ARMOUR

First published in Great Britain in 1989 by
Arms & Armour Press Ltd., Artillery House,
Artillery Row, London SW1P 1RT.

Distributed in the USA by Sterling Publishing Co Inc.,
2 Park Avenue, New York, NY 10016.

Distributed in Australia by Capricorn Link (Australia) Pty. Ltd.,
P.O. Box 665, Lane Cove, New South Wales 2066.

British Library Cataloguing in Publication data:
Katz, Samuel.
Follow me! a history of Israel's military élite.
1. Israel, Tseva haganah le-Yisra'el, 1948–
I. Title
355′.0095-694
ISBN 0-85368-784-6

Typeset and artwork by Graphicraft Typesetters Ltd.
Printed in Great Britain by
Anchor Brendon Ltd, Tiptree, Essex.

Title page illustration: Chief Paratroop and Infantry
officer Brigadier-General Amos Yaron observes the
battle for Sidon. 9 June 1982. (IMoD)

Jacket illustrations: Front, a paratroop
grenadier inches his way towards a firing
position (Michael Giladi). Back, always
marching and always laden with equipment,
a GOLANI squad heads for the hills. (Courtesy
IDF spokesman/Jonathan Torgovnik) Badges
and insignia, left to right, top to bottom:
campaign ribbons for 1967 (left half) and
1973; Master Parachutist wings; infantry beret
badge; GOLANI badge; SAYERET HARU badge;
Lebanon campaign ribbon; and Naval frogman's
badge.

CONTENTS

MA'ARACHOT
'FOLLOW ME!'

Dedicated to the 1,259 TZANHANIM dead,
and their families . . .

PREFACE

THE history of the Israeli Defence Forces (IDF) is the history of the state of Israel; and élite units created the IDF. In conventional terms, the IDF does not maintain a separate 'Special Forces'. No single military formation enjoys such unique status because the concept of bestowing special pride and responsibility on a single unit has been historically disdained by the Israeli military. Instead, small independent units have made up what are collectively known today as the IDF's élite or HA'YECHIDOT HANIVCHAROT (the 'chosen units').

The selecting of units to be characterized as 'chosen' or élite has been a difficult task when examining an army which in the past 40 years has been victorious in five major wars, and countless security operations. While certainly *all* the IDF's combat arms have performed in an above the average manner, and some units, such as the Israeli Air Force, have achieved a reputation as the world's best, their size, organization, and operational mandate fail to categorize them as élite units, no matter how spectacularly they have fought.

What makes units like the PAL'MACH and the TZANHANIM (paratroops) élite is that they were formed as small independent fighting formations, for specific, sometimes almost impossible tasks. Many of the IDF's numerous SAYEROT or reconnaissance formations were established with a single specific military task in mind; the completion of which led to their demobilization. Units are also classified as élite in accordance with their combat history and combat assignments; including the GOLANI and GIVA'ATI Infantry Brigades, as well as the reserve paratroop brigades, which have traditionally outperformed their conscript counterparts. Although the Air Force, Army, and Navy are under a unified command, each service maintains several élite units as well.

As in any examination of the IDF, security remains a paramount concern. The names, official designations, and organizational character of many such units must remain classified; from those of the pre-independence struggle to those in present operation. Although the focus of much of this book lies with the élite unit commanders, the names of many must remain restricted to initials of surnames. In conclusion, several 'hearty' words of thanks are in order for a loyal group of friends and associates who insured the realization of this book: Miki Kaufman, Bat-Sheva, and the staff at the IDF Archives who as always were more than helpful; Brigadier General Ephraim Lapid and Major Dvora Takson of the IDF Spokesman office and Major General Amos Yaran and Major Gad at the Washington, D.C., embassy. Mr Lee E. Russell, and a special word of thanks to Mr Joseph P. Bermudez Jr and Mr Andreas Constantinou, for their patience, and unlimited assistance. In addition, I wish to offer very warm thanks to my sister-in-law Ms Shiri Elyakim for keeping me informed on current events; and special thanks to my father-in-law, Mr Nissim Elyakim, for his tireless efforts and running back and forth to the Censor's Office on my behalf. Last, but not least, I wish to offer a very loving TODAH to my sweet wife Sigalit, who by helping with translations, graphics, logistics, and most of all for calming down a highly strung author', made the completion of this book possible.

Samuel M. Katz

INTRODUCTION

AT 11.00 hours on 13 March 1987, KIBBUTZ EIN HAROD ME'UCHAD buried one of her sons: Captain Rami Ben-Tzvi, killed a day earlier in southern Lebanon while leading his company in a fire-fight against Shi'ite guerrillas.

Like all Israelis, Rami was conscripted into the Israeli Defence Force on his eighteenth birthday. Like many from the KIBBUTZIM, he volunteered for service with the paratroops. The rigours of the often brutal paratroop basic training posed little challenge for Rami, who excelled as a soldier and as a leader. Half-way through the Squad Leader's Course, the IDF invaded Lebanon, and Rami found himself part of the amphibious force landing on the Lebanese coast at Sidon. He fought against Palestinian guerrillas all the way to Beirut where he watched many of his friends fall in battle.

Rami's commanders considered him a 'natural', and he was sent off to the Officer's Course. Passing with flying colours, he was given command of a paratroop reconnaissance platoon and sent once more to the madness and confusion of Lebanon. His unit was given the dangerous task of protecting armoured convoys, by acting as bait for the inevitable guerrilla ambushes. Engaging a fanatical enemy which all too often sought martydom, they found themselves the target of suicide bombers and booby-trapped explosive devices, suffering heavy casualties. In this campaign, Rami proved his worth as a soldier and an officer, risking personal safety on many occasions to bring his wounded men to shelter. As platoon commander, he faced the grim responsibility of visiting the families of men who had fallen, and needed to look after his men lying maimed in hospital. Slowly, Lebanon took its toll on Rami. When the opportunity arose, he left the army.

Rami found civilian life after Lebanon full of disillusionment. He embraced Orthodox Judaism, worked with the KIBBUTZ live stock, wrote poetry and painted. But Rami

---

◄ A paratrooper grenadier pauses on the road to Beirut, during the advance on the Lebanese capital. (IMoD)

was a soldier, a finer officer, and he missed the army. The IDF fascinated him, and he enjoyed being the decisive factor in the day to day problems of his men. A 'soldier's officer', he availed himself little of the privileges of rank. He ate only after he had made sure that all his men had been fed; he rarely went home on leave, and lovingly called his soldiers 'children'. He signed for another year of military service, and received the command of an infantry company from the reborn GIVA'ATI Brigade which by 1986 had developed into the IDF's premier infantry formation; outbattling even the paratroops and the élite GOLANI Brigade in inter-service exercises. The company was everything for Rami, and he requested that GIVA'ATI extend his tour of duty for an extra nine months. Once again however, he found himself in Lebanon.

On 12 March 1987 at 02.30 hours, Rami's company came into contact with a band of guerrillas near the town of Hari't on the border of the security zone which now separates Israel from Lebanon. As always Rami was in the vanguard, and he was the first to be hit. He took a 7.62mm burst from an RPK light machine-gun in the chest, and died shortly afterwards. He was 26 years old.

Captain Rami Ben-Tzvi was more than just another of the 700-plus Israeli combat fatalities in Lebanon since the 1982 invasion. His military career and death personify the role and true nature of the élite unit commander in the Israel Defence Force. For Israel's history is filled with men like Rami, who through their courage and self-sacrifice have insured the preservation and survival of the state of Israel.

The history of Israel's élite combat formations is a history of courage and leadership. From humble beginings, they provided the basis from which the entire Israel Defence Force would later develop. They created a new breed of military leader, who forsook the traditional military rituals of parading, saluting, and boot-shining, opting instead for a regiment of combat proficiency, ingenuity, and improvization. These were men who believed that leading from example and self-sacrifice was the 'privilege' of command. These officers were friends to their subordinates; brothers in arms, who ate the same food, and slept in the same quarters. Officers were called by their first name, and little formal military discipline existed. In battle, however, the military authority they represented was absolute.

The élite unit commander has developed into one of the fundamental cornerstones of the Israel Defence Force. Men like Meir Har-Zion, Arik Sharon, Raful Eitan, Yoni Netanyahu, and the current Chief of Staff, Dan Shomron, are Israel's most famous soldiers, men whose names reappear in the countless accounts of 'impossible' missions. It is interesting to note that almost each IDF Chief of Staff has been a veteran of an élite unit; the last seven to have served in that post being highly decorated paratroopers. Most of the IDF's Generals, in fact, began their military careers in élite units, where their courage and intelligence received the most exacting scrutiny, and where many potential commanders lost their lives.

The men these officers command, however, are an even more instrinsic element in the history of the élite units of the IDF. They are the machinery, whose training, skill, and determination has been the decisive factor in achieving victory in all of Israel's conventional and covert military campaigns. In these units, a deep rapport exists between soldier and officer. The conventions of military behaviour are eagerly discarded in an atmosphere of trust. Each comprehends that the unit is a *team* made up of players with varied skills and united functions.

Israel is not a nation of supermen. It does not possess a political, social or economic élite which expects its sons to undergo the transformation into 'supreme' fighters at the age of eighteen. It is, however, a nation that has never known the joys of peace; and as a result has compulsory military conscription for all its citizens. Those with the requisite physical and psychological attributes, who understand the extent of the national need, volunteer for one of the few very special units. For patriotism, prestige and glory, countless newly inducted soldiers line up to volunteer to serve with the paratroops, the Naval Commandos, and the other IDF élite. They will undergo arduous physical and mental examinations before being accepted. Acceptance guarantees only the beginning of a process where abilities are pushed past the human limit; from torturous 100-kilometre forced marches in basic training, to lying in ambush deep in enemy territory.

Men like Captain Rami Ben-Tzvi are products of a military history rich in self-sacrifice and heroism. They are élite because they realize that theirs is a very special role in assuring the survival of the country they love – from the young Private marching 100 kilometres with full pack, to the officer leading his men under heavy fire with the immortal battlecry of 'Follow Me!'

▼ Reconnaissance paratroopers train with a Bell-212 helicopter in the Jordan Valley, June 1981. (IGPO)

1
THE FATHERS OF THE ISRAEL DEFENCE FORCES
The first élite, 1936–48

THE FO'SH AND THE SPECIAL NIGHT SQUADS

ISRAEL'S élite military units trace their roots back to September 1907 and BAR-GIORA, a secretive, watchman organization named after a famed zealot who fought the Romans in AD 70. BAR-GIORA'S main objective was the transformation of the Jewish settler into a fierce warrior, one whom the Arab would fear enough to let live in peace. They trained hard, and with great enthusiasm; practising marksmanship, horsemanship, and ambush skills in the inhospitable Galilee wilderness. In 1909 BAR-GIORA expanded into a large, better organized force known as HASHOMER, or 'Watchman'. HASHOMER's volunteers were the élite of the Second ALIYAH (the period of Jewish migration to Palestine 1904–14), and were men and women of exceptional motivation who maintained a deep bond between working the land and military prowess. They not only engaged in the defence of their agricultural settlements, but conducted daring retaliatory raids against Arab villages. Although HASHOMER established the the first KIBBUTZ (communal settlement) at Degania in lower Galilee and created a fledgling arms industry, it was most noteworthy for demonstrating the potential of the Jewish fighter.

During the First World War, the Jews of Palestine actively supported the British. The successful Jewish N'I'L'I espionage ring, and a British-sponsored Jewish military force, known as the 'Jewish Legion' were testaments to this support, and they brought political rewards for the Zionists who received tacit recognition for the nationalistic aspirations in the Balfour Declaration of 2 November 1917. Palestine's Arabs were also showing signs of political nationalism, and vehemently opposed the creation of a Jewish state in a land where they were the majority. Anti-Jewish riots broke out in 1920, and the British appeared unwilling and quite unable to quell the Arab violence. With no alternative short of starting a national Jewish self-defence force, the HISTADRUT (Zionist General Federation of Labour) disbanded HASHOMER and created the HAGANAH or 'Defence'.

The HAGANAH had all the trappings of a conventional army, except for proper weapons, equipment, and well-trained soldiers! As an underground force, it had to conduct its training under the cover of sporting and cultural activities, and on the whole proved to be an ineffective defence organization. During the murderous Arab riots of 1929, the HAGANAH was unable to defend Jewish lives and property, and the YISHUV was forced to rely on British protection. When the Arabs rioted once again in 1936, the British found *themselves* incapable of protecting Jewish lives. They sanctioned what they had feared most, the arming of the Jews for self-defence, and the forming of a special Jewish police force; known simply as NOTRIM (Guards). This was tantamount to the quasi-legalization of the underground, as almost every policeman belonged to the HAGANAH.

At first, the NOTRIM made only a symbolic appearance. They were issued with British .303 SMLEs, although some units armed themselves with stolen and locally produced guns, and hand-grenades and Lewis guns. The NOTRIM provided the HAGANAH with ideal camouflage. NOTRIM operations cleverly concealed HAGANAH training, patrols, and illegal activities. The NOTRIM also attracted the élite of the YISHUV's youth; men like Moshe Dayan and Yigal Allon, NOTRIM sergeants, all native-born Sabras with high military ambitions.

The persistent Arab riots of 1936 prompted the HAGANAH to renounce its policy of HAVLAGAH (self-restraint) towards Arab provocation and to seize the military initiative. At the forefront in this endeavour was one of HAGANAH's most innovative commanders, a burly Crimean named Yitzhak Sadeh. Known simply as

HAZAKEN ('old man') Sadeh, the one-time commander of HAGANAH's Labour Battalions, had by 1936 most vividly symbolized the fighting spirit of the underground. A military visionary of profound proportions, he preached an offensive approach to the YISHUV's defensive concerns.

In 1936 Sadeh formed small, mobile patrol units called NODEDOT to help defend the isolated settlements around Jerusalem. Prior to his arrival, the settlement's defenders had been forced to fire from inside the protective fences of their positions to beat off Arab attacks. Sadeh gave them grenades and Mauser 7.63mm pistols, trained them, and took them 'beyond the fences'. They conducted spectacular surprise attacks, raiding Arab villages at night. The first NODEDOT unit consisted of 70 young men who wore khaki drill, and British sun helmets obtained through dubious means. Sadeh trained these idealistic men hard, taking them on forced marches and then navigation and terrain familiarization. Sadeh's main objective was to train his men to operate freely and effectively in the Arab's domain – night!

In 1937, the notion of élite mobile units was enhanced when the HAGANAH formed the FO'SH, an unconventionally trained unit capable of immediate mobilization wherever its services were required. The FO'SH (the Hebrew abbreviation for 'Field Companies' or PLUGOT SADEH) was commanded by Yitzhak Sadeh, who at last was able to fulfill his dream of having the Jews assert themselves militarily. Sadeh handpicked each of the FO'SH fighters, choosing men from the NOTRIM, NODEDOT, and other British-sanctioned police units who had proved their military worth. Sadeh looked for physically capable soldiers, who showed strong signs of dedication and comradeship.

▲ A FO'SH patrol passes through an Arab village in Galilee, 1937. Their distinctive *kolpak* hats were intended not only to prove their 'élite' status, but to instil fear into the hearts of the local Arabs. (HAGANAH Archives)

From its headquarters in an unobtrusive house in Tel Aviv's Rotschild Boulevard, Sadeh commanded the FO'SH in concert with the HAGANAH's regional commands. Funding for the FO'SH was taken from the KOFER HAYISHUV (a tax levied against the Jews of Palestine to finance HAGANAH activities), though money was always in acutely short supply. The FO'SH did without proper uniforms, sufficient equipment, and adequate supplies and rations. Nevertheless, by March 1938, there were more than 1,000 FO'SH fighters divided into thirteen regional commands; with a further 500 ready for full-scale training.

Sadeh had grand designs for 'his' FO'SH. He organized a quartermaster's unit, as well as a topographical and educational corps; more advanced and capable than anything the HAGANAH could deploy. Most impressive of these 'bastard' units was an Arabic-speaking intelligence service whose agents were recruited from the 'Arab diaspora': Jews who had immigrated to Palestine from Arab lands, who were fluent in the local dialects, and could easily pass for Arabs. They were infiltrated into sensitive localities throughout Jerusalem and Galilee, and reported accurate, invaluable intelligence pertaining to pending Arab military activities.

In battle, FO'SH fighters proved their worth. They openly attacked Arab guerrilla concentrations, and prided themselves on their innovative military approach. Making the most of their meagre resources, the FO'SH relied upon

skill, ingenuity, and courageous commanders who led outnumbered and inexperienced fighters against numerically superior forces. Sadeh and the FO'SH had their opponents in the conservative HAGANAH High Command! It was argued that the FO'SH, by openly confronting the Arabs, was destroying the basis for 'legal Jewish self-defence' within the British Mandatory system, as well as potentially sabotaging any chances for Jew and Arab to co-exist peacefully. Most importantly, there were fears that the FO'SH constituted an élite force which was politically undesirable; and the FO'SH was disbanded.

Despite Sadeh's achievements with the FO'SH, they were still considered as a ragtag, though well-intentioned underground force. Only when an eccentric young *professional* British Captain named Orde Charles Wingate appeared on the scene in 1936 did the HAGANAH take the potential of a military élite seriously. Wingate had been assigned to Palestine in 1936 in order to utilize the irregular warfare skills he had acquired in the Sudan to halt repeated Arab guerrilla attacks on the Iraqi Petroleum Company's pipeline which ran to the Haifa refineries. A devout Christian reared on the Bible, Wingate was a passionate supporter of Zionist aspirations, and took on his assignment in Palestine with great zeal and fervour. He thought very highly of the Jews, especially those from the agricultural settlements and KIBBUTZIM, of whom he wrote in a letter to his cousin, Sir Reginald Wingate: 'I have seen the young Jews in the KIBBUTZIM. I tell you they will provide a soldiery better than ours. We have only to train it.'

Wingate travelled throughout Palestine, convincing his British superiors of the need to arm the Jews, as well as offering himself to the Jewish Agency as commander of a legalized Jewish Defence Force. The Jews at first approached Wingate with great scepticism, though his persistent mannerisms and frustrated attempts to speak Hebrew helped gain their loyal confidence. He became known simply as HAYEDID, 'the Friend', and with Jewish trust in his sincerity, he approached the Commander-in-Chief of the British forces in Palestine, Sir Archibald Wavell, with a plan to stem Arab guerrilla activity against the pipeline. He proposed the formation of mixed English-Jewish counter-guerrilla units, to be known as the Special Night Squads (SNS, though known in Hebrew as the PLUGOT HA'ESH or 'Fire Companies'). Wavell gave the young Captain his blessing; and sanctioned what Wingate believed was to be the embryo of a Jewish Army.

Like Sadeh, Wingate handpicked his soldiers with great care, requesting the HAGANAH's most courageous and intelligent soldiers. He undertook long journeys on foot throughout northern Israel to familiarize himself with the territory, armed with two SMLEs, an English-Hebrew dictionary and a letter of safe passage from HAGANAH Commander-in-Chief, Eliyahu Golomb. One of the sites which impressed Captain Wingate most was the settlement of Hanita. Located on the Lebanese border, Hanita was founded on 21 March 1938 by four hundred FO'SH fighters supported by 100 uniformed NOTRIM (commanded by Sadeh, and two of his lieutenants; Moshe Dayan and Yigal Allon), who overnight set up a tower and stockade. For

more than a week, Arab guerrillas attacked Hanita, but the settlers stubbornly stood fast. Wingate arrived at Hanita in April 1938, and pursuaded the settlers to initiate 'mobile ambushes'.

Yitzhak Sadeh met Captain Wingate at Kibbutz Ein Harod (one of the HAGANAH's most important bases), and these two unlikely brothers in arms succeeded in making the SNS operational by May 1938. Wingate trained the eager HAGANAH soldiers in the art of unarmed combat, and the use of bayonets and grenades, while his British NCOs taught small arms proficiency and night-fighting techniques. SNS fighters studied 'commando techniques' long before their importance was accepted by the traditional military mind. The SNS found sanctuary in the KIBBUTZIM of northern Galilee, where they blended into the landscape by day, to be unleashed at night with stealth, speed and force. It is important to note that British support for the SNS was minimal, and almost every SNS operation had to be 'covertly' reinforced by HAGANAH units. In fact, Wingate was often forced to borrow weapons from the severely limited HAGANAH arsenals. This caused Wingate to insure that the SNS operated in total secrecy; from the Arabs as well as from the British.

On 13 September 1938, the SNS's first course for Jewish NCOs began at Kibbutz Ein Harod. During the commencement ceremonies, Wingate sternly addressed the men in Hebrew and said: 'We are here to found a Jewish Army', then switching to English, he lectured the young cadets as to the responsibilities of command. In fact, Wingate's influence on Israel's future military experience, especially in leadership and the use of élite units, was monumental. He enforced the importance of command through personal example; whether through leadership displayed during combat, or by being first and fastest during a forced march. Although a harsh disciplinarian, he prided himself on treating his subordinates as intelligent equals; and prior to each operation would conduct pre-planning discussions ensuring that each soldier understood the purpose of the mission. He enthusiastically invited lower ranking soldiers to assume command in accordance with changing conditions in battle, and to make their own independent battlefield decisions. Most important however for future Israeli military thought, he

was the *official* devotee of 'carrying the war into the enemy's territory', by having commando forces leave the sanctuary of the settlements to head out on long-range penetration raids. Wingate deeply influenced Israeli military thought, and would be the inspiration behind the creation of most of Israel's élite units.

In the field, the SNS enjoyed a brief though successful tenure of duty. The squadsmen, wearing their distinctive blue shirts and Australian-type slouch hats, carried out dozens of raids and ambushes against Arab villages, and the bases from which the guerrillas operated; the most memorable being the battle for the village of Dabburiyah, in which Wingate himself was wounded. SNS patrols were characteristic of their unconventional and often ruthless nature. In essence, they quelled the riots which had begun in 1936. In making the Arab fear the night, the SNS succeeded in securing the oil pipeline as well as the Teggart Wall, the defensive barricade along the northern frontier with Lebanon. It was built by Jewish workers, protected by the FO'SH and the SNS. During the SNS's first months of operations, the number of attacks against the pipeline dwindled to only two! Military successes aside, the conservative British regarded Wingate as a pariah. His eccentric behaviour and passionate love for the Jews frightened his commanding officers. The British disbanded the SNS, the graduates of the second Jewish NCO's course at Ein Harod became Privates in the British Army, and Wingate left Palestine in 1939, being noted as a 'good soldier, but a security risk!'

Wingate's departure and the end of the riots marked the end of the military marriage of convenience between the British and the Jews. The HAGANAH underwent a major expansion, and the FO'SH was replaced by the larger HI'SH or HEYL SADEH (Hebrew acronym for 'Field Force'). The HI'SH had a sizeable reserve force, and was the true predecessor of the Israel Defence Force. It was, however, illegal, and without Wingate, the British clamped down on HAGANAH activities. On 5 October 1940, the British, in an endeavour to show impartiality to both Jew and Arab, arrested 43 HAGANAH members (including Moshe Dayan) on trumped-up charges of participating in an illegal HAGANAH commander's course. All 43 were released sixteen months later and invited by the British authorities to contribute their military expertise in the fight against Hitler.

THE PAL'MACH

'With this weapon deposited safely in my hands by the
'HAGANAH'
I shall fight the enemies of my people and my country.
With no surrender, with no recoil of fear.
With the dedication of my soul.'

The PAL'MACH Oath of Allegiance

THE Second World War created the second military marriage of convenience between the British and the YISHUV, even though the 1939 White Paper curtailing Jewish immigration to Palestine created hostilities between the two sides. Nevertheless, both the moderate HAGANAH and right-wing IRGUN TZVAI LEUMI (IRGUN) conceded that the common enemy was Hitler; eloquently summarized by David Ben-Gurion when he vowed: 'We shall fight the war as if there were no White Paper and we shall fight the White Paper as if there were no war.' The British also understood the importance of the YISHUV in the oncoming struggle against Germany. Palestine was of enormous strategic value to the British Empire, and with Arab sentiments evidently pro-Nazi, the Jews were their only true ally in the region.

Winston Churchill had been a persistent advocate of arming the Jews for a combat role, though both the Foreign and War Offices advised against it. In fact, throughout Palestine, thousands of young Jewish men and women lined up to volunteer for service in the British Army. The Zionist Executive urged the British Military to accept these eager recruits to combat postings, but they were instead directed to the Auxiliary Military Pioneer Corps (AMPC) which, together with Palestinian Arab volunteers, 'filled sandbags' along the Maginot Line! Little effort was paid to the notion of a formal Jewish Army. Instead, agreements were reached with the British to train HAGANAH fighters for special operations. Secrecy was absolute, all details handled by MI4 and the Special Operations Executive (SOE). In late 1940, three SOE agents, Arnold Lawrence (T.E. Lawrence's brother), Nicholas Hammond, and Henry Barnes, came to Palestine to launch a 'Jewish Army' from a hotel room on Mt Carmel. It was a fantastic irony; but one year earlier, the British had been at war with the HAGANAH.

The relationship between British intelligence and the HAGANAH's intelligence, counter-intelligence, and internal security service SHA'I (SHERUT YEDIOT or 'Information Service') was fruitful. The British received an excellent calibre of recruit, while the HAGANAH received British funding, weaponry, and training. While the Jewish agents worked on behalf of 'King and Country', they at the same time pursued HAGANAH interests. SOE and MI4 realized this, and a cooperative working relationship existed. SOE officers and their 'deputized' HAGANAH liaison officers went so far as to help gain the release of HAGANAH fighters interned by the British. Abba Eban, one such liaison

officer and a former Israeli Foreign Minister, utilized his SOE card not only to gain the release of comrades arrested on weapons charges, but to travel freely throughout Palestine transferring legal SOE weapons to illegal HAGANAH arsenals. In fact SOE officers urged the HAGANAH to fool the Mandatory authorities, and overtly assisted in the effort to 'switch recruit identity numbers', increasing the number of fighters sanctioned for training.

Throughout the KIBBUTZIM all over Israel, special intelligence, sabotage, and demolitions courses were conducted by the SOE, and a training-school code-named 'ME 102' was operated for German-speaking Jews to be dropped into Nazi-occupied Europe. The HAGANAH replied in turn by supplying invaluable intelligence of their own. Their linguistic experts (something SOE desperately lacked) interrogated new arrivals from Europe, gathering masses of information at SHA'I HQ in Haifa. The SOE had 'special operations' in mind for the HAGANAH operatives. The first known to be a planned attack on the Roumanian freighter *Iron Gate* on the Danube, blocking off the river supply route to Germany. There was also a cancelled plan to switch HAGANAH agents with Roumanian refugees, who would soon form an anti-German underground. The British had high expectations from their Jewish agents.

As the Germans pushed through Europe, the Balkans, and North Africa, the British feared that a possible Axis push towards India through Syria and Iraq was imminent. The YISHUV had far more consequential concerns about German threats. With Europe as an example, the possibility of Palestine under German control had fatalistic conclusions. The Jewish Agency pleaded with the British to develop a firm Jewish military potential; but the British balked, refusing to form a 'Jewish Brigade'. Instead, the British agreed to sponsor what the HAGANAH High Command had urged for most, an independent, mobile, permanently mobilized task force to act as a guerrilla army should the Axis forces reach Palestine. It was to be an élite volunteer force accepting only the most physically and psychologically fit HAGANAH fighters, and centred around a cadre of professional FO'SH and SNS veterans. On 14 May 1941 the PAL'MACH (PLUGOT MAHATZ, or 'Strike Companies') declared its existence.

The PAL'MACH's two-fold objective was to protect the YISHUV from Axis invasion, and internal Arab attack. Should the British lines crumble and the Axis, led by the Arabs, invade Palestine, the PAL'MACH was to disrupt enemy lines of communication, and destroy enemy airfields. Trained as guerrillas, and taught to operate in small decisive units, they developed into experts in reconnaissance, and demolition. The largest PAL'MACH unit was a company, and six companies were established immediately. It was obvious to the HAGANAH High Command who should lead this élite force, and Yitzhak Sadeh was named PAL'MACH Commander.

Organizational and logistic problems aside, the British required the immediate services of the PAL'MACH. The SOE had been disappointed by their Arab agents, whose performance on the whole was dismal. A group of Arab operatives who were dispatched into Lebanon to destroy a Vichy French communications system, abandoned their assignment, and sold their issued explosives to Galilee Black Marketeers! With pending plans to attack the Vichy French in Syria and Lebanon only days away, Special Operations Commander Group-Captain Donville turned for help to Moshe Shertok, Head of the Jewish Agency's Political Department. Shertok turned to the HAGANAH, and SHA'I and PAL'MACH operatives were infiltrated into the Levant. In fact, HAGANAH cooperation with the Free French had been under way ever since the fall of France. From the Haifa flat of HAGANAH agent, David Hacohen, Captains Raymond Schmittlein and François Coulet operated the Free France radio station, which broadcast Gaullist psychological warfare programmes throughout the Levant.

In November 1940, the SOE trained a special unit of the HAGANAH's best fighters in amphibious warfare for commando raids on the Lebanese and Italian coasts. In Tel Aviv's Exhibition Park, the unit trained in the production and use of limpet mines, while undergoing naval and amphibious assault training on Tel Aviv's murky River Yarkon. The HAGANAH commandos displayed admirable enthusiasm and skill, and by the spring of 1941, the unit was operational. To coincide with the Allied invasion of the Levant, 23 of these fighters, now the cutting edge of the newly formed PAL'MACH, volunteered for an impressive operation planned by SOE, an amphibious assault on the oil refineries at Tripoli. They embarked in the *Sea Lion* (a motorized British Coast Guard ship carrying three light landing craft) on 18 May 1941 with an SOE liaison officer, Major Anthony Palmer. After leaving Haifa and heading west into international waters, *Sea Lion* made her last communication before radio silence was observed. *Sea Lion* never reached Tripoli, the fate of the 23 and Major Palmer remaining a mystery to this day. Some reports indicate that the men were captured by the Italian Navy, others claim that the bodies of twenty seamen had been washed up on the Lebanese coast. In keeping with the strict secrecy shrouding the incident, the families of the 23 men were not immediately informed of their deaths. It was a tragic beginning for the PAL'MACH, losing their most capable fighters in a single unsuccessful operation.

Following the *Sea Lion* incident, Sadeh suggested new possibilities for the PAL'MACH, and days before the Allied invasion of Syria and Lebanon, the PAL'MACH went into action. Reconnaissance groups were dispatched nightly on intelligence-gathering missions, while other groups concentrated on sabotage, destroying communication lines, and blowing up bridges. When the Allies invaded on 8

▼ Carrying sticks instead of guns, a squad from the PAL'MACH's 'German Platoon' enjoy the hot Israel sun during a forced march in the Jezreel Valley, July 1941. (HAGANAH Archives)

► Preparing for the worst of all possible scenarios. PAL'MACHNIKs practise urban assault techniques. Although their numbers were minuscule in the light of the crucial task they would have to perform it the Germans reached Palestine, their existence did instil confidence among the YISHUV. (HAGANAH Archives)

June, the PAL'MACH was in the vanguard; in 'pure' Jewish units or as scouts for Allied forces, most notably the Australian 7th Division. One scout unit commanded by Moshe Dayan was to undertake preliminary reconnaissance patrols, locate enemy positions, and report which roads could handle heavy military traffic. On the eve of the invasion, Dayan's unit was ordered to reach the Lebanese village of Iskenderun, nine kilometres from the Israeli frontier, and seize a nearby bridge on the Beirut coastal highway. For this task Dayan recruited volunteers from the KIBBUTZIM of northern Galilee familiar with the border region, as well as enlisting the services of Circassian and Druze Muslim guides. The small advance force was made up of five PAL'MACHNIK's (Hebrew for male PAL'MACH fighter) and ten Australians, who prepared for the final border crossing at their temporary HQ at KIBBUTZ Hanita. On the night of 7 June, the bridges were seized, though during a fire-fight at a nearby police fort Moshe Dayan suffered a permanent injury to his left eye; the most well-known war wound in history since Nelson's!

In a similar operation commanded by Yigal Allon, a small reconnaissance party infiltrated across the border, capturing a bridge over the River Litani, and four French prisoners. An Australian colonel, quite impressed by the PAL'MACHNIKS, promised to award commendations to Allon and his unit. Allon politely declined, requesting instead to keep 'his POW's captured weapons'. The Colonel not only agreed to Allon's odd wish, but offered him a large stockpile of arms captured from other French troops. HAGANAH transport was summoned, and the guns, grenades, and ammunition carted off to safe-keeping. Four years later, they were to be used against the British. Throughout the campaign the PAL'MACHNIKs proved their worth as execellent scouts, effective night fighters, and cunning saboteurs.

That summer, two PAL'MACH bases were established at KIBBUTZ Ginosar and Beit Oren. The men lived in the most spartan of conditions, sleeping outdoors, without the services of cooks, quartermasters, or orderlies. Sadeh was determined to maintain the 'underground' nature of the PAL'MACH. He realized that with the termination of a British need for Jewish fighters in the Mediterranean campaign, the PAL'MACH would have to regroup and go underground! Sadeh's was a visionary prediction, and with dried up funds, and Syria and Lebanon secured, the PAL'MACH was ordered to disband its bases, and to send its soldiers home. The PAL'MACH refused to fade away, and Sadeh kept the fighters attached to their units. Training was carried out only six days a month, consisting of only the minimal: squad size target practice and routine mar-

ches. Nevertheless, the PAL'MACH companies retained their strong sense of of unit cohesion and purpose.

As Rommel's Afrika Korps advanced towards the Egyptian frontier, the British drew up contingency plans for evacuating from the Middle East. Once again turning to the PAL'MACH, British GHQ set up an elaborate plan for espionage and sabotage operations against the Germans should the expected thrust into Palestine materialize. The preparations to meet the German Army offered PAL'MACH commanders the unique opportunity to develop indigenous tactics, which would not only be employed against an Axis invasion, but would prove invaluable during the struggle for Israel's independence. A desperate plan to turn the area between Mt Carmel, and the mountain

► Yerucham Cohen, commander of SHACHAR, the PAL'MACH's 'Arab Platoon', seen during the campaign against the Vichy French in Syria. (HAGANAH Archives)

chains of western Galilee into a modern day Metzada (the fortress overlooking the Dead Sea, where 960 Jewish zealots beseiged by the Romans committed suicide rather than submit to slavery) was formulated. The 'fortress', defended by the HAGANAH was to shelter 500,000 Jews. It was to be supplied by ship and submarine from the port of Haifa, and by air at a series of airfields. The siege plan was labelled TOCHNIT HACARMEL or the 'Carmel Plan', and was to act as an enclave from which the PAL'MACH could operate against the Germans. It was less a military solution, than a 'solution for Jewish civilization'.

The British supported 300 PAL'MACHNIKs for extensive commando training, though the HAGANAH utilized the British funding to train almost three times as many. In June 1942, a large-scale training course in sabotage and guerrilla warfare was conducted in a forest near Kibbutz Mishmar Ha'emek in the Valley of Jezreel. The military courses personified the PAL'MACH military doctrine which would later determine the characteristic of the Israel Defence Force. The PAL'MACH was taught to fight with what manpower and material was available, rather than what was tactically advisable. At Mishmar Ha'emek, the PAL'MACH fighters learned the skills required to conduct a successful guerrilla campaign. Considerable effort was also made to teach the young men and women the latest techniques in demolitions. As the PAL'MACH lacked large-calibre weapons, explosives became their artillery. They perfected assault techniques as small shock units, and operations as individual saboteurs. Each PAL'MACH soldier considered that the ultimate PAL'MACH unit was a single fighter and his weapon!

Courses were also given in long-range reconnaissance, intelligence gathering, communications, and weapons proficiency. The PAL'MACHNIKs learned to operate almost every conceivable weapon they might come in contact with, from German rifles and grenades to French light machine-guns. They became experts in the personal weaponry and equipment of the Axis soldier, and were trained to field strip a German MP-38 with the same ease as their issued Sten guns. Intensive marksmanship sessions were conducted daily, the men being taught to shoot with great precision as ammunition was scarce. Weapons too were in short supply. The funding the British provided could not arm the thousands of men who wished to be trained. Guns were borrowed from HAGANAH emergency arsenals, and when these proved insufficient, brooms, branches, and walking-sticks provided the closest resemblence to the real thing!

Martial arts training was not neglected, and the art of cold killing received serious attention. The PAL'MACHNIKs developed their own brand of Judo called KRAV MAGA ('Close Quarter Battle'), and knives, truncheons, and fists became deadly weapons. PAL'MACHNIKs were even pre-pared for the worst scenario, including capture, interrogation, and torture at the hands of the Gestapo.

Its role as a guerrilla force provided the PAL'MACH with a fair degree of flexibility, which bred innovation. In accordance, three distinctive language based units were created. The first was SHACHAR ('Dawn'), or as they became commonly known, the 'Arab Platoon' or HAMACH-LAKA HA'ARAVIT. These Jews from the Middle East diaspora were taught to act and think as Arabs, learning their heritage, and mannerisms. Commanded by Yerucham Cohen (who had a fair complexion and red-haired beard no less!), all courses and communications were not only carried out in Arabic, but in the proper local dialects. The Arab Platoon operated as a covert Allied intelligence force in Syria, Lebanon, Trans-Jordan, though mainly among the Arabs of Palestine. Despite successful infiltration, there were some problems of identity, as Arabs from Damascus to Beirut noticed strange discrepancies; ranging from improper slang to wearing shoes made in Haifa! Although trained as agents and saboteurs, they received intensive commando instruction as well. When and if the Germans invaded, the Arab Platoon was to interdict enemy lines, and operate as an internal Arab Fifth Column, causing mass confusion and destruction.

HAMACHLAKA HAGERMANIT, or 'German Platoon' was made up of fair-haired PAL'MACHNIKS from Germany and Austria, and was to infiltrate behind enemy lines disguised as Wehrmacht soldiers. German was the only language spoken, and the soldiers were taught every detail about being a German soldier. In the classroom, the role the German soldier was studied, from basic training to service in the Western Desert. They were proficient with every piece of weaponry and equipment in the German arsenal, and were taught the intricacies of German military life and day to day procedures, from rank insignias, to military salaries, to the most popular brothels. SOE instructors, defecting German soldiers, and Afrika Korps POWs all offered their knowledge in the effort to transform the Jewish fighters into unlikely '*Deutscher soldaten*'. The brightest pupils were sent into British POW camps and mingled among the prisoners to gather intelligence, while others fought with the Long Range Desert Group in the Western Desert. An audacious plan even called for 'German Platoon' commandos to infiltrate deep behind German lines in the desert, and blow up Rommel's headquarters! Luckily however, the 'German Platoon' never had to see action inside Palestine.

A 'Balkan Platoon' was also formed, and it saw action along with British SAS and SOE formations in the Aegean and Yugoslavia; and a 'Roumanian Platoon' was rumoured to have existed with the specific purpose to raid the oil fields at Ploesti. The main PAL'MACH effort however remained the defence of Palestine. The British Eighth Army succeeded in halting Rommel at El Alamein, and the Middle East was secured from Nazi domination. This led to the disintegration once again of the relationship between the British and the HAGANAH. Even though the PAL'MACH had expanded, with the battalion being introduced as a tactical unit (four PAL'MACH compaines were commanded by a Battalion Commander), support behind it dwindled. By the spring of 1943, the alliance ended with ill-will, as British troops confiscated PAL'MACH guns and ammunition. A few nights later, however, a PAL'MACH detachment stole the weapons back without being detected. Clearly the PAL'MACH had been excellent students of commando techniques, and were determined not to let their distinctive military education go to waste. The HAGANAH High Command still comprehended its overall military weaknesses, and although the PAL'MACH was an élite formation, conventional means of conducting a military campaign such as deploying infantry, artillery,

armour, and engineering forces were severely limited. It was successfully argued that the YISHUV's Jewish men should volunteer for conventional service with the British Army, in the hopes of one day achieving a Jewish Brigade; eventually realized on 20 September 1944, with the formation of the 5,000 man Jewish Brigade Group which saw active duty in Italy and Belgium.

After two years of training and operating in an overt manner, the PAL'MACH found its new anonymity and illegal status most difficult to accept. Without British funding, the HAGANAH found it virtually impossible to support the PAL'MACH, which by 1943 exceeded 1,000 fully trained fighters. Saving the PAL'MACH from termination was a noble concept, dating back to HASHOMER. The KIBBUTZIM adopted two PAL'MACH platoons each. The PAL'MACHNIKS worked on the KIBBUTZ for fourteen days a month, while the remaining days were devoted to military training. The KIBBUTZIM were to provide the PAL'MACH with ideal cover, while at the same time installing a strong sense of community and moral obligation necessary in the inevitable military struggle for Israel's independence. The KIBBUTZ would introduce the élite PAL'MACH fighters to the notion of dual responsibility in an embattled society. This 'work and fight' ethic would carry over years later into the IDF with the creation of NA'HA'L (Hebrew acronym for 'Fighting Pioneer Youth').

Working the land for a living did not please many of the PAL'MACHNIKS. They regarded theirs as an élite status, and felt degraded by their forced labour. Many disgruntled fighters even defected, volunteering for service in the élite formations of the British Army. Others chose to remain, and collectively they fashioned a distinctive character at the communal settlements. The famed PAL'MACH KUMSITZ ('get-together') around the camp fire late at night, singing martial songs, became a fundamental element of Israeli folklore. The PAL'MACH's élite reputation in fact enhanced itself in the KIBBUTZIM, where the remainder of the YISHUV was offered the opportunity to observe their resolve and dedication. Life in the KIBBUTZ opened many doors for the PAL'MACH's women fighters as well. Although women had always been an integral element of the HAGANAH and SHA'I, in the PAL'MACH they received the same intense commando training as the men, taking on an equal role. In SHACHAR, women from traditionally conservative and 'old-fashioned' Middle Eastern families took the forefront of responsibility, becoming invaluable intelligence operatives and saboteurs. The equality women shared in the KIBBUTZ reinforced this 'sisters in arms' ethic; although in 1943 women were segregated into their own units, removing them from front-line service. The presence of women in the PAL'MACH underground 'obviously' decreased the harshness and stress of the all-male military atmosphere. Their active participation in the defence of their nation turned the PAL'MACH into a true people's army; and during the 1948 War of Independence, women PAL'MACH soldiers served with distinction as intelligence analysts, wireless operatives, nurses, even snipers. The death in combat of

▲ Since the days of the PAL'MACH, women soldiers have served Israel's élite forces with distinction. Here, a parachute-rigger makes a final check on a parachute under the banner: 'Their lives are in your hands!' (IDF Archives)

extensive amphibious training, assisting illegal immigration required the formation of a naval force, and in 1943 the PAL'YAM (PLUGOT YAM or 'Sea Companies') was established. Four courses were offered by the PAL'YAM: naval sabotage, naval transport, amphibious assault, and naval guerrilla warfare (the utilization of small craft for unconventional military tasks). The PAL'YAM was manned by PAL'MACHNIKS from the fishing villages along the Mediterranean coast, who had some sea-going experience, as well as sea-worthy craft.

In 1943, the PAL'MACH took to the air as well, with the formation of the PAL'AVIR (PLUGOT AVIR or 'Air Companies'). It was a bold attempt at planting the seeds for a conventional air force, and it used civilian flying clubs as cover for military training, Although the PAL'AVIR possessed only simple gliders and a few Piper Cubs, they managed to formulate air assault strategies in expectation of combat against the RAF and Arab Air Forces. Together with Palestinian Jews who had flown with the RAF (such as Ezer Weizmann), the crudely equipped PAL'AVIR formed the basis for the world's most combat-effective air force which would develop years later. In fact throughout the Second World War years, the PAL'MACH served as the HAGANAH's field laboratory. New systems of organization and training were researched and perfected through each PAL'MACH operation. More importantly, the creation of an Israeli command cadre emerged throughout the PAL'MACH, and the training routine PAL'MACH officers received and administered deeply affected the future character of the IDF.

By the end of the Second World War, the PAL'MACH order of battle consisted of four well-organized, well-trained, and well-disciplined battalions. In its programme of expansion, a formal reserve system was instituted, which later formed the basis of the IDF's impressive reservist army character. Every 'Private' released from active duty after his two years' service was posted to a reserve unit. Squad and section commanders (NCOs) were required to serve three years, junior officers four years of active duty before being attached to reservist formations. Only 'senior commanders' were retained for unspecified periods in 'regular units'. Reservists were called up for training a few weeks a year, and were required to be on permanent alert. By the spring of 1945, the PAL'MACH boasted more than 2,000 fighters.

many women PAL'MACH fighters served as notice to the future IDF as to the sociological price a nation must pay which maintains women combat soldiers.

With the fight against Hitler no longer a primary objective for the PAL'MACH, they now devoted their meagre resources towards the realization of the Jewish homeland. A major 'military' task ahead against the British would be assisting the death camp survivors in reaching Palestine illegally (Britain's restrictive White Paper was still valid) by sea. Although each PAL'MACH fighter had to undergo

THE STRUGGLE AGAINST THE BRITISH

BY spring 1945, bloodshed in Palestine was inevitable. With Palestine's internal differences between Arab and Jew exacerbated by British indifference towards the thousands of Holocaust survivors yearning to reach the land of Israel, the YISHUV's three underground armies sprang into action. The HAGANAH was clearly the most moderate, most popular, and best equipped of the three, with more than 10,000 fighters, and the élite PAL'MACH strike companies. The IRGUN, led by Menachem Begin, had oddly enough supported the British during the war, conducting sabotage and intelligence operations against the pro-Nazi Rashid Ali al-Gailani in Iraq. The IRGUN had an extensive network in Iraq, and its demolitions unit proved invaluable during the campaign, especially in the liberation of Habaniya by British forces (in which IRGUN officer David Raziel was killed in a Luftwaffe air raid). In 1944 it mobilized its 3,000 fighters, and 1,000-man Battle Corps (HEYL KRAV) for full-scale war against both the British and Arabs. The LE'H'I (LOCHAMEI HERUT YISRAEL or Israel Freedom Fighters) more commonly known as the 'Stern Gang', was a fanatical right-wing terror group which claimed more than 500 hard-core fighters or terrorists. It considered Britain as the true enemy, and had even contacted German and Italian intelligence for military assistance during the Second World War.

While IRGUN and LE'H'I policies against the British were clear, the HAGANAH faced an operational dilemma. As an ethical 'defence' force obedient to Jewish moral codes, it could not condone acts of terror against the British. It could not ignore British policy either. In the end it opted for a strategy of resistance known as the 'struggle'. The 'struggle' consisted of a three-pronged assault involving illegal immigration, illegal settlement, and *military action*. It was a strategy of constructive engagement which involved all aspects of Jewish aspirations for a state of Israel. The HAGANAH was careful to attack *only* military targets, in order to maximize political objectives with the minimum of British casualties. In addition, only those military targets which directly threatened illegal Jewish immigration were to be targeted, such as Royal Navy ships, radar stations, and police forts. The military aim was not to introduce a British body count of horrendous proportions, but to convince London of the importance of Zionist aspirations. In May 1945, the HAGANAH unleashed the PAL'MACH for action.

The PAL'MACH struck on land and sea, in Palestine and in Europe. One of the PAL'MACH's primary objectives was the support of BRICHA ('Operation Flight'), the smuggling of Europe's surviving Jews to Palestine. Hundreds of clandestine routes were established throughout Europe, in which the survivors of Hitler's Final Solution' trekked hundreds of miles to waiting vessels of dubious seaworthiness for the voyage to Palestine. Escorting these refugees were machine-gun toting PAL'MACHNIKs, who guarded this precious human cargo. PAL'MACH night training was extensively utilized during BRICHA, and mountain passes successfully regotiated under the most arduous of conditions. The PAL'MACHNIKs were aided by the MOSSAD or 'Institution' (an intelligence service set up by the HAGANAH to facilitate this underground railway), as well as by Jewish Brigade soldiers who furnished transport and cover for MOSSAD operations, and by sympathetic South African and Australian soldiers, and friendly Italian partisans.

The successful transport of the illegals (MA'APILIM) to Palestine required breaking through the British naval blockade, a task assigned to the PAL'YAM. A major training facility was established at KIBBUTZ Sdot Yam near Caesarea to instruct PAL'YAM personnel to operate MA'APILIM ships, as well as counter British ships attempting to intercept them. Many ships were intercepted, and their 'human' cargo interned in detention camps in Cyprus. Nevertheless, the PAL'YAM crews displayed exemplary skill and courage, especially against British boarding parties, and succeeded in bringing to Palestine thousands of future Israelis.

In the waters off Palestine and Cyprus, the PAL'YAM's small underwater demolitions unit sabotaged numerous British naval vessels. On 21 August 1946 a limpet mine severely damaged the patrol craft *Empire Rival*; on 13 February 1947 three Royal Navy coast guard ships were sabotaged, and on 3 March 1947 a limpet mine was attached to HMS *Ocean Vigour* off the Cyprus coast by PAL'YAM officer Yosef Dror. These operations were carried out by courageous underwater warriors supplied with inadequate equipment, and assigned impossible tasks. Many divers wore wet suits which neither kept out the water or cold, while others operated with dubious homemade explosives.

Once on land, the PAL'MACH defended the landing beach, until the MA'APILIM had been got to safety. Security prohibited the mentioning of a landing zone until but hours before the landing, and as a result, PAL'MACH security details were required to march long and fast in order to reach any proposed landing site within hours. Once the immigrants had been loaded on HAGANAH transports, the PAL'MACH would initiate its British-taught guerrilla tactics to delay pursuing British forces!

Not only was the PAL'MACH operating as the strike arm of the HAGANAH, but also in cooperation with the IRGUN and LE'H'I, with whom a unified 'Jewish Resistance Movement' was formed in October 1945. Its first combined operation was the 'Night of the Railways' on 1 November 1945 when 153 acts of sabotage against railway installations nationwide were carried out. The PAL'MACH opposed 'joint-military action', especially with the LE'H'I terror group. Its main strength, however, was operating alone, and it did so in spectacular fashion. These ranged from the freeing on 10 October 1946 of 203 illegal immigrants held by the British at Atlit, to incessant raids against British supply convoys in search of weapons and ammunition. It should be noted, that as a result of the PAL'MACH's limited conventional capabilities, most attacks had to be carried out at night. These operations not only required a great degree of physical and psychological stamina for the individual soldier, but an extensive degree of tactical logic on the part of PAL'MACH officers. It included the ability to operate as small units (squad to platoon size), or in coordination with larger forces (in company to battalion strengths). Training for such operations were conducted in the vast emptiness of the Negev Desert, where the PAL'MACHNIKS were able to practise marksmanship and demolitions, and experiment with new tactics safe from British eyes.

Protesting Britain's Jewish immigration policy, the PAL'MACH acted in spectacular fashion, cutting off all British land points of access into Palestine. On the night of 17/18 June 1946, the PAL'MACH staged its largest operation ever, attacking eleven road and rail bridges leading into the country. They attacked the Metula (two bridges), B'not Ya'akov, El Hawa (across the the River Yarmouk), Sheik Hussein, Ed-Damieh, Allenby, and Gaza bridges, with no PAL'MACH casualties. The only difficulties were encountered at the Keziv Bridges (two medium bridges over the River Achziv). Arab watchmen spotted the PAL'MACH sapper squad, and opened fire. The PAL'MACHNIKS fought tenaciously, reaching the bridge and setting off their charges (at the same time evacuating Arab civilians nearby). A fierce fire fight, and a mishap with the explosive charges resulted in the deaths of thirteen PAL'MACHNIKS.

On the night of 20/21 July 1947, a PAL'MACH platoon commanded by Haim Bar-Lev (a future IDF Chief of Staff) attacked two British coastal radar stations on Mt Carmel, the western near the Stella Maris monastery; the eastern near Harival; both defended by detachments from the British 6th Airborne Division. By 22.30 hours on 20 June, the PAL'MACHNIKS, wearing khaki, carrying rucksacks loaded with explosives and fatigues, faces darkened for the Mediterranean night, began their protracted infiltration into the eastern base's outer defences. The squads got to within 20 metres of the radars, until discovered by British sentries. A fierce 20-minute fire-fight ensued in which the PAL'MACHNIKS, armed with TMTs (a crudely produced HAGANAH copy of the Sten), pistols, and SMLEs, directed accurate fire against the British defenders, pinning them down, aiming to wound, not kill! The PAL'MACH withdrew, suffering one dead and numerous wounded. The attack on the western position also met with stiff resistance, but the inner defences were breached and the radar destroyed. Both operations were typical of PAL'MACH moves against the British at that time. The concern for casualties on both sides of the fence was compounded only by concern for weaponry. Each PAL'MACH order of battle, operational report, and statistic included the number of weapons each unit possessed. Often death-defying efforts were conducted to retrieve lost weapons as well as wounded comrades. It must be noted that the 3,000-man PAL'MACH possessed only 656 rifles!

The British reacted strongly against such acts of PAL'MACH, IRGUN and LE'H'I provocation, and on the morning of Saturday 29 June 1946, they imposed a general curfew throughout Palestine. It was known as 'Black Saturday', and resulted in the incarceration of many of the YISHUV's top leaders; although the HAGANAH succeeded in going totally underground. Massive searches for arms caches were also conducted by the British, and the KIBBUTZIM were searched. In KIBBUTZ Yagur, the British uncovered 325 rifles, 96 mortars, 78 pistols, 425,000 rounds of ammunition, 5,000 grenades, and 800 pounds of high-explosives. While the HAGANAH laid low, the IRGUN acted in decisive fashion. Jerusalem's King David Hotel, the seat of the Mandatory Government in Palestine, was the target of IRGUN explosives on 22 July 1946, resulting in 91 deaths. This shocking act ended the reality of the 'Jewish Resistance Movement'; but also led the British to lose the will to remain in Palestine. They were the targets of bloody acts of terror from Jewish underground groups, and their harsh reaction bred only more destructive violence in return. Disillusioned, the British turned the Palestine question over to the newly formed United Nations. The troubles in Palestine entered international debate. The Arabs prepared for an inevitable fight, while the HAGANAH mobilized the YISHUV for total war.

THE 1948 WAR OF INDEPENDENCE, AND ITS AFTERMATH

O N the night of 29 November 1947, the United Nations decided the fate of Palestine. One by one, the nations sounded their voice, as the entire population of Palestine listened in on radio. Thirty-three nations were in favour, thirteen opposed, and ten abstained on the motion to partition Palestine into an independent Jewish and an independent Arab state with Jerusalem as an international city. On 30 November 1947, war erupted throughout Palestine.

The first Jewish nation in 2,000 years would have to be achieved through military force, something which weighed heavily in the Arab's favour. By November 1947, the HAGANAH order of battle consisted of the 9,500-man HI'SH (18–25-year-old conscripts), the 30,000-man HI'M (HEYL MISHMAR or Guard Corps), and the 9,500 teenagers of the GAD'NA 'Youth Battalions'. This manpower was divided into five territorial infantry brigades: (A) LEVNONI–Galilee, Jezreel Valley and Haifa (in February 1948 split into the 1st GOLANI Brigade, and the 2nd CARMELI Brigade); (B) ALEXANDRONI (3rd Brigade)–the midlands between Jerusalem and Tel Aviv, and including one IRGUN battalion; (C) KIRYATI (4th Brigade–the Tel Aviv area, and including one IRGUN battalion; (D) GIVA'ATI (5th Brigade)–the lowlands between Tel Aviv and Jerusalem, and southwards; and (E) ETZIONI (6th Brigade)–Jerusalem and its surrounding hills.

In March 1948, the PAL'MACH, commanded by Yitzhak Sadeh's prize pupil Yigal Allon, had expanded from a brigade-size force to three brigades also divided along territorial lines. The two battalions positioned in the Negev Desert ('Negev South' and 'Negev North') were reinforced with two additional battalions ('Beer-Sheva' and the 'Raiders') to form HATIVAT HANEGEV (Negev Brigade). In the north, the GALIL and E'MEK Battalions were expanded to form HATIVAT YIFTACH (YIFTACH Brigade), and in Jerusalem, HATIVAT HAREL (HAREL Brigade), was formed consisting of the SHA'AR HAGAI and 'Jerusalem' battalions; as well as the HAPORTZIM ('Breakthrough'), 4th, or HQ Battalion which commanded the PAL'YAM and PAL'AVIR. The PAL'YAM consisted of 200 full-time Naval Commandos and frogmen with dozens of landing and civilian type craft, while the PAL'AVIR fielded only eleven single-engined aircraft; with forty licensed pilots, including twenty RAF combat veterans! There were a total of fifteen PAL'MACH Battalions (eleven mobilized, four in reserve); boasting 3,100 men and women. A fourth PAL'MACH Brigade, ODED, was formed in April 1948 in conjunction with Operation 'YIFTACH', the PAL'MACH offensive in Galilee which secured Sassa, Safed, and much of Galilee in preparation for the inevitable Syrian offensive which would follow the British withdrawal from Palestine.

Being the only mobilized and battle-trained force in the HAGANAH, the PAL'MACH was forced to assume a conventional military role. This displeased many PAL'MACH officers including Allon, who firmly believed in maximizing the PAL'MACH's commando capabilities. Even though the nature of the fighting did not call for the PAL'MACH to operate as an *independent* strike force, certain operations not only typified its élite combat status, but reflected its importance on the future development of IDE élite forces.

In the north, the YIFTACH Brigade was instrumental in the Seizure of Safed (one of the Galilee's northernmost towns, with 12,000 Arabs and only 1,500 Jews) in bitter fighting against the guerrilla force of Adib as Shishakli. In the Negev Desert, many of the isolated MOSHAVIM and KIBBUTZIM defended by the PAL'MACH were supplied at regular intervals by the PAL'AVIR, then known as the SHERUT AVIR ('Air Service'), the predecessor of the IDF/Air Force. Small, mechanically questionable Piper Cubs and Austers made weekly desert landings and para-drops, supplying food, medicine and, most importantly, ammunition to the beleaguered positions. When the Egyptian Army attacked through the south on 15 May, the PAL'MACH was instrumental in halting them, using their speed and perseverance to inflict harsh losses on the ill-prepared Egyptian infantry and armour formations. They were the inspiration too behind the GIVA'ATI Brigade's (commanded by PAL'MACH veteran Shimon Avidan, founder of the 'German Platoon') 54th Battalion reconnaissance group known simply as SHU'ALEI SHIMSHON, 'Samson's Foxes'. Copying PAL'MACH experience in the LRDG during the Second World War, SHU'ALEI SHIMSHON was equipped with jeeps fitted with MG-34 light machine-guns and PIAT anti-tank weapons.

In the Jerusalem and midlands area the HAREL Brigade (commanded by future Chief of Staff Yitzhak Rabin) fought the most bitter battles of the war against the guerrilla armies of Abdel-Kader Husseini and Hassan Salameh (in the vicinity of Lydda-Ramle), and the professional Arab Legion of Trans-Jordan. During the first stages of the fighting, the principal military objective was the securing of the supply routes between Tel Aviv and Jerusalem, and between Jerusalem and the four Gush Etzion settlements in the Hebron Hills. Gush Etzion had been under siege since the U.N. declaration, and persistent attempts to bring in supplies had met with failure, and horrendous casualties.

On 27 March 1948, a convoy guarded by 140 HI'SH fighters and 100 PAL'MACHNIKs attempted to reach Gush Etzion, which had'nt been supplied for four months. The convoy set out on the Sabbath morning hoping to achieve

---

surprise. It failed, and Arab guerrillas managed to inter-dict the convoy outside the village of Nebi Daniel south of Bethlehem. A brutal close-quarter battle ensued, which lasted 30 hours and involved more than *3,000* Arab guerrillas. The HI'SH fighters set up secondary lines of defence, while the PAL'MACHNIKs heroically assaulted the Arab firing positions, engaging them in hand-to-hand fighting. Urgent pleas were made to HAREL HQ in Jerusalem for reinforcements, though the British were the first to appear on the scene. An arrangement for safe passage was reached in exchange for the peaceful confiscation of all the arms, which were duly spiked! A similar convoy set out from Jerusalem the next day to relieve the settlement of Yechia, and met a worse fate. In a single bloodetting, 42 PAL'MACHNIKs were killed in savage fighting. Only one supply lorry reached Yechia that day!

Supply attempts to Jerusalem from Tel Aviv were just as hard fought. The only road, a narrow uphill trail surrounded by towering hills and majestic pines was successfully cut at numerous places, most notably in the valley of Sha'ar Hagai (Bab el-Wad) by well-entrenched guerrillas who enjoyed good firing positions. To overcome these field of fire roadblocks, the HAGANAH deployed a force of home-made armoured cars (civilian lorries armoured with cumbersome steel plating); and a force of courageous PAL'MACH (including both men and women) volunteers who met with death during every convoy. Today, these armoured skeletons still lie where they were stopped along the Tel Aviv–Jerusalem Highway, monument to the PAL'MACHNIKs who sacrificed their lives so that Jerusalem could survive. The situation was intolerable, and a zealous offensive was planned. It was known as Operation 'NACH-SHON', and involved an unprecedented 1,500 mobilized fighters. The battle which best characterized the brutal nature of the fighting was that for Kastel, a village, eight kilometres west of Jerusalem, which towers above the

route. The rocky approaches to the village were well-protected by Abdel-Kader Husseini's men, and after eight days of brutal combat in which the village changed hands several times, as well as resulting in the death of Husseini, Kastel was seized by the HAREL Brigade.

The declaration of the State of Israel on 14 May, and the subsequent invasion of the newly created Jewish nation by the combined armies of Lebanon, Syria, Iraq, Transjordan, and Egypt turned the fighting into a conventional military struggle. Although the PAL'MACH had by now been fully incorporated into the newly created TZAVA HAGANAH L'YISRAEL or Israel Defence Force (formally established on 31 May 1948), the notion of spectacular operations conducted by highly specialized élite units was not lost. Yitzhak Sadeh, commander of the newly created PAL'MACH's 8th Armoured Brigade, sanctioned the creation of a mechanized 'commando' battalion to be based loosely along the lines of the LRDG. The unit was designated the '89th Assault Battalion', and was commanded by Moshe Dayan.

The 89th was comprised of four distinct companies, each characterized by regional or political affiliations. One company was made up of young men from the KIBBUTZIM and MOSHAVIM, and included many PAL'MACH defectors; one group was recruited just from Tel Aviv residents, another of IRGUN and 'Stern Gang' volunteers; the fourth from overseas volunteers (mainly Jews from South Africa) known as MA'HA'L. The 89th Battalion was not well equipped; they were issued with lightly armed second-hand jeeps and Scout Cars. During the IDF's five brigade-sized offensives, codenamed Operation 'Danny' (10–19 July), the battalion (in conjunction with the PAL'MACH YIFTACH Brigade commanded by Moulah Cohen) captured the airport at Lydda (Lod), and seized the nearby town of Ramla in a lightning assault against crack Arab Legion units on 12 July. On 17 July, the reinforced battalion (now equipped with twelve lightly armed jeeps, four open scout cars, a captured Arab Legion armoured car with a 2-pounder gun dubbed the 'Tiger', and two home-made armoured cars) assaulted Egyptian positions deep in the Negev Desert, beginning to close the ring around the Egyptians in what is now known as the 'Faluja Pocket'. Together with the jeep-mounted SHU'ALEI SHIMSHON, and the PAL'MACH's Negev Beasts' company, the 89th managed to interdict enemy counter-attack efforts, with quick, mobile strikes. These jeep-mounted forces were instrumental in the eventual capture of Beer-Sheva, and the expulsion of all Egyptian forces from Israeli territory, reaching as far as El-Arish in Sinai during Operation 'HOREV' (25 December 1948 – 7 January 1949). Perhaps the most important result of these mechanized commando forces operations was the leading example from which the IDF Armoured Corps anti-tank reconnaissance formations (SAYERET SHIRION) would develop years later.

On the naval front, the PAL'YAM operated against both Syrian and Egyptian shipping in two spectacular commando operations. The first was a series of three operations known as 'SHALAL ('Loot') 1, 2, and 3', conducted at three different stages against a single target: the arms the Arabs had purchased from Czechoslovakia 'SHALAL 1' was the search at sea for the weapons aboard the Italian ship *Lino*, preventing them from reaching the intended destination of Beirut. It was carried out by the PAL'MACH's 4th Battalion, which commanded the PAL'YAM. On the night of 2 April, the HAGANAH ship *South Africa* headed out towards Rhodes with 25 PAL'YAM naval commandos. The ship searched for the *Lino*, but after three days received word that *Lino* had dropped anchor in the Italian port of Bari. This intelligence was handed over to RECHESH (HAGANAH intelligence squads which roamed the world in search of weapons), and MOSSAD officers in Italy, who acted immediately.

On the night of 9/10 April the mission, now termed 'SHALAL 2' was carried out, commanded by Yosef Dror who two years earlier had been instrumental in PAL'YAM sabotage operations against the Royal Navy. Dror and his second in command Benny Kravitz, attached limpet mines to *Lino*'s stern, and in the ensuing explosion, the ship sank. The Italian government, however, salvaged *Lino*'s cargo, and returned it to its rightful owners. The Arab League dispatched Syrian Colonel Mardam Ba'i (later to be executed for his failure) to oversee the transfer of the weapons to the cargo ship *Argero*. The original plan called for PAL'YAM personnel to board the *Argero* disguised as crewmen, and then seize control of the ship on the high seas; diverting her precious cargo to Israel. Last-minute logistical snags led to a more adventurous plan. 'SHALAL 3', carried out by PAL'YAM officers David Ben-Horin and Oved Sadeh, called for a clever use of Italian uniforms, and close cooperation with IDF/Navy warships. Ben-Horin and Sadeh aboard a rented fishing vessel, followed *Argero* and boarded her disguised as Italian Naval Officers. They assumed command of the vessel, but when near Crete surrendered *Argero* to two 'enemy' IDF/Navy ships (I.N.S. *Wedgewood* and *Haganah*) which had appeared 'fortuitously'. On 26 August 1948, the final crate of weaponry was transferred from the *Argero* to the IDF/Navy; and on 29 August, the 8,000 rifles and 8,000,000 rounds of ammunition reached Haifa.

At this time the IDF/Navy deployed two 'naval commando' units; the frogman unit commanded by Yosef Dror, and a 'sabotage craft unit' commanded by Yochai Ben-Nun, employing Italian MTM-type explosive craft, which carried 250 kilograms of high-explosives. The sabotage craft unit underwent intensive manoeuvres on the Sea of Galilee, and then were transferred to the port of Yaffo to receive instruction from an Italian instructor, Fiorenco Caprioti. Just before the start of Operation 'Yoav' (a 5-brigade IDF offensive – 5–12 October– commanded by Yigal Allon, which expelled the Egyptians from the Negev), the unit intensified its training efforts, preparing to attack Egyptian naval vessels in the area, although none were found. On 21 October, the Israeli fleet (consisting of four ships, and which ferried the naval

saboteurs) set out towards Gaza in search for two Egyptian ships, rumoured to be in the area. During the mission, the naval task force received notification of a cease-fire, although one hour later the Egyptian Navy flagship RENS *Emir Farouk* was spotted with an escorting minesweeper. After a series of indecisive messages which ordered then aborted the attack, the final order was finally issued from IDF HQ to attack *Emir Farouk*, 'with indiscriminate force'.

At 21.10 hours, three MTM craft and a collection vessel were discharged from the INS *Maoz*. They were commanded by Yochai Ben-Nun, Zalman Avrahamov, and Ya'akov Vardi; and each headed stealthily towards their intended targets. Ben-Nun, the commander of the operation, ordered Avrahamov to attack *Emir Farouk*, Vardi to attack the minesweeper, and he would later decide which target required *his* deadly load. The saboteurs wore infrared reflectors upon their khaki caps, and would be picked up in mid-water by the collection vessel, equipped with special visual devices.

Avrahamov aimed his MTM at *Emir Farouk* and headed point-blank for his target. Although unable to release himself from the speeding MTM, with the floatation device, he managed to jump off moments before *Emir*

▲ A mobile convoy from the GIVA'ATI Infantry Brigade's élite 54th Battalion SHU'ALEI SHIMSHON ('Samson's Foxes') reconnaissance force, 1948. A direct descendant of the British Long Range Desert Group, the heavily armed, jeep-mounted SHU'ALEI SHIMSHON proved deadly to Egyptian forces, particularly in the Faluja Pocket. (IDF Archives)

Farouk took a direct hit and began to list towards one side. Vardi (for an unknown reason) also directed his craft towards *Emir Farouk*, and also encountered difficulties releasing himself from the MTM, even though the explosive mechanism's three-minute timer had already been activated. Egyptian sailors aboard the listing *Emir Farouk* meanwhile directed fire at Vardi. He accelerated his craft, jumped without the floatation device, and a second explosive missile hit the *Emir Farouk*. Ben-Nun now directed his efforts against the minesweeper, but found himself the target of concentrated Egyptian machine-gun fire. Courageously he continued towards the target, and although he too encountered difficulties, managed to free himself in time, and the minesweeper took a direct hit. At 23.10 hours, the 'sabotage craft unit' returned to the safety of the INS *Maoz*. 25 years later to the day, Brigadier-General

(Res.) Yochai Ben-Nun would lead a similarly spectacular 'naval commando' mission against an Egyptian *Komar Fac* in the Red Sea.

Although the PAL'MACH, and its subordinate units had been an integral element in Israel's victory in the 1948 War of Independence, plans for its demobilization had been under way for some time. Israel's first Prime Minister and Defence Minister David Ben-Gurion feared that separate military organizations threatened the bond which held the Jewish state together; and indeed the PAL'MACH was an 'independent' combat formation. It had its HQ and intelligence organization separate and independent from that of the IDF, and its fighters considered themselves to be far superior to their HI'SH and IDF counterparts. Already in the newly created state there had been sentiments of civil war between the IDF and the IRGUN following the *Atalena* incident (in which an IRGUN ship ferrying immigrants and arms was ordered to be shelled off the Tel Aviv coast with heavy casualties). Israel desperately needed a unifying military entity capable of closing the ranks and protecting the frontiers. Most importantly, Ben-Gurion feared the politicization of the IDF, especially by PAL'MACH officers, many of whom leaned to the political left. Many PAL'MACHNIKs supported the MA'PA'M Party (an amalgamated left-wing party opposed to Ben-Gurion's MA'PA'I party), and a potential political threat by an élite military force would have perilous consequences for the infant Jewish state. On 15 October 1948, after intense and heated political debate, PAL'MACH HQ was ordered to disband.

The PAL'MACH clearly contributed to its own demise by being such an élite and independent entity. Although it was *not* the force of singing partisans, dressed in khaki that folklore has created (morale in many PAL'MACH units since 1945 was dangerously low, and many soldiers even deserted!), it was the best the Jews could field at the time. Nevertheless, many top PAL'MACH officers, including Yigal Allon, believed that PAL'MACH HQ should have been retained as the command of a special operations force directly responsible to the IDF Chief of Staff. The nation-building importance of a PAL'MACH-type force had not been overlooked, however, and a new unit called NA'HA'L (Hebrew acronym for 'Fighting Pioneer Youth') was created as an apolitical IDF force to mandate Ben-Gurion's dream of an 'army of farmers'.

Independence did not bring peace to Israel's frontiers; and the vacuum created by the PAL'MACH's disappearance as 'role model' effected IDF performance, which in 1949 was dismal at best. Although Ben-Gurion had dreamed of an egalitarian society without 'élite', military realities across Israel's frontiers dictated the contrary.

2

THE LEGENDS ARE BORN
The Paratroops, 1948–67

THE FIRST YEARS: 1949–53

ACHAREI HATZANHANIM – 'AFTER THE PARATROOPERS'

The Paratroops' Banner

IN 1942 HAGANAH commander Eliyahu Golomb proposed the formation of a 100-man Airborne PAL'MACH detachment to jump deep into Europe in a desperate attempt to save as many Jews from the death camps as possible. The British refused to sponsor this company-size force, offering to support only a token sized unit. Although there had been other British trained 'Israeli' paratroopers, mainly PAL'MACHNIKs from the Balkans and Central Europe, who jumped into Yugoslavia to aid SOE and partisan operations, this force's primary objective was to establish Jewish underground and resistance movements in Roumania, Hungary, and Slovakia, and to assist escaping Allied pilots and POWs, A total of 240 PAL'MACH and HAGANAH fighters volunteered for the force, though only 32 (including three women) were finally chosen. They were subjected to intensive parachutist, commando and intelligence training by British and HAGANAH instructors, and were issued with British uniforms and rank insignias to be worn in the event of capture. These would be of little avail.

Some of the paratroopers succeeded in their tasks. The first to go, Peretz Rosenberg, jumped with a British detachment into the Yugoslav mountain region of Chernagora and even reached the HQ cave of Tito himself. Others met with tragic fates. Hannah Szenes from KIBBUTZ Sdot Yam was captured as she crossed the Yugoslav frontier into her native Hungary. Dragged off to Gestapo headquarters in Budapest, she was subjected to brutal torture, and executed. In all twelve paratroopers were captured and seven killed, including Abba Berditchev, captured in Slovakia and put to death in the Mauthausen concentration camp; Enzo Sereni in Italy, and Haviva Reik, captured and killed and in her native Slovakia. Although

they did not save one Jew from the gas chambers, theirs was a mission which broke through the desperate barrier of hopelessness.

The order to establish an IDF paratroop force was issued on 10 May 1948. At a secret meeting held at PAL'MACH HQ, Yigal Yadin (HAGANAH Operations commander), Aharon Remez (Air Force OC), and Yisrael Galili (a senior HAGANAH commander) decided to form a paratroop/commando type force capable of executing special operations deep behind enemy lines. Two PAL'MACH companies were to be the nucleus of this force, but their removal from the front lines was militarily impossible. Nevertheless, on 3 June 1948 (four days after the Israel Defence Force declared its existence), Air Force HQ ordered the opening of a paratroop jump school at the Ramat David airfield. The IDF did not maintain sufficient manpower for an operational training school so it was decided to open a jump course in a most unlikely location.

Since the end of the Second World War, Czechoslovakia had been the only country openly assisting Zionist aspirations with moral support and arms supplies. Czech arms secured the success of Operation 'NACHSHON', and the first IDF/Air Force combat fighters were Czech AVIA 199s. Czechoslovakia was also the main HAGANAH, RECHESH and MOSSAD 'operations centre' in Europe, especially in the recruiting of overseas and refugee volunteers willing to fight for Israel. Captain Haim Guri, the PAL'MACH's noted poet, commanded the Czech Operation, and organized a force made up of volunteers from Central Europe, the United States, and Palestine. After careful physical and psychological scrutiny, forty volunteers were selected, and their training took place at a former SS base in the Carpathian Mountains.

▲ Graduates of the HAGANAH's parachutist course in Czechoslovakia; now fully-fledged TZANHANIM in the Israel Defence Forces, parade for inspection prior to a training jump in 1950. (IDF Archives)

The first phase of the training concerned weapons, sabotage and communications. This was followed by the long-awaited 'jump' proudly witnessed by Yisrael Galili, and other HAGANAH and IDF officials. The course lasted four weeks (some personnel remained behind in Czechoslovakia on a parachute rigging course), and included three jumps, and squad and platoon level exercises. One of the most important elements of the course was an introduction to the brief though impressive history of airborne forces during the Second World War, and the campaigns of Crete, Normandy, and Arnhem were studied religiously. The graduates of the course joined other volunteers in Israel, and on 2 September 1948, IDF Directive No. 87 ordered the formal establishment of YECHIDAT HATZANHANIM, or 'Paratroop Unit', which numbered 28 officers and 238 men.

The man chosen by IDF Chief of Staff, Lieutenant General Ya'akov Dori, to lead this first paratroop unit was Yoel Palgi. In 1944, Palgi had parachuted into Yugoslavia, and crossed the border into his native Hungary. He was arrested by the Gestapo, interrogated, tortured, and sent to the gas chambers. He escaped, and returned to Budapest where he joined the Jewish underground. Palgi remained in Europe after the war, serving the MOSSAD until 1948 when he was sent to South Africa to recruit pilots and aircraft.

YECHIDAT HATZANHANIM was initially composed of three distinct elements: IDF volunteers, foreign volunteers (including many non-Jews from America, France, South Africa and Belgium), and the 'Czech Brigade'. Their first home was the former British commando base at Ahuza on the slopes of Mt Carmel. The international character of the unit created unique espirit de corps; the foreign volunteers displaying exceptional skill and morale. Most notable of the 'Jewish Foreign Legion' were the jump instructors: French Captain Shocoran, whose Hebrew vocabulary consisted of the three words 'who's drinking wine?'; the Austrain Jews Karl Kahane, ex-LRDG and ex-SAS, and Marciel Tuvias, ex-Austrian Army and French Foreign Legion. The battle-hardened, patriotically inspired PAL'MACHNIK veterans were also of exceptional stock, but the unit suffered from serious difficulties. Training conditions at the Ahuza base were primitive, equipment was second-hand (including the British X-Type parachutes on their way to the shirt factory), while the C-46 Commando pilots (American volunteers) had dubious experience.

The paratroopers' second Israeli training jump on 16 November 1948 was marked by the tragic death of Captain Itamar Golani. A PAL'MACH veteran (he had commanded a squad in the June 1946 radar raid on Mt Carmel), Golani was considered an outstanding officer with a promising career ahead of him. His death served to show how little faith many volunteers had in their new-found 'élite' unit. Other training fatalities led many to reconsider their participation in the unit, and morale reached a dangerously low level. The aborting of a proposed jump into El Arish during the closing stages of the 1948 War led the most combat-able among the force to lose heart. They saw their participation as an exercise in futility and many requested immediate transfer. Commanders soon lost control, military discipline vanished and chaos reigned throughout the

▶ The paratroops' second and most influential commander, Major Yehuda Harari, proudly stands by a C-47 transport during a distribution of wings ceremony (MISDAR KNAFAYIM) at Tel Nof. (IDF Archives)

Ahuza base. Realizing that he had failed in his task, Palgi resigned his command.

In March 1949, Chief of Staff Dori summoned Yehuda Harari, a captain in the 7th Armoured Brigade, to his headquarters in Tel Aviv. The bespectacled Dori told Harari: 'The paratroops are dying, and something has to be done immediately!', and Harari was *volunteered* into the paratroops! The Hungarian-born Harari had reached Palestine as a refugee in 1938. He joined IRGUN, and volunteered for the British Army in 1940. He served with the Jewish Brigade's 2nd Battalion where he proved his worth as a courageous soldier, and an exemplary leader. Following the war, he was part of Haim Laskov's (a company commander in the 2nd Battalion) 'Vengeance Unit' which hunted down Nazi criminals throughout Europe. During the 1948 fighting, Harari served as a company commander in the 7th Brigade, and was severely wounded on 31 May 1948 at the Latrun bloodletting.

Harari was disgusted by what he found when he reached Ahuza in April 1949. There was no guard at the gate, the perimeter fence was barely standing, and the base was littered with rubbish. Most of the paratroopers were either working at the Haifa shipyards (where they held jobs by day, returning to Ahuza at night for a hot meal and a place to sleep), or carousing at a Women's Corps base nearby. Those who remained in camp were either drunk or sitting half-naked playing pinochle. Harari's response was immediate. Of the 400 paratroops at Ahrza only a dozen or so officers, jump instructors, and riggers were retained.

In May 1949 Harari erased all traces of Palgi's organization. He realized that the formation of a paratroop force depended on its élite character forged from the successful mastering of jump and fighting techniques. To achieve this, discipline, and command would be of paramount importance. The insolence and neglect that had been the norm at Ahuza was over. Harari was a stern officer, whose 'battlefield' justice was legendary. To deter the numerous thefts and fights characteristic of the unit, Harari challenged the largest and most notorious soldier to a 'fair fight' behind the base canteen. Harari gave no quarter, severely beating the hapless man. Discipline in the paratroops was soon secure!

Jump instruction was given meticulous attention. Harari's chief jump instructor was a British volunteer named David Apple (an alias), who had run the SOE jump school in Yugoslavia, and who many believed to be a British agent! The paratroops moved from Ahuza to the Tel Nof airfield near Rehovot, and began to take the job seriously. Although the facilities at Tel Nof were primitive and neglected, the force of zealous 'soldiers of the sky' managed to get the base operational in days, while the Air Force provided their precious few C-46 and C-47 transports for jump training. In an impressive military ceremony on the Tel Nof tarmac in January 1950, the graduates of the first IDF jump instructor's course were awarded the coveted

---

▼ Having saved his life in one of the all-too-frequent accidents which plagued the paratroops' first years, Yeshayahu Dor (left) shakes the hand of Sami Rafael. Following the mishap, both men jumped again to instil confidence into the ranks of new volunteers looking on. (IDF Archives)

white and black cloth parachutist wings by Prime Minister Ben-Gurion.

In November 1950, the General Staff decided to upgrade the company size unit to a battalion, designated the 890th Airborne Infantry (Paratroop) Battalion. The expansion presented Harari with a severe manpower problem. At the time, the cream of Israel's youth tended to volunteer into NA'HA'L infantry units, while the paratroops generally received new immigrants, and 'second-class' conscripts. For the 890th to become a crack force, it would need not only qualified jump instructors, but daring young men commanded by courageous officers. After careful thought, Harari gave all IDF officers the opportunity to undergo jump training, where one could 'sharpen physical fitness as well prove one's courage'. Harari knew that the adventure parachuting offered would entice the type of commander he was looking for, and indeed many soon volunteered. In January 1951, Harari's 'A' Company was joined by a newly formed 'B' Company; though the battalion could still muster only 180 fighters.

Attempts to forge the 890th into an élite unit proceeded slowly. Several training jumps ended in tragedy, or in near fatal accidents, when heroic efforts were made to retrieve dangling comrades from the tails of C-47s. Such incidents did little to enhance the élite image the force was supposed to maintain. Equipment was still second-rate, and jumping

in the inherited British practice of using only one parachute was taking its toll of the small force. Nevertheless, Harari recruited, and received Class A material. Under the disciplinarian control of ex-Legionaire, Marciel Tuvias (who had killed a British soldier in the Western Desert after being called a 'dirty Jew'), all basic trainees underwent a brutal indoctrination into the battalion. Its physical aspect was the most difficult, as long forced marches were conducted daily. In fact, Harari actively sought athletes, wrestlers, boxers, and 'thugs' for the battalion. It would be the top-quality officers volunteering for the paratroops that would secure its élite and legendary status.

In 1952 'A' Company jumped in the course of large-scale exercises. The paratroopers conducted their mission brilliantly, reaching their target and destroying it quickly and effectively. In the field, however, operational assignments given to the 890th often ended in confusion. There was little coordination among the paratroopers, and command echelons, and they were often issued equipment

---

▼ Officers from the 890th Paratroop Battalion pose for a group portrait in 1953. Major Harari (seated, third from right in bottom row) is flanked by two of his Second World War veteran officers who helped shape the TZANHANIM's image: Karl Kahana (bottom row, second from right), and Marciel Tuvias (second from left). (IDF Archives)

such as parachute harnesses and heavy mortars for routine patrols along sensitive border areas. These incidents clearly illustrated to many the dire need for the General Staff to declare the military objectives of the 890th. While Harari envisaged the creation of an IDF version of the US 82nd and 101st Airborne Divisions, many top IDF officers intended the paratroopers to emulate a post-independence version of Wingate's SNS; an élitist force of cross-border raiders.

Clearly the military threat of cross-border infiltration into Israel had been a decisive factor behind this debate in military disposition. In 1952 alone, there were more than 3,000 border incidents involving Arab *fedayeen* (guerrillas) crossing into Israel from the Syrian, Jordanian and Egyptian frontiers. The paratroops, the best equipped, trained, and paid of the IDF combat units, found themselves incapable of dealing with the threat this infiltration posed.

From the summer of 1952 until January 1953, the paratroops engaged Jordanian forces along the Jerusalem border in a covert campaign of sniping and ambushes. They were backed up by large formations from the GIVA'ATI, and GOLANI Infantry Brigades which were unable to force a decisive engagement. Their efforts were hindered by constricting regulations which screened 'official'

IDF involvement. The men were ordered to wear civilian clothing, carry weapons not traceable to the IDF, and were forbidden to pursue the infiltrators into their own territory. Operation 'OFRA' (25–26 January 1953) marked the opening of the large-scale paratroop retaliatory raids. The operation, in concert with a force of GIVA'ATI infantrymen, attacked the Jordanian villages of Falma and Eidna in the Hebron Hills. The attack was intended as a warning to Jordanian authorities and local civilians of the consequences of supporting the *fedayeen*, but the IDF force failed to achieve total surprise and the attack failed. Harari had trained his men for operations deep behind enemy lines, *not* for small cross-border penetration raids which was what the IDF needed at this time; Harari's methods and his mandate were threatened.

Harari's tactical vision of large-scale paratroop operations were cancelled by the military threat the *fedayeen* posed. Instead, a small guerrilla-type force for cross-border retaliatory raids, similar to those carried out by the SNS, was established for commando operations. This force was to be made up almost exclusively of young volunteers from the agricultural cooperatives, whose love for the land would motivate them to perform spectacular feats on the battlefield.

THE LEGEND OF 'UNIT 101'

THERE had been several attempts to organize small, specifically tasked, élite units similar to the NODEDOT and SNS. The main catchments for such units were among the 'minority' soldiers (Bedouins, Druze, and Circassians) who, during the 1948 War, had displayed the resolve to fight for the Jewish state. During Operation 'YIFTACH' (May 1948) an Arab unit from the Bedouin tribe of Arab el-Heib joined the PAL'MACH in its offensive against Safed and Rosh Pina, while Circassians were recruited into the GOLANI Brigade's BARAK Battalion. Following the war, the minorities continued to volunteer for the IDF, where they served in 'UNIT 300', a small scout force positioned in the Negev Desert, where their inherited skills of tracking and navigation were maximized. Their main operations were against Bedouin criminal gangs infiltrating into Israel from Jordan and the Sinai Desert.

Another attempt to form an SNS-type unit was a mysterious, short-lived SAYERET or reconnaissance formation known as 'UNIT 30'. This was the brainchild of Moshe Dayan (then attached to IDF Southern Command) and was intended to be a special operations force dedicated to long-range reconnaissance patrols, securing Israel's eastern frontier in the Hebron Hills and Negev Desert. As opposed to the paratroops, 'UNIT 30' was made up completely of conscripts who served in the unit from day one in the IDF to their release from active service three years later. This insured unit cohesion, and a masterful knowledge of the terrain they would patrol.

The unit's ranks were drawn from conscripts who had volunteered for other units (such as Pilot's Course and the Paratroops), and whose pre-military psycho-technical examination scores had been exceptional. On a blistering summer's day in August 1951, a military truck carrying thirty soldiers wearing work clothes arrived at the Beit Jubrin Police Fort, the training base for IDF Southern Command. A young officer awaiting the truck ordered the soldiers to leave their kitbags behind, to lie flat on the sand and crawl! The soldiers intuitively followed the command, not realizing that their finish line was more than 200 metres away. 'UNIT 30' was born.

▼ 'UNIT 101' veterans, now senior NCOs in the 890th Paratroop Battalion, exchange battle stories on a captured Arab Legion Land-Rover near Hebron, 1954. (IDF Archives)

The 200-metre crawl was the beginning of a brutally intensive training routine which lasted for four months. It consisted of weapons proficiency, squad combat instruction, demolition, sharpshooting, mountain and urban combat, and infiltration; and was concluded by parachute jump training. 'UNIT 30' was a neglected entity, however, and not one senior commander observed or supervised its training. The sergeants ran the course using discarded British commando manuals and training films. To insure an élite status, the 30 soldiers were not issued with the regular issue Sten guns and Czech K98 Mauser rifles, but carried Finnish Suomi M1931 9mm submachine-guns with 71-round drum magazines, Bren guns, and 2-inch mortars. They had no issue uniforms, but wore local Arab garb and camouflage uniforms purchased on the black market.

From 1951 to 1952, Arab infiltrators freely crossed into Israel, and carried out numerous acts of theft, sabotage, and murder against the agricultural settlements of the area. 'UNIT 30' was sent in, and together with its Bedouin, Druze, and Circassian scouts (borrowed from 'UNIT 300' and a similar unit in Southern Command known as YECHIDAT SHAKED, or 'Almond Unit'), they ousted heavily armed Bedouin squatters, as well as conducting numerous cross-border raids interdicting infiltrator and smuggler routes inside Jordan. 'UNIT 30' also operated as an intelligence and counter-intelligence force, conducting topographical surveys from the River Jordan to Gaza, as well as pursuing Egyptian military intelligence agents on both sides of the border. Their largest operation was a retaliatory raid against the Jordanian port city of Aqaba, and they were also involved in the defence of the adjacent Israeli port city of Eilat. The IDF General Staff did not know how to develop or utilize the unique talents and motivations of 'UNIT 30', and Southern Command disbanded the 28 fighters (two had fallen in battle) in late 1952. 'UNIT 30' was the IDF's first attempt to form an élite fighting force capable of cross-border preventive and retaliatory operations. It was an experiment which led to the creation of the IDF's most famous, and least understood, commando force, 'UNIT 101'.

The man who invented 'UNIT 101' was Colonel Mishael Shaham, Commander of the 16th Jerusalem (Reserve) Brigade. His vicinity had been hardest hit by the Arab guerrilla attacks, and the practised response of complaining to the United Nations did little to prevent enemy activity. Shaham raised the notion of developing a retaliatory strike force capable of dealing with the Arab bandits, but officers (Operations Chief Dayan included) indifferent to the questionable successes of 'UNIT 30' balked at the idea. Undaunted, Shaham appealed to Ben-Gurion, and Ben-Gurion contacted Dayan. The go-ahead for the force was issued.

In August 1953, Shaham summoned 25-year-old reserve Major Ariel 'Arik' Sharon from his studies at Jerusalem's Hebrew University. Sharon had been a platoon commander in the ALEXANDRONI Brigade's 32nd Battalion and had been severely wounded in the Battle of Latrun. The burly Sharon was a known 'maverick'. His intelligent, though boisterous and overbearing personality was legendary; and perfect for the command he was about to receive. Shaham explained to him that his services were needed to help destroy the home of a notorious Arab murderer (Mustapha Samueli) in the Jordanian village of Nebi Samuel (6 kilometres north-west of Jerusalem). Shaham told the young major, 'There are those that study the feats of others, and the others will study yours!'

For the raid on Nebi Samuel, Sharon selected seven men, all friends from the 1948 War and from the university, whose fighting ability and trust he held in high regard. Most notable of these were Shlomoh Baum, a Company NCO of the GOLANI Brigade's small recon force; Yosef Sa'adiah, a former PAL'MACH sapper, and Yitzhak Ben-Menahem (nicknamed 'Gulliver'), a childhood and university friend of Sharon's who had served with him in the 32nd Battalion. After careful observation of Nebi Samuel from the safety of Camp Schneller in Jerusalem, the 'Seven' set out with their Thompson submachine-guns, grenades, commando knifes, and Molotov Cocktails. They reached the village undetected, and set their explosive device by Samueli's door. The TNT proved ineffective, however, exploding with a thud but causing little damage. Discovered, the 'Seven' improvised, throwing grenades into the house, and raking it with .45 calibre fire before withdrawing. They crossed back into Israeli territory, raised glasses, and commented on their 'lovely night's outing'.

Shaham reported to Prime Minister David Ben-Gurion, who after studying the fallout from Nebi Samuel, authorized Chief of Staff Mordechai Makleff to form a retaliatory strike force to conduct top-secret operations for the General Staff. On 5 August 1953 'UNIT 101' (a direct reference to the US Army's 101st Airborne Division) was established, commanded by Major Sharon, and to be manned by only fifty fighters.

'UNIT 101' began with four reservists (including Baum, who would be appointed as Sharon's deputy and 'Gulliver'), all 1948 War veterans who would command 'sections', or squads of conscripts, mainly KIBBUTZNIKIM and MOSHAVNIKIM dissatisfied with service in the paratroops or NA'HA'L. The unit's first conscript volunteer was also its most famous: the ex-NA'HA'L scout, Meir Har-Zion. Prior to his joining the NA'HA'L in 1952, Har-Zion was known regularly to short cut through Jordanian territory on trips from Jerusalem to the oasis at Ein Gedi. He was considered a natural in the field, a tracker of supreme talent who at the age of eighteen had already obtained a reputation throughout the IDF. Volunteers soon brought in other volunteers. Ex-paratroopers, ex-armour soldiers, and ex-'UNIT 30' fighters rushed to the new unit where military unconventionalities were the accepted norm. Sharon also 'threw in' a few ex-PAL'-MACHNIKs to balance things out.

The unit was divided into four-man 'recon sections',

each commanded by an officer or senior NCO. Physical, mental, and combat training was intensive, with round-the-clock sabotage, judo instruction and forced marches by night which often strayed into enemy territory. Their base at Camp Staph near Jerusalem was set up as an Arab village, so that the fighters could familiarize themselves with the physical appearance of an enemy target. Camp Staph also resembled a 'Wild West' town. Groups of unkept men with weapons roamed the perimeter, while explosions were heard around the clock. Pigeons made ideal moving targets, and the concept of exploding grenades in empty oil drums allowed many to witness their destructive effect. The favoured weapon of the unit was the 'Tommy Gun', its large calibre and harsh recoil providing as 'macho' a weapon as could be found in a submachine-gun. The familiarization of the soldier's personal weapon was a most important training objective for the unit. It was no secret to Sharon and Baum that 90 percent of all soldiers *never* fire weapons in combat, and most of those that do either fire at the sky or into the ground. Sharon wanted his men to know and understand their weapons, to respect them and, most importantly, to hit their targets. The dozens of dead birds, punctured ration tins, and shattered beer bottles which littered Camp Staph were a testament to the proficient use of those weapons. Cold killing, and the use of knives, clubs and fists were also given due place. The fighters of 'UNIT 101' quickly learned that 'war is not for vegetarians'.

The informal environment at Camp Staph led many to consider 'UNIT 101' as an undisciplined force. The men wore civilian and or non-issue military clothing, they favoured sandals, did not sport military haircuts, and most boasted 'wild beards'. There were no standard conducts of military discipline either, as officers, NCOs, and the lower ranks enjoyed a working relationship similar to a friendship. There was no saluting, no parading, and very little attention to the spit and polish Harari had instituted into the 890th Battalion. 'UNIT 101' was, however, a highly disciplined fighting force, in which every man knew his combat role. As a commander, on the other hand, Sharon was an interesting paradox. Although he demanded, and received the absolute loyalty and respect of his men, he *rarely* displayed the same to his superiors. It was common for Sharon to yell obscenities at or about senior IDF officers and government officials. Ever since the terrible Israeli military blunders at Latrun (at which Sharon was wounded and lost many of his men), he held 'pencil-pushing' commanders in great contempt. This bitterness was much to the taste of the fighters of 'UNIT 101', who viewed Sharon 'as one of the boys'. Sharon nevertheless expected much of his men, and two unwritten laws existed in 'UNIT 101': no one 'returned' to base if a mission had not been carried out, and each operation required a descriptive and honest report. The reward for observing these rules was a feast of delicacies provided to each returning patrol.

Three weeks after the order to establish 'UNIT 101', 25

of its fighters set out for its first large-scale operation. The plan called for two sections (commanded by Sharon and Baum) to attack the El-Breij Refugee Camp in the Gaza Strip and eliminate a guerrilla force, while a third section commanded by Shmuelik Merchav went to destroy the house of Colonel Mustapha Hafez, the head of Egyptian Military Intelligence in the area, and controller of *fedayeen* activity in the region. One member of the attack force, Shmuel Falah, objected to raiding a refugee camp with 6,000 inhabitants, claiming it was against the TOHAR HANESHEK ('purity of arms') ethic he had been taught so zealously in the PAL'MACH. Not allowing dissention to grow, Sharon attached Falah to the section heading for Hafez's house.

On the night of Saturday, 30 August 1953, Sharon and Baum's sections reached the camp's perimeter. Sharon quickly silenced one of the guards (breaking the butt of his French MAS-49 carbine in the process), and the attack began. Sharon and Har-Zion raced through the pitch-black alleys, wiping out a machine-gun position with their bare hands, as both Sharon's carbine, and Har-Zion's Thompson failed to operate. The other sections fired into houses suspected of harbouring guerrillas. Baum meanwhile had set an ambush on the Khan Yunis-Gaza road, to block the expected Egyptian counter-attack. After the night's damage had been inflicted, Sharon ordered his unit to break contact, and head back to Israeli territory, while he and Har-Zion secured their withdrawal. On the Israeli border, a command car from 'UNIT 101' eagerly awaited the fighters' return.

That same night, Merchav, Falah and 'Miki' the sapper reached Colonel Hafez's HQ in Gaza and destroyed the building with explosives, but Colonel Hafez was not at home. In July 1956 A'MAN (AGAF MODE'IN or IDF Military Intelligence) operatives assassinated Colonel Hafez in the course of a meticulous operation.

Almost every night 'UNIT 101' crossed the border freely into Egypt or Jordan, conducting reconnaissance and retaliatory operations. Before the incorporation of electronic detection devices, field radars, and infra-red vision equipment, 'UNIT 101' made the night their own. Successful patrols and retaliatory raids increased the unit's combat expertise, as well as self-confidence. The raid on El-Breij had established their reputation as excellent fighters, but there were many in the IDF who questioned whether 'UNIT 101' could operate with the same success against conventional forces. The doubters would soon have their answer. On the night of 12/13 October 1953, a group of infiltrators threw a hand-grenade into the house of the Kanias family in the border town of Yahud. Two children (2-year-old Reuven and 18-month-old Shoshana), were killed, the remaining family members severely wounded. Their deaths brought the number of victims murdered by infiltrators from Jordan to 124, since the armistice agreement signed with Jordan in 1949. Israel *had* to retaliate and a large raid was authorized which combined the services of 'UNIT 101' and the 890th Battalion's

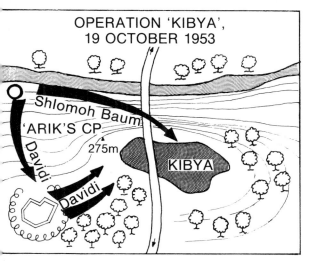

'B' Company commanded by ex-PAL'MACHNIK, Captain Aharon Davidi. The eventual meeting of minds between Sharon and Davidi would change the role of paratroops forever. Sharon would become the true leader of the 890th, Davidi his loyal pupil, and the paratroops, the IDF's cutting edge.

The target chosen was the village of Kibya, but two kilometres from the Israeli border. Intelligence reports claimed the attackers had originated from Kibya, and the villagers would now pay the price. It was, however, home to 2,000 civilians and defended by thirty Jordanian soldiers concentrated in two heavily fortified positions. For Operation 'Shoshana', Sharon (the mission's overall commander) enlisted the services of 103 paratroopers and 'UNIT 101' fighters divided into six attack sections: (A) a 'UNIT 101' force of twenty men led by Baum was to 'hit' Kibya from the east; (B) a strike force of twenty paratroopers commanded by Davidi which would break through western Kibya, neutralizing the Jordanian firing position; (C) a forty-man paratroop sapper force, equipped with 700 kilograms of high-explosives; (D) a blocking force of five 'UNIT 101' fighters which would prevent a Jordanian counter-attack from Budrus, while also preventing the civilians from fleeing; (E) an advance reconnaissance section of five 'UNIT 101' fighters commanded by Meir Har-Zion, which would later block off eastern Kibya; and (F) the support force of 'UNIT 101' fighters, providing artillery cover with 120mm mortars.

On the night of 14 October, the 103 soldiers gathered in the Ben-Shemen woods. Davidi's company was made up mainly of new immigrant conscripts from North Africa who had yet to be tested in battle. To raise his men to battle pitch, Davidi read excerpts from the newspaper AL-HAMISHMAR recounting the murder at Yahud. These soldiers were only too familiar with Arab brutality in their native lands, and in a frenzy, they raised their clenched fists and shouted vengeance. Sharon, Baum, Har-Zion and the men from 'UNIT 101' looked on at the display in silence.

Har-Zion's section crossed the border first, heading towards the nearby village of Shukba to set up an ambush. In an olive grove forty metres from Kibya, a father and son looking after their crops were spotted. To kill the two would be murder, so Har-Zion tied them up and gagged them, but they managed to free themselves and ran screaming into the darkness. The Israelis gave chase but lost them. In the end, they fired their weapons and awakened the village. Har-Zion would have to sit tight in the grove, and race towards Shukba only once the Kibya attack was under way. For two hours, Har-Zion engaged the confused villagers and army regulars in brief unyielding fire-fights. At 02.00 hours he led his men back across the border into Israel. Har-Zion blamed the 'failure' on himself, but Sharon greeted him as a hero, proudly proclaiming the operation at Kibya a victory. An ambush was never needed at Shukba.

Baum on the other hand led his forces fully prepared for a fierce battle; he was carrying eighteen hand-grenades, ten 'Tommy Gun' magazines, and two Molotov Cocktails. The force entered Kibya from the east, utilizing Bangelore torpedoes to break through the thick barbed wire which surrounded the village. The force encountered heavy small arms fire, but managed to seize the village, while Davidi's paratroopers neutralized the Jordanian machine-gun nest in the western approaches. The sappers prepared the houses for demolition while the 'UNIT 101' fighters assembled the villagers, sending them off to the neighbouring hamlet of Budrus. So many villagers had fled Kibya at the beginning of Har-Zion's encounter, that the attack force believed the village empty, and no effort was made to search the houses thoroughly. In the course of two hours, 45 homes (mainly of the rich and influential) were destroyed. No cries were heard from the rubble, and the attack force returned to Israeli territory at dawn. Sharon issued the official report claiming that between 8–12 Arabs had been killed in the operation.

The next morning, the nation of Israel awoke to the news that 69 men, women and children had been killed in cold blood in the village of Kibya. Prime Minister Ben-Gurion immediately summoned Sharon and the senior commanders of 'UNIT 101' to his office in Jerusalem. For almost an hour Ben-Gurion interrogated Sharon about his past, family, and ambitions, while questioning the moral character of his soldiers. Ben-Gurion, however was pleased with the events at Kibya, and said: 'It's not important what the rest of the world will say, important is the response of the local Arabs, and in this respect, the operation was a success.' Ben-Gurion later told the world that the assault on Kibya had been carried out by local settlers enraged by the murders at Yahud. No longer would the IDF sit with its hands tied in the face of Arab infiltration and acts of sabotage. The IDF (mainly the paratroops who had just completed their first operational victory) revelled in a glow of self-confidence. The ante of violence in the Arab-Israeli conflict had been raised.

The exoneration of 'UNIT 101' in Ben-Gurion's eyes

led Sharon and his subordinates to feel themselves above the law, even that of the Military Police. On a Friday night in November 1953, three MPs stopped the military vehicle driven by Yitzhak Jibli, an ex-PAL'MACHNIK who had volunteered into Unit 101 as a result of the Kibya raid. He had not yet been issued with uniform or papers, and was taken to MP HQ in Tiberias on the Sea of Galilee. An MP NCO named 'Yitzhak' and four other soldiers greeted Jibli with blows to the head. Jibli identified himself as a 'UNIT 101' fighter, but 'Yitzhak' called the unit a 'girls force' and the beating continued. Jibli managed to reach a telephone, and contacted Camp Staph. Sharon immediately contacted Dayan, and Jibli was released next morning.

When Jibli returned to Camp Staph the following day, his comrades were shocked by the sight of their bruised buddy. After hearing the story in detail they vowed revenge, and Sharon contacted Moshe Dayan. Dayan understood only too well the violent implications of Major Sharon's telephone rampage, and authorized a 'raid' on Military Police HQ, Tiberias 'as long as no one is killed'. Two weeks later, Shlomo Baum led 'UNIT 101' sections towards the intended target. The operation was treated as a raid on an enemy position and was preceded by countless reconnaissance and intelligence-gathering patrols. A fully armed detachment surrounded the base, prepared if necessary to use force on any interfering party, while Baum's attack force broke through and seized control of the building. Jibli identified his attackers, and Master Sergeant 'Yitzhak' and his men received such a savage beating, that they required a week's hospitalization. Ever since the 'Tiberias Incident' IDF combat soldiers have been courted with the respect and consideration their uniforms and deeds deserve.

Although 'UNIT 101' had secured a revered reputation, Arab attacks continued. Responding to the murder of two IDF soldiers near the Jordanian border in December 1953, Sharon dispatched Meir Har-Zion and his 'reconnaissance section' (HULIYAT HASAYRIM) deep into Jordanian territory. Their task: the killing of four policemen outside the central mosque in the biblical town of Hebron, 21 kilometres from Israel. At twilight on 24 December, the four-man section crossed into Jordan to begin their relentless march through the icy Judean Hills. After negotiating the difficult terrain for four hours, the section reached Hebron, where every house concealed at least one rifle! Manoeuvring

slowly in the deep snow, the force was finally discovered before it reached the mosque, and began to fire at any available target. What now appeared to be a suicide mission developed into a confusing fire-fight. After killing several local military personnel, the section disengaged, and raced for the cover of darkness. Four hours later, they had crossed another 21 kilometres, reaching the Israeli border and an anxious Sharon. Hebron was one of 'UNIT 101's most daring exploits, a feat of remarkable self-confidence and physical skill considering the vast territory covered on foot in harsh winter conditions. It was no wonder that 'UNIT 101' was often called 'Arik's Suicide Force'!

By January 1954, the capabilities of 'UNIT 101' had peaked. Their responsibilities had outgrown their small size, and newly appointed Chief of Staff, Lieutenant General Moshe Dayan had long envisaged a merger between 'UNIT 101' and the 890th Battalion; turning 60 commandos into 6,000. In his address to the fighters of 'UNIT 101' informing them of their imminent incorporation into the paratroops, Dayan said: 'Maybe you are the chosen, but it is your responsibility to join forces with the paratroops and show them what the IDF is really about!' Dayan was also adamant as to who should command the enlarged paratroop force, and Major 'Arik' Sharon became the paratroops' third commander.

'UNIT 101' had been existence for only five months, but in that short period it had succeeded in transforming the military perception that the IDF had of itself. It was the first step that was to lead the IDF to favour the formation of élite units. The dozens of reconnaissance units known as SAYEROT were all established in the shadow of 'UNIT 101's meticulous execution of operations, camaraderie, and command. Not since the days of Orde Wingate and the PAL'MACH era had commanders portrayed such devotion and courage to their tasks, and over the men they led in battle. Command was an honour by example only, and it was 'UNIT 101' which transformed the PAL'MACH battle cry of 'Follow Me!' into an IDF institution.

▶ Two paratroop officers discuss the success of their ambush of *fedayeen* terrorists near Gaza, April 1955. (IDF Archives)

FROM BATTALION TO BRIGADE: THE YEARS OF RETRIBUTION, 1954–6

THE incorporation of 'UNIT 101' into the 890th Paratroop Battalion proved to be a most difficult transition. The disciplined paratroopers regarded Sharon's 'ragtag' army as self-glorifing guerrillas; while the paratroops were viewed as mere parade soldiers, smartly dressed in their pressed olive uniforms and red berets! This open animosity was exacerbated by the appointment of Sharon over Harari as battalion commander. Harari had been responsible for upgrading the paratroops into an élite force, and was highly regarded as a commander. His subsequent resignation resulted in mass defections by loyal officers and jump instructors, creating a command vacuum which was quickly handled by Sharon who filled the vacant postings with 'UNIT 101' comrades, and outstanding NA'HA'L officers he actively recruited into the battalion.

'UNIT 101's influence dictated the course of the 890th Battalion; its outstanding combatants and heritage forming a role model against which future standards would be measured. Meir Har-Zion was commissioned without

attending the officer's course (Chief of Staff Dayan correctly argued that sending Har-Zion to 'BA'HA'D 1'-the IDF's Officer Candidate School – was futile, especially since Har-Zion could teach the instructors more than he himself could learn), and with ex-PAL'MACH officers newly arrived from the NA'HA'L (Captains Danni Matt and Sa'idiyah Elkayam) the conventional sized unit retained its 'scouting' character. In addition, commanders such as Yirmi Bardanov (the unit's sapper officer), who remained with the battalion after Harari's departure, proved themselves among the much vaunted '101' and NA'HA'L fighters. Captain Aharon Davidi meanwhile reinforced the conventional nature of the battalion, his often brutal training routine installing a well-defined unit identity. Sharon had difficulties mastering the logistics of command for such a large force, and appointed himself the battalion's 'Foreign Minister', taking contingency plans for retaliatory strikes to the General Staff, and the KNESSET (Israel's Parliament) for approval.

As *fedayeen* attacks into Israel continued, Davidi pre-

pared his battalion for operations. Once government approval reached Tel Nof (home of the 890th Battalion), Davidi raced through the camp, and assembled his kit and soldiers for battle. A famous raid in 1954 was the attack on the Jordanian Legion's camp at A'zun: Operation 'BARUCH I', 29–30 June 1954. Seven paratroopers commanded by Davidi and led by Har-Zion crossed the border, and reached the base after a dangerous march through enemy territory. They attacked the base, throwing grenades at Jordanian soldiers asleep in their tents. During their withdrawal, Yitzhak Jibli was hit in the leg by a .303in bullet, and rendered immobile. Har-Zion and Davidi took turns to carry their injured comrade, but it slowed them dangerously. They were faced with a dilemma: to leave Jibli behind and reach the Israeli frontier, or take the risks and continue with him. In a field decision that would forever influence IDF battlefield behaviour, Davidi (urged on by Jibli's stubborn persistence) left Jibli behind, and he was taken prisoner. Although several subsequent 'Kidnapping' operations secured Jibli's release months later, the lessons of Operation 'BARUCH I' were absolute. Wounded or fallen

▲ With his German MP-40 close at hand, Lieutenant Meir Har-Zion, 'UNIT 101's and the 890th Paratroop Battalion's most famous soldier, briefs men of the battalion's reconnaissance company, SAYERET TZANHANIM, prior to an intelligence-gathering patrol. (IDF Archives)

▶ 890th Paratroop Battalion Commander, Major Ariel 'Arik' Sharon (centre) displays Russian-made weaponry captured by the paratroopers for Chief of Staff, Lieutenant-General Moshe Dayan (right). Lieutenant Har-Zion stands at Major Sharon's right; and attempting to peep at the goings-on is young Captain Rafael 'Raful' Eitan, the paratroops' most famous warrior. (IDF Archives)

soldiers have never since been abandoned on the battlefield, no matter what casualties their retrieval incurred.

In June 1954, Captain Mordechai 'Motta' Gur's NA'HA'L 'D' Company was incorporated into the 890th Battalion. A renowned desert warrior, Gur had gained his reputation for physical strength and courage in the PAL'MACH's HATIVAT HANEGEV, and was considered an

outstanding officer. He made 'D' Company into an élite within an élite, comparable in skill and motivation to the battalion's reconnaissance company (SAYERET TZANHANIM) commanded by Har-Zion, and later by Danni Matt.

In the autumn and winter months of 1954, the battalion carried out frequent large-scale manoeuvres and parachuting became less a display of personal courage, and more a platoon and company-sized affair. Free fall jumps over the Mediterranean were introduced as a 'reward' for outstanding performance, and the city of Ramat Gan even adopted the unit, offering it home-cooked meals, and a strong sense of belonging, absent since the days of the PAL'MACH.

On 28 February 1955, after months of training, aborted missions, and *fedayeen* attacks, the battalion received approval for a large-scale retaliatory strike. Code-named Operation 'CHETZ SHACHOR' (black arrow), a reinforced paratroop force crossed the border and attacked the Egyptian military base at Gaza, together with the adjacent water tower and railway station. Captain Sa'idiyah Elkayam's 'A' Company attacked the military installations, while Gur's 'D' Company took control of the railway station. Securing the assault force was the battalion SAYERET, commanded by Captain Matt.

Operation 'CHETZ SHACHOR' was the first operational test for the newly issued UZI 9mm submachine-guns. The UZI's ease of handling and massive though accurate firepower made it an ideal weapon; but the paratroopers received no artillery support, and the UZI proved itself in the desperate close-quarter fighting that ensued. 'A' Company met with initial difficulties, making a wrong turn and mistakenly attacking the village of Beni Suheila, adjacent to the military installations. During the assault on the camp, Elkayam was killed, and command of both 'A' and 'D' Companies developed on Gur, who ordered the sappers to raze the area. The wounded were carried back to the battalion aid station in an orderly and professional fashion, as was the attack force's withdrawal. Securing the withdrawal was Captain Matt and the SAYERET, whose 'offensive ambush' employing land-mines and high-explosives killed thirty pursuing Egyptian troops. Egyptian President Nasser would later claim that the raid on Gaza prompted an escalation in hostilities which drew his country closer to the Soviet Union. In Israel the para-

▼ Senior paratroop officers pose with the IDF top brass following Operation 'EGED', the raid on the Kuntila Police fort, 28 October 1955. Standing, from the right: OC, Southern Command, Major-General Asaf Simchoni; Musa Efron; Captain Danni Matt; Chief of Staff, Lieutenant-General Moshe Dayan; 890th Battalion Commander, Major 'Arik' Sharon; Lieutenant Meir Har-Zion. Kneeling, from right: Captain 'Raful' Eitan; Ya'akov Ya'akov; Aharon Davidi. (IDF Archives)

troops, and most notably the SAYERET became an overnight sensation. An expanded combat role for the battalion was inevitable.

For the first months of 1955, Gur's 'D' Company conducted numerous, small retaliatory raids against Egyptian military and *fedayeen* targets, but attacks against Israel continued. Responding to a *fedayeen* attack on a water installation near the Gaza Strip on 25 August, Sharon prepared a large-scale operation against the headquarters of the 'Palestine Brigade' (elements of the Egyptian military forces made up of hapless Palestinian volunteers) at Khan Yunis. The main thrust of the operation has originally been entrusted to 'E' Company until the death of its commander Captain Avraham Marcus, killed by an Egyptian land-mine on 28 August as he surveyed the crossing-point. Assuming command of 'E' Company was a 26-year-old reservist Captain named Rafael 'Raful' Eitan. Born in MOSHAV Tel Adahim, a PAL'MACHNIK at the age of 19, 'Raful' served as a platoon sergeant with the HAREL Brigade's élite 4th Battalion, the most battled-scarred of all PAL'MACH units. During the savage battle for Katamon in Jerusalem, he had proved his worth as a fearless and innovative commander. Together with his platoon commander, David 'Dado' Elazar (the IDF's 9th Chief of Staff), 'Raful' set out with 120 men, and returned with a handful of survivors, himself critically wounded. Together with Sharon and Gur, Eitan's appointment to the regular paratroops was to change Israel's military future.

The raid on Khan Yunis, 30 August 1955 (code-named Operation 'Elkayam' in memory of Captain Elkayam killed at Gaza) was the paratroops' first true mechanized operation, deploying from M3 Halftracks. The operation was masterfully executed, and although Gur received a serious leg wound from grenade fragments, the operation resulted in the deaths of 72 Egyptian and Palestinian soldiers, at the cost of one Israeli fatality.

Following two successive raids against Egyptian targets (Operation 'EGED' the raid on Kuntilla on 27 October 1955, where Eitan was awarded the I'TUR HA'OZ decoration for courage for his command under fire, and a major raid on the Egyptian facilities at A-Zabha in Operation 'HA'AR GA'ASH', 2 November), the special talents of the battalion were required up north. On the night of 8/9 December, five paratroopers and GOLANI infantrymen on a covert mission for A'MAN (IDF Military Intelligence) to replace the battery in a listening-post attached to Syrian military lines were captured. Ben-Gurion wanted the men back (one had already committed suicide in the notorious Al-Mazeh prison at Damascus rather than submit to further torture), and the paratroops prepared for action. Syrian artillery harassment of Israeli boats on the Sea of Galilee provided an ideal excuse for punitive measures. On 11 December 1955, the IDF struck.

Operation 'ELI-ZAIT' called for a combined GIVA'ATI and NA'HA'L force led by the paratroops to attack the intricate series of Syrian military fortifications on the eastern bank of the Sea of Galilee; while SAYERET TZANHANIM would

'kidnap' as many Syrian soldiers as they could bring back to Israel. H-Hour was 22.00 hours, and at 16.10 hours Davidi's task force (led by Eitan's 'E' Company, and consisting of a NA'HA'L contingent and a reserve paratroop force commanded by Marciel Tuvias) crossed the muddy fields and the stormy River Jordan into Syria. After crossing the frontier, Eitan split his force into three, and attacked the alerted positions, destroying their barbed wire defences with Bangalore torpedoes. Although many of the fighters were only fresh out of basic training, Eitan rallied them, and in a wild charge against extremely heavy and accurate Syrian fire, they neutralized all the enemy positions with machine-gun and bazooka fire.

'Force 2', commanded by Lieutenant Har-Zion, consisted of the SAYERET and a platoon of NCOs and officers which ran the battalion's basic training commanded by Levi Hofesh. It set out from the banana fields at KIBBUTZ Ein-Gev at 17.45 hours, and in bone-chilling rain reached the target (the 'KURSEI' fortifications) 90 minutes before H-Hour. As Har-Zion's men began to cut through the barbed wire perimeter fence, a Syrian patrol approached, unaware of their uninvited guests. Har-Zion grasped his commando dagger, and prepared to eliminate the patrol, But one of the Israelis fired his rifle accidently and Har-Zion ordered the assault. The SAYERET split into three, Har-Zion headed towards the central pillbox, where he observed three Syrian captains playing cards. A satchel charge was thrown in, and the position was captured minutes later. A squad commanded by Lieutenant Micha Kafusta seized another pillbox with bazooka and rifle-grende fire, while the third force commanded by Lieutenant Oved Ledijinsky seized a third in just two minutes. At 03.00, the SAYERET was ordered back to Israel.

Although Operation 'ELI-ZAIT' resulted in the deaths of six Israeli soldiers (including Captain Yitzhak 'Gulliver' Ben-Menahem, one of 'UNIT 101's original 'seven'), and twelve wounded (included Eitan), the raid was a complete success. Fifty Syrian troops were killed, and 29 taken prisoner. In March 1956, the exchange of POWs between Israel and Syria occurred. Operation 'ELI-ZAIT' was the largest paratroop raid of the period, and its first amphibious deployment. It was also their last operation as a battalion.

By the end of 1955, Lieutenant-Colonel Sharon was in command of a force larger than a battalion. Although standard IDF companies maintained 120 men, Sharon preferred smaller units, and each paratroop company was limited to 60 men. As Sharon insisted, 'In any event, the recon troopers and the commanders attack first taking care of the nasty business. So what's the difference if after them follow one hundred and five or forty-five soldiers?' But by 1956 there was already a reserve paratroop battalion (the 28th, later re-designated the 771st, commanded by Major Yisrael Cohen, one of the commanders of the PAL'MACH's 'Negev Beasts' in 1948), and a third battalion, the NA'HA'L's 88th, was incorporated into the paratroops, commanded by Major 'Motta' Gur. Chief of Staff Dayan

◀ Paratroopers from Major Mordechai 'Motta' Gur's (centre without helmet, on steps) 88th Battalion during Operation 'SHOMRON', the raid on the Jordanian Police fortress at Kilkilya, 10 October 1956; only weeks before the jump at Mitla. The raid was one of the first coordinated actions of the expanded 'UNIT 202', the forbearer of HATIVAT HATZANHANIM. (IDF Archives)

wished to form a paratroop brigade commanded by his protégé, Colonel Rehavam 'Gandhi' Zeevi, but the undaunted Sharon appealed personally to Ben-Gurion who secured his status as 'warlord' of the TZANHANIM. Dayan retaliated by refusing to authorize Sharon command of a 'formal' paratroop brigade (and with it the rank of colonel), but an 'almost' brigade, designated 'UNIT 202'. Major Yitzhak 'Hacka' Hofi (a future IDF Major-General and Chief or MEMUNEH of the MOSSAD), a calculating and obedient officer, was named as Sharon's deputy, and Major 'Raful' Eitan was given command of the 890th Battalion. SAYERET TZANHANIM was given an expanded role as well, and Har-Zion was given the task of transforming his reconnaissance scouts into intelligence-gathering commandos, on 24 hours' alert for 'special' operations.

Har-Zion had little chance to develop the expanded SAYERET. During Operation 'YEHONATAN' (the paratroop raid on the Jordanian Police fort at A-Rawha, 11 September 1956) Har-Zion was struck in the throat by a Jordanian bullet, his life barely saved by dramatic battlefield surgery. The IDF's finest soldier was never able to return to active duty. During the next two weeks, the paratroops conducted two major retaliatory strikes against Jordanian targets.

Operation 'Gulliver' (the 13 September attack on the Jerandel Police Fort), and Operation 'LULAV' (a coordinated attack by the 890th and 88th Battalions against the Hussan Police Fort on 25 September), which resulted in heavy enemy casualties.

The last and largest of the retaliatory strikes was Operation 'SHOMRON', the raid on the Kilkilya Police Fort on the night of 9/10 October 1956. Although by October 1956, the IDF was busy preparing itself for the forthcoming invasion of the Sinal Peninsula, and Britain (Israel's covert partner in the conflict) had warned against further punitive actions against Jordan, a *fedayeen* attack from her territory warranted a harsh military response. For the first time in the paratroops' operational history, they received armour (a unit of AMX-13s), and artillery (a battery of mortars and 25-pounder guns) support. The assault on the police fort was a masterful display of coordination between the 890th and 88th Battalions. After a desperate closequarter battle, the fort was seized and destroyed by the sappers. The heavy combat resulted in the deaths of thirty Jordanians, and eighteen paratroopers. Also killed in the raid was former 890th Battalion sapper officer, Captain Yirmi Barnadov, who only days earlier had been released from active duty. In an all too typical IDF fashion, Yirmi joined his unit of his own accord, and while rescuing injured comrades from a damaged M3 Halftrack, was fatally wounded by Jordanian fire.

Two weeks later, the brigade would be fighting for its life in the inhospitable sands of Sinai. For the TZANHANIM an era had ended.

DEATH IN THE MITLA PASS

ISRAEL'S invasion of the Sinai Desert on 29 October 1956, initiating the 1956 Sinai Campaign or Operation 'KADESH', was a direct product of the *fedayeen* raids, and their subsequent retaliatory responses. The situation on Israel's borders was intolerable, and British and French plans for the Suez Canal provided the catalyst for decisive military action. Planning for the attack had been under consideration for some time. There had been Operation 'YARKON' (on 9 July 1955, six officers from the GIVA'ATI brigade's 51st Battalion had been infiltrated into Sinai, to determine routes of passage throughout the eastern half of the desert peninsula), and the aborted Operation 'OMER' (capturing the strategic Straits of Tiran, seized by Nasser months before). On 5 October 1956, when planning for the invasion was receiving serious scrutiny, Chief of Staff Dayan urged a central task for his 'UNIT 202', which by October 1956 had expanded into the 202nd Paratroop Brigade.

At 13.30 hours on 29 October, Major 'Raful' Eitan reviewed his 890th Battalion at Tel Nof. Wearing their parachutes and carrying their equipment, the men were eager for their forthcoming step into history. Their target, the strategic Mitla Pass (150 kilometres from Israel, and 70 kilometres from the Suez Canal), the gateway towards central Sinai and the Suez Canal. At 16.59 hours, in the amber light of sunset, the sixteen C-47 Dakotas ferrying the battalion broke from their low-level flight pattern, and prepared to discharge their human cargo. When the green light went on, Eitan and his 395 paratroopers jumped from the aircraft. The operation was accompanied by ten IAF Meteors flying close cover.

The battalion landed unopposed, but were five kilometres from their intended drop zone at Parker Memorial (a local landmark). After receiving some congratulatory *a'hawe* (coffee) from unsuspecting Egyptian workmen; Eitan brought his men to the eastern approach to the pass. At 21.30 two 120mm mortars, four 106mm recoilless anti-tank rifles, and eight reconnaissance jeeps were dropped by air. Eitan ordered his men to dig in for the expected Egyptian counter-attack.

The original war plan for Operation 'KADESH' ('KADESH 1') had called for the 890th Battalion (considered the élite of the 202nd Paratroop Brigade) to jump at El-Arish, but its proximity to the Israeli frontier could bring few military rewards. The strategic Mitla Pass on the other hand, facilitated the advance of the main IDF strike force into the Sinai. Originally the 890th was to have jumped at the western entrance to the pass, but aerial reconnaissance photographs had shown some Egyptian military activity. Although a jump at the eastern entrance would initiate the precarious crossing of the pass, Egyptian resistance was not considered serious enough to prevent such an undertaking. To make the jump appear (if discovered) as a mere retaliatory strike, Sharon and the remainder of the 202nd

Paratroop Brigade pre-positioned itself along the Jordanian frontier; offering the Arab Legion the impression of a pending attack. At H-Hour minus 10, the 202nd headed south, crossing into Egyptian territory just as the 890th Battalion's chutes were opening. They were to link-up with Eitan following the successful neutralization of the Egyptian positions at Kuntilla, Themed, and Nakhle. Accompanying the 202nd were two mechanized battalions, field artillery, and a company of AMX-13 light tanks. Time was of the essence, as Colonel Meir Amit (Chief of Operations, and future MOSSAD chief) fully comprehended that Eitan and his men could not withstand a determined Egyptian effort.

On the morning of 30 October, the Egyptian 2nd Infantry Brigade was dispatched to deal with the Israeli intruders; and by noon, the 890th Battalion was being subjected to heavy mortar fire. A few hours later, the Egyptians mounted an uncoordinated infantry assault which was beaten off by accurate fire from Eitan's men, as well as close air support provided by a flight of IAF M.D.450 Ouragans. After dispersing the Egyptian infantrymen, the Ouragans headed towards the Mitla Pass, and destroyed the menacing mortar positions, at the same time attacking vehicles and secondary positions. The flight commander reported that they had hit an entire battalion, and its men were escaping towards the Suez Canal. In fact, only the brigade's senior officers fled, while the remainder of the force deployed in the pass, and prepared well-concealed firing positions to meet the Israeli onslaught.

In the light of the uncertain intelligence available, Eitan dispatched a force from his reconnaissance company commanded by Captain Oved Ledijinsky to scout the pass, only to receive reports of 'heavy enemy military activity'. Eitan decided to sit tight, and await the arrival of the remainder of the 202nd Paratroop Brigade.

At 22.30 hours, the 202nd's mechanized convoys reached Parker Memorial, having fought their way through the desert for 36 hours. Sharon had not been privy to the General Staff's planning of the operation, and was under the impression that the paratroops' task was to reach the Canal at lightning speed. He immediately ordered the brigade to prepare for the assault through the pass, and to the Canal. Lieutenant-Colonel 'Motta' Gur, Commander of the 88th NA'HA'L Battalion, urged Sharon to allow *his* unit to spearhead the breakout, as his men were jealous of the 890th's historic jump. Sharon ordered the advance to commence at 04.30 hours on the 31st, but a telegram from Southern Command forbade him from entering the pass.

Throughout the night of 30/31 October, Southern Command engaged in heated debate with Sharon over strategy. Chief of Staff-Southern Command, Colonel Rehavam Zeevi (Sharon's past rival for command of the 202nd) did not want the brigade to engage in a pointless and costly battle, while Sharon vehemently opposed the futility of having an entire brigade sitting idly in the desert sands. Communications by Morse code were difficult, and in the end Southern Command relented, and permitted Sharon to send in *only* a small patrol. Sharon sent in the entire 88th Battalion, later arguing, 'the paratroops go on patrol as if heading towards major battle'. All subsequent commands were issued in writing and in triplicate, so as to absolve both junior and senior officers from any possible incrimination!

As the NA'HA'L paratroopers passed the 890th's Forward Command Post at the 'Fork Position' near Parker Memorial, Eitan's men grumbled bitterly. It was *their* jump, *their* fight, and now victory was being snatched from *their* grasp. The 88th's lead reconnaissance M3 halftrack commanded by Lieutenant Arik Caspi noticed 'unidentifiable' troops racing along the slopes of the pass, and requested permission to engage. Permission was denied (his company commander insisting that they were 'friendlies' from the 890th Battalion), and the advance into the pass continued. Fifty yards later, Caspi's M3 became the target for hundreds of anti-tank rounds, and small arms fire opened up from all sides. The battle for the Mitla Pass was under way.

Gur, unconvinced as to the strengths and determination of the Egyptian forces, ordered the advance through the pass to continue. Indeed, elements of the 88th Battalion, commanded by deputy brigade commander Yitzhak 'Hacka' Hofi, got four kilometres through and out of the pass, but were unable to make contact with its sister force cut off behind. Egyptian fire intensified in the narrow valley of the pass. Caspi's driver suffered a fatal head wound, and the M3 lurched off the road. From that moment on, the battle became a rescue operation, as opposed to the swift assaults the paratroops had been trained to execute. Gur personally led another unit from his battalion into the pass to reach Caspi's beleaguered force, only to find himself cut off and pinned down under murderous fire. Gur sent his communications officer, Dan Shalit, to reach a high spot in the pass (the mountainous *wadi* prevented audible radio transmittion) and contact Lieutenant-Colonel Davidi, who was with the SAYERET at the eastern entrance to the pass. The SAYERET, commanded by Micha Kafusta, raced to save Gur, whose situation was becoming precarious.

During this chaotic and desperate struggle, Sharon remained behind at the Parker Memorial. Gur would later bring charges against Sharon (and against numerous other paratroop officers including Eitan) for cowardice. Accusations of cowardice were also raised against Davidi and Eitan (and his deputy, Moshe Levy, a future IDF Chief of Staff) for not entering the pass to save the NA'HA'L force.

▶ Portrait of a stoical paratroop medic clutching his UZI 9mm submachine-gun, with Major 'Raful' Eitan's 890th Battalion prior to the jump at Mitla, 29 October 1956. (IGPO)

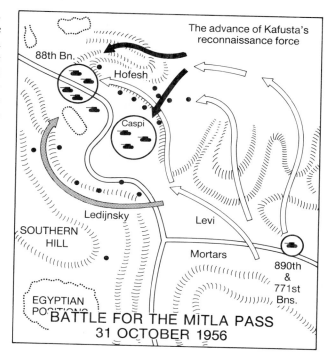

The advance of Kafusta's reconnaissance force

88th Bn.

Hofesh

Caspi

Ledijnsky

SOUTHERN HILL

Levi

Mortars

890th & 771st Bns.

EGYPTIAN POSITIONS

BATTLE FOR THE MITLA PASS
31 OCTOBER 1956

Gur was also blamed for leading an entire battalion into a trap.

For the next ten hours the battle raged. The NA'HA'L's SAYERET, skilfully led by Kafusta, climbed the steep slopes surrounding the pass in an attempt to outflank the Egyptians. They suffered horrendous casualties, from well-entrenched snipers and a brief though deadly MiG strafing run. The Egyptians fought tenaciously, forcing the paratroops to fight twice as hard in order to attack their deeply embedded positions in the labyrinth of caves and sepulchres. It must be noted that throughout the battle, the paratroopers displayed supreme courage, especially in bringing their wounded comrades to safety.

As night fell, Davidi and Eitan sent their best fighters, including their respective SAYERET companies into the mêlée, and the bitter process of eliminating the Egyptian positions one by one began. The main difficulty was in locating the hidden firing positions, and in an act of heroism characteristic of the paratroops at Mitla, a young conscript volunteered to drive a jeep to draw and locate enemy fire. He was killed moments later. The fighting was brutal, and often hand to hand. Grenades were used at close quarters and although achieving destructive results, they resulted in numerous Israeli deaths as well. (Captain Ledijinsky was killed by his own grenade which, thrown from a bunker, rolled back on him.) Once the paratroopers had achieved the initiative, however, victory was secure. In the manner in which they had been trained, the exhausted but indefatigable TZANHANIM systematically cleared all the bunkers and caves of enemy resistance.

At 22.00 hours, the Israeli flag was hoisted above the towering cliffs. The ten hours in the pass had cost the brigade 38 dead and 120 wounded; the Egyptians suffered 260 dead. On 3 November, two companies from the 88th Battalion, and two companies from the 771st parachuted into A'tur in southern Sinai, securing a desert airstrip. Theirs was a symbolic action, unifying the brigade in the common experience of a combat jump. Days later, the jump at A'tur enabled the entire brigade to receive the red (combat) background to their silver metal parachutist wings, issued at an emotional ceremony, as fallen and wounded comrades were mournfully honoured. The battle at Mitla remains one of the most controversial of all IDF actions in its 40-year history. Although debate as to the military worth of the battle continues today, one fact remains absolute; a lesser unit could not have salvaged itself in the face of such determined opposition. As their banner has boasted ever since, 'after the paratroops!'

BETWEEN THE WARS, 1957–67

THE débâcle at the Mitla Pass ended an era for the paratroops. Theirs had been a costly victory which sparked bitter internal debate. In the ensuing military investigation, Sharon, Hofi, Gur, and Eitan were all scrutinized and criticized. Sharon bore the brunt of the indignation, a scapegoat of command and a victim of poor military judgement. He was 'voluntarily removed' as the TZANHANIM's warlord, and put 'on ice' for a number of years. He returned to prominence years later commanding an armoured division to victory in Sinai during the 1967 War, and was considered by many *the saviour of Israel* during the 1973 Yom Kippur War. Although his 'UNIT 101' mentality prevented him from achieving his life's dream of becoming IDF Chief of Staff, politically he evolved into Israel's most controversial Defence Minister, leading Israel through its most controversial war: the 1982 and continuing war in Lebanon.

Although Mitla was traumatic for the paratroops, it did not destroy them. In early 1957, their name was changed from 'UNIT 202' or the 202nd Paratroop Brigade to simply HATIVAT HATZANHANIM or 'The Paratroop Brigade', and Colonel Menachem 'Mann' Aviram (liaison officer between the TZANHANIM and General Staff during Oper-

ation 'KADESH') was appointed its commander. Lieutenant-Colonel Gur was appointed deputy brigade commander, Lieutenant-Colonel Eitan retained command of the 890th, Major Matt assumed command of the NA'HA'L's 88th, and Lieutenant-Colonel Davidi was given authority over the reservists. The years of Aviram's command were quiet, and afforded the brigade time to expand its airborne and combat capabilities. Brigade jump exercises were held at frequent intervals, and for the first time in its history, the paratroops trained to seize enemy airfields; a skill it would later utilize with spectacular results.

The most important feature of Aviram's period in command was the expanded role the brigade SAYERET (SAYERET TZANHANIM) assumed. Under the command of Captain Yair Peled, one of the most outstanding of all the

▼ Independence Day, 1963. Paratroopers from HATIVAT HATZANHANIM ('Paratroop Brigade') march through the main street of Ramat Gan, the Tel Aviv suburb which adopted the paratroopers. Note large-scale wings and 'winged snake' standard displayed above review stand. (IDF Archives)

▲ A senior NCO jump instructor wearing the white 'master's' background to his jump wings, makes a final check on one of his 'pupils' prior to a training jump from a Noratlas in 1964.(IDF Archives)

▲ Heavily laden with equipment, including main line and reserve chutes, and ammunition packs, paratroopers assemble their gear before boarding their Noratlas transports. (IDF Archives)

paratroop junior officers, the SAYERET developed into a true commando force. The requirements for service in her ranks were upgraded to almost impossible levels, with only the most exceptional fighters surviving the rigours of training long enough to sport the coveted SAYERET 'recon' wings. As HATIVAT HATZANHANIM's operational scope grew, so did the military importance of the SAYERET. More than a mere reconnaissance force, the SAYERET now enjoyed a dual role as an intelligence and commando force, and hundreds of daring covert cross-border sabotage and intelligence-gathering missions were carried out. During one such operation near the Egyptian border on 6 September 1959, Captain Peled was brutally murdered by Bedouins.

Under Aviram's guidance, SAYERET TZANHANIM initiated the arrival of helicopters into the paratroops' arsenal. The SAYERET quickly adapted to its new-found mobility, and developed new and innovative assault tactics. The incorporation of the helicopter virtually ended the military importance of parachuting, as targets could now be reached quickly without the complex planning and logistics which combat jumps entailed.

From 1960 to 1965, the paratroops were commanded by Colonels Eli Zeira (a company commander in the 890th Battalion during the early retaliatory strikes, and the luckless Chief of Military Intelligence, A'MAN, during the

1973 War), and Yitzhak Hofi. Although these years were uneventful, they saw the formation of HA'AN TZANHANIM, the paratroops' own engineering and sapper force, and a greater degree of tactical cooperation between the paratroops and the Armoured Corps.

In 1964, Colonel 'Raful' Eitan became the commander of HATIVAT HATZANHANIM. Eitan, who in the interim years had undergone a command course with the United States Marine Corps, introduced a massive expansion programme. He formed an additional conscript battalion (the 202nd, commanded by Major Ephraim Hiram), and in 1965 two paratroop reservist brigades were formed: the 80th, commanded by Colonel Danni Matt, and the 55th, commanded by Colonel 'Motta' Gur. Also in 1965, Chief of Staff Lieutenant-General Yitzhak Rabin ordered the creation of a unified command coordinating the activities of paratroop and infantry forces, and Colonel Aharon Davidi was appointed as the IDF's first KA'TZ'HA'R, Chief Paratroop and Infantry Officer.

The expansion of IDF paratroop and élite infantry capabilities directly coincided with renewed *fedayeen* attacks from across the Jordanian frontier. These *fedayeen* from the newly formed Palestine Liberation Organization's *el-Fatah* (military arm) were quite unlike their counterparts of the 1950s. They were better equipped and trained, and had clear military objectives.

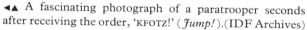

◄▲ A fascinating photograph of a paratrooper seconds after receiving the order, 'KFOTZ!' (*Jump!*).(IDF Archives)

◄ Standing in front of an intimidating symbol of greatness, HATIVAT HATZANHANIM's Commander Colonel 'Raful' Eitan addresses an assembly in 1965. 'Raful' modernized the paratroopers, drawing upon much of the PAL'MACH's heritage of innovation for inspiration. Wearing the officer's peaked cap, and standing behind 'Raful' is Chief of Staff, Lieutenant-General Yitzhak Rabin, himself a former PAL'MACH officer, and the current Israeli Defence Minister. (IDF Archives)

▲ A new generation of élite unit officers stand to attention at their graduation from officer's course ceremony, 1964. The two cadets pictured here (a paratrooper on left, a GOLANI cadet on the right) wait for their instructor (foreground, standing proudly) to remove the white tape covering their commission insignia. (IDF Archives)

▲► The founder of the 202nd Paratroop Battalion, Major Ephraim 'Pihutka' Hiram (front, right) discusses the success of Operation 'MAGRESA', the paratroop raid on Samua, 13 November 1966, with his smiling deputy, Captain Dan Shomron, a decorated reconnaissance officer who commanded the rescue at Entebbe, and is the current IDF Chief of Staff. (IDF Archives)

Their guerrilla attacks warranted a new round of retaliatory strikes by the paratroops, who were also quite unlike their predecessors of the 1950. By 1965, the TZAN-HANIM were true first-generation Israelis, SABRAS* who were not limited by the refugee or Holocaust survivor mentality. Israel was the only home these men knew, and they were prepared to defend it no matter what the personal sacrifice. The first test of this new breed came on 28 May 1965, in Operation 'TZUK SELA'. The target – the Jordanian town of Kilkilya.

In October 1956, Kilkilya had been the site of the paratroops' final retaliatory strike prior to the 1956 Sinai Campaign. The decision to attack it once again in 1965 announced a clear and ominous message: clearly warning 'Here we stopped, here we'll continue!' On the night of 27/28 May 1965 a combined task force from the 202nd and 890th (commanded by Major Tzuri Shaguy) Battalions crossed the border into Jordan, and proceeded to destroy civilian and military targets in the town of Jenin, and Kilkilya. The raid was executed with meticulous precision, and although heavy Jordanian resistance was encountered, the paratroops suffered no casualties. On the night of 4/5 September, the 202nd Battalion returned to Kilkilya, destroying eleven wells in response to *fedayeen* attacks against Israeli settlements. One of the young officers who

---

*The name which characterizes all native-born Israelis; taken from the desert cactus fruit with a hard, sharp shell, and a soft and sweet interior.

distinguished himself for courage and leadership was the 202nd Battalion's deputy commander, Captain Dan Shomron, Chief Paratroop and Infantry Officer commanding the famous Entebbe raid, and the current IDF Chief of Staff.

On the night of 11 November 1966, a jeep on a routine patrol near the Arava Desert bordering Jordan struck a land-mine, killing three paratroopers. It was the thirteenth guerrilla attack originating from the Hebron Hills, and the TZANHANIM's own brand of vengeance was required. They struck two days later.

Code-named Operation 'MAGRESA', it was the largest operation of the period, as well as the paratroops' first ever daylight raid. Three battalions: a force from the 202nd commanded by Lieutenant-Colonel Yoav Shacham; the 50th NA'HA'L Paratroop Battalion commanded by Major Shmuel Pressberger; and two SAYERET formations assisted by Centurion tanks from the élite 7th Armoured Brigade attacked the Jordanian village of Samua, five kilometres from the Israeli border. After crossing the border, the convoy headed towards the Police Fort at Ha'Rafat, while a SAYERET force led by Yoav Tel-Tzur headed together with the 202nd's unit to Samua. The Jordanian 29th Brigade was called in and bitter fighting ensued. Under heavy fire, the paratroops cleared the village of its inhabitants, while the SAYERET prepared 60 homes for demolition. In the day-long mêlée, nineteen Jordanian troops and Palestinian guerrillas were killed. The lone Israeli fatality was Lieutenant-Colonel Shaham, hit by a sniper's bullet as he led his forces in the assault. Other casualties were ferried to safety by helicopters, which evacuated the wounded under heavy fire.

It is interesting to note that immediately following the raid on Samua, the paratroops received more conscript volunteers than could be absorbed. The TZANHANIM now bore the task of living up to its legendary status. By 1967, however, the paratroops were not the IDF's only élite. Their success as excellent role models led to the creation of several specifically tasked élite formations, while larger more established forces regrouped, and upgraded their capabilities.

3

THE OTHER ELITE
The Golani Brigade and the Territorial Reconnaissance Forces

A FAMILY OF FIGHTERS: THE GOLANI INFANTRY BRIGADE

IN its forty years of existence, the GOLANI Infantry Brigade has secured for itself an honoured position among Israel's forces, yet its evolution into an élite fighting force was hard fought, and paid for in blood. One of the original six HAGANAH territorial infantry brigades, 1st GOLANI's operational zone was the Galilee and Jezreel Valley region. It enjoyed an impressive combat reputation, and participated in numerous campaigns throughout the war, including the conquests of Rosh Pina, Tiberias, and Eilat. GOLANI's manpower was conscripted from the local KIBBUTZIM; men of impressive calibre who maintained a strong sense of military discipline and purpose. They were known for their courage under fire, and an unusually high proportion of GOLANI fighters were awarded bravery decorations. When the 1948 War ended, however, they were demobilized, and GOLANI's ranks were filled with a different type of soldier.

In 1949 Israel was a nation flooded with immigrants. As hundreds of thousands of Jews from all over the world flocked to the 'promised land', the IDF became Israel's 'melting-pot', absorbing immigrants from more than 60 nations into the new nation's only common experience. Conscription into the IDF offered many their only chance to escape the misery of the squalid 'transit camps', as well as the opportunity to learn Hebrew. The IDF's educational capabilities helped these new arrivals in a remarkable fashion, but these 'students' in uniform still had to become soldiers. In 1949, the IDF's approach to training was simple: 'break the raw recruit and rebuild him later in the desired mould'. This brutal approach did not go down well with the immigrant conscripts, and their reluctance became the lack of resolve to soldier.

During this period, GOLANI received a disproportionate number of immigrants, mainly the illiterate, undisciplined and unwilling. The best arrivals at BA'KU'M (the IDF's 'absorption and assignment' base for conscripts) were coerced into volunteering for the Air Force, Naval Commandos or TZANHANIM, while others of high psychological and physical make-up were sent to the 7th Armoured or GIVA'ATI Infantry Brigades. The remainder ended up in GOLANI. Discipline at the brigade's home base at Camp Zemach was non-existent. Brawling, desertions, alcohol and drug abuse, and thefts were common place. Not all this activity was criminally motivated. One morning a company of recruits awoke only to find their boots missing; sold by a soldier who sent the money home to his impoverished family. GOLANI commanders understood their unique problems, and vowed to make the most of the human resources at their disposal. Nevertheless, GOLANI obtained the negative stigma as the 'IDF's trash bag'.

Operational performance did little to improve GOLANI's image. Although the brigade's training routine was intense, including forced marches, and ceaseless practice assaults against dummy targets, its combat capabilities were limited. The equipment issued to GOLANI was substandard, causing morale in the unit to slide to dangerous levels. On 2 May the GOLANI Brigade was called in to repel Syrian forces which had crossed into Israeli territory near the Sea of Galilee at Tel Motile. At first only a company was called for, then a battalion, and eventually the entire brigade was involved. In the ensuing four days of brutal combat, the Syrians were beaten back into their own territory though at the heavy cost of forty GOLANI dead and 72 wounded.

The battle for Tel Motile transformed the character of the GOLANI Brigade. While GOLANI was eventually victorious, something had gone terribly wrong with the standards of leadership and discipline. As a member of the General

Staff wryly commented following the military's investigation: 'the best GOLANI fighters were those killed first'. While the conduct of the brigade's senior officers was commended, the battlefield performance of junior officers and NCOs left much to be desired. Although they led, going through the motions of command, the men did not follow.

The General Staff concluded that if the brigade was ever to perform as a Class A unit, drastic and revolutionary solutions would be required. As a result, KIBBUTZNIKIM and MOSHAVNIKIM who had proven their capabilities as commanders in the Paratroops and NA'HA'L were immediately transferred into GOLANI's ranks. The young junior officers and NCOs held in disdain the distance of command which had been the norm prior to their arrival, and they soon established their own rules of military behaviour. In a remarkably short period, revolutionary changes were implemented at Camp Tzemach. The restrictions which had separated commander from simple soldier were torn down. As had been the practice in the FO'SH, SNS and the PAL'MACH, soldiers began to receive the respect of the commanders, and officers now ate, slept and trained with their subordinates. Callousness was replaced by caring, and the families of soldiers with problems received visits by platoon and company commanders. Within two years, GOLANI became a family built on pride.

The success of the GOLANI Brigade's efforts were directly connected to the fanfare surrounding 'UNIT 101' and later the 890th Paratroop Battalion. These two units succeeded in raising the standards for the entire IDF to emulate. The paratroops provided GOLANI with a goal, the reaching of which would bring justified recognition. GOLANI's training routine was increased, its pace accelerated, and the men were pushed beyond normal levels of human endurance. On paper, the brigade looked brilliant, in the field, it was still delegated to routine security duty in the northern region, or to act as back-up for patrols and forays into enemy territory.

During the Sinal Campaign, GOLANI was finally offered the chance to prove itself, being assigned the task of securing the strategic Rafah crossroads in northern Sinai. The operation called for a three-battalion assault led by the 72nd HABOK'IM HARISHONIM Battalion, commanded by major Meir Pa'il (today the IDF's foremost historian), through an extensive outer perimeter minefield and then the dislodging of the stubborn Egyptian defenders from their vast network of fortified positions. The historic photograph taken shortly after Rafah's capture, where GOLANI Commander Colonel Binyamin Jibli stood victoriously with his officers, earned the brigade its rightful share of public attention and praise. Fame had a stiff price, however; fourteen GOLANI riflemen were killed at Rafah.

Although the victory at Rafah brought GOLANI due

notice, the brigade was still frustrated by the assumption that only the TZHANANIM could handle the most difficult of military tasks. In an endeavour to compete with their red beret comrades, GOLANI commanders decided to upgrade the potential of its reconnaissance company, SAYERET GOLANI, into a commando force. Although HANAMER HAME'UFAF ('Flying Leopard', the nickname given to SAYERET GOLANI because of its winged leopard recon wings) had been in existence for quite some time in one form or another, as did the Brigade's reconnaissance force, it had yet to acquire the type of capabilities that made 'UNIT 101' and Har-Zion's SAYERET TZHANANIM legendary. With the ultimate aim of becoming the IDF's premier reconnaissance formation, SAYERET GOLANI vowed to be different. Unlike other SAYEROT, SAYERET GOLANI did not accept conscript volunteers. Instead, its volunteers were the best GOLANI had to offer; soldiers and NCOs who had proved their combat ability. They were the only ones allowed to qualify for the gruelling trial week or GIBUSH which tested the candidate's mental, physical and psychological limits. Those passing, underwent further examinations, and a further six months training, the successful completion of which permitted 'formal' volunteering into the SAYERET. This strict recruitment procedure, which continues to this day, made SAYERET GOLANI one of the IDF's premier reconnaissance units.

SAYERET GOLANI's training routine was brutal, and included 100-kilometre forced marches with 50kg packs through the most inhospitable terrain imaginable. Intensive firing exercises were held daily, and the men of the SAYERET were taught to use every type of weapon in the Arab as well as the IDF's arsenal. SAYERET GOLANI did not accept supermen, nor did it produce them. Instead it installed a deeply felt emotional bond between soldier, commander and unit; typical of all IDF élite units, and one of the contributory factors in their combat proficiency. They set an example which the entire brigade followed closely; and within a year of its inception, the GOLANI Brigade's other battalions: 1st BARAK ('Lightning') Bn., HABOK'IM HARISHONIM ('First Conquerors') Bn., GIDEON Bn., and the NCO's Course Company, ARAYOT HAGOLAN ('Golan Lions'), had their first opportunity to 'prove' their new-found combat proficiency in Operation 'HARGOL'; the raid on the Syrian mortar positions at Tewfiq on 31 January 1960.

The deserted village at Tewfiq, towering above the Sea of Galilee and KIBBUTZ Tel Katzir, had provided Syrian artillery with its observation and fire-support base for bombardments against Israel. When Syrian troops disguised as peasants infiltrated a demilitarized zone near Tel Katzir, supported by a day-long 120mm mortar bombardment, an Israeli military response was inevitable.

◄ The GOLANI Brigade goes to war, 6 October 1973. While the GIDEON Battalion held the forward line, GOLANI reinforcements clogged the Golan Heights arteries leading to the battle. (IDF Archives)

Although the paratroops had prepared an assault on Tewfiq, Chief of Staff Lientenant-General Tzvi Tzur opted to provide GOLANI with a true test under fire. At 23.20 hours on 31 January, a column of GOLANI riflemen from ARAYOT HAGOLAN and SAYERET GOLANI crossed into Syria followed by M3 halftracks carrying explosive charges. Following a brief fire-fight with the village's startled defenders, lower Twefiq was secured by 23.50 hours. While SAYERET GOLANI prepared the positions for demolition, a heavy Syrian bombardment commenced from the heavy guns nearby at Upper Tewfiq. A fierce artillery and tank fire duel raged for almost three hours, until the orders were issued to SAYERET GOLANI to raze the area. The M3s which had ferried the destructive explosives to their targets headed home filled with booty, including dozens of Goryunov machine-guns. A recipient of the I'TUR HA'OZ decoration for courage for his bravery under fire was a young platoon commander, Lieutenant Amir Drori. Twenty-three years later, during the 1973 War, Drori served as GOLANI Brigade OC during its darkest hour, and was OC Northern Command during the 1982 Lebanon invasion.

Operation 'HARGOL' brought the brigade its long overdue recognition. A further boost to the brigade's image was the 1961 appointment of Colonel Mordechai 'Motta' Gur as GOLANI Commander. His transfer from the TZHANANIM (following a stint at the French War College) was ordered by Chief of Staff Tzur who wanted GOLANI upgraded to the paratroops' combat level. Indeed Gur brought with him many of the paratroops' élite traditions, and worked feverishly to develop a close-knit bond between the command echelon and the ranks. As Sharon had instituted in 'UNIT 101' and later in the 890th Battalion, routine forced marches were conducted inside enemy territory; a precarious though effective way of raising a soldier's self-confidence. In an effort to upgrade the combat status of the brigade even further, Gur offered parachute training to the most outstanding men.

For years, the Sea of Galilee had been a disputed body of water. Although Israel owned the entire sea, the international border with Syria ran along a 10-metre stretch of its shoreline: hence the hostilities in a region where even a metre of disputed earth leads to bloodshed. In late 1961, Syrian artillery attacks against Israeli fisherman on the Sea of Galilee increased in intensity and accuracy. These attacks worried Ben-Gurion, but no action was taken. On 16 March 1962, the Syrians hit an Israeli police launch with machine-gun fire from their postions near the village of Nuqieb. Retaliation was ordered. Chief of Staff Tzur did'nt think twice as to which unit should be selected. Colonel Gur was summoned, and informed that the GOLANI would attack Nuqieb and its adjacent village that very evening! Code-name, Operation 'SNUNIT'.

On the evening of 16 March 1962, the GOLANI Brigade was enjoying a concert put on for them in the town of Tiberias. The men, dressed in Class A uniforms, were enjoying the sweet sounds of music when the sudden appearance of their officers signalled an ominous development. Quickly the soldiers were assembled, equipped, and briefed. Although Gur was apprehensive about delegating the task to GOLANI on such short notice, he had supreme confidence in his men. He had inherited GOLANI a year earlier from the capable hands of Colonel Aharon Yariv (who would later mastermind Israeli intelligence activities as the head of A'MAN), and the brigade was, many considered, at the peak of its operational capabilities.

The Nuqieb gun emplacements were only three kilometres north of KIBBUTZ Ein Gev, on a small unobtrusive hill accessible by only three routes: northern, southern, and the western route which was the only one wide enough for halftracks. Its position being tactically unfavourable, Nuqieb would have to be attacked in a wide flanking move, the assault force moving in from the east. This task was given to GOLANI's best, SAYERET GOLANI, commanded by the charismatic Major Tzvi 'Tzvika' Ofer, and ARAYOT HAGOLAN led by Major Beni Enbar. Although the brigade's other battalions were capable forces, their competence was not of the same order as that of the SAYERET and the NCOs in training. In the final assault plan, SAYERET GOLANI was given the mission of silencing the gun positions from the west, while ARAYOT HAGOLAN would first silence the village of Nuqieb, and then proceed to support the SAYERET, attacking from the east. A two-company force from the GIDEON Battalion would wait in reserve, preventing a Syrian military response from the north.

At 21.00 hours, the SAYERET left Ein Gev. It was a clear night with a brilliant full moon, which brought the danger that their advance would be discovered even before they crossed into Syria. Major Ofer had trained his boys well, however, and in speed and silence the recon fighters reached their target's outer perimeter defensive ditch. The attack force split into three: Ofer's force ('Force Tzvika') to attack the southern and most heavily fortified of the positions, while the remaining platoons would attack the central and northern fortifications. As the lead elements approached the barbed wire fence, shots were heard. Things were not going according to plan.

Awaiting ARAYOT HAGOLAN in ambush was a strong Syrian force equipped with heavy machine-guns and mortars. As Enbar's force took cover, they noticed to their horror dozens of men, women and children in night attire fleeing into the fight, screaming 'yahud! yahud!' (Jews!) With the element of surprise lost, Enbar ordered his men to assault the Syrian gun positions, but to avoid the civilians if possible. The Syrians on the other hand used *their* fellow countrymen as cover, and countless were mown down. ARAYOT HAGOLAN suffered many wounded, including Lientenant Yodke Peled, who was hit in the chest by a tracer bullet and rushed back to Israel for emergency surgery. Major Ofer was forced to backtrack towards the village, and lead elements of the company towards the operation's primary target. The remainder of ARAYOT HAGOLAN cleared the village of its Syrian defenders, the homes of known soldiers being destroyed. The Syrians resisted stoutly, and each house and room had to be fought for. The GOLANI fighters cleverly attached their German-made flashlights to their UZI submachine-guns and FN FAL assault rifles, and managed to overcome the the tenacious defenders, and proceed towards the main battle.

The assault proved to be more difficult than expected. The narrow confining bunkers, filled with immobilizing mud from recent rain were difficult to get through in the face of heavy machine-gun fire and grenades. Concentrated fire from fortified bunkers claimed the lives of five of the SAYERET's best men. In fact, almost every officer and NCO leading an assault team ended up a casualty. Dozens of 'private', close-quarter encounters raged. Soldiers were drowned in the mud as rifle butts, shovels, and fists were used with fatal effect. The battle developed into a routine of tossing in a grenade, followed by a burst of fire which emptied the magazine. In the confusion, only the SAYERET's password 'HANAMER HAME'UFAF' identified friend from foe.

Although the Syrians defended their turf stubbornly, the two-company assault was overwhelming. Slowly they began to give ground, as anti-tank rifle-grenades were used with great effect to destroy the sand-bagged fortifications, and the destructive capabilities of Bangalore torpedoes were maximized brilliantly. At dawn, the GOLANIs returned to Israeli territory, followed all the way by Syrian heavy artillery. Fifty-three Syrian soldiers were killed at Nuqieb, countless others wounded. Operation 'SNUNIT' cost the GOLANI Brigade seven dead and 43 wounded. Four fighters were decorated for their courage under fire, including Ofer, whose perseverance and care for his men secured victory.

Nuqieb was GOLANI's rite of passage. It propelled the brigade beyond its second-class position into the forefront of IDF attention. Although many argued that they had still to achieve parity with the Paratroops, the success at Nuqieb disproved all negative sentiments directed against the brigade. It subsequently received new equipment, new 'lizard' pattern camouflage fatigues, and a new sense of pride. The northern towns of Acre and Nahariya adopted the units, and the KIBBUTZIM of the north gladly offered the men hot showers and meals during breaks in training. Syrian harassment of the northern settlements continued, however, and GOLANI vowed to silence the Syrian guns forever should the opportunity arise.

'ALMOND', 'WALNUT' AND 'CAROB': THE TERRITORIAL RECONNAISSANCE UNITS

WHILE the Paratroops basked in the glory of their feats, and the GOLANI Brigade feverishly developed a similar image of their own, three unique reconnaissance forces worked round the clock securing Israel's boundaries. They were small units, built around a cadre of Bedouin and Druze trackers, and a highly disciplined force of long-range reconnaissance commandos. Their work was lonely, arduous, and received little fanfare back home. Nevertheless, the IDF's three territorial SAYEROT (SHAKED, EGOZ and HARUV) maintained an unrivalled combat record.

Before examining these remarkable though neglected units, a brief synopsis of the status of Israel's closed borders is required. Surrounded by enemy states, Israel has been forced to quarantine her international boundaries with massive barbed wire defences protected by mines, and early-warning stations. During the early 1950s, the securing of such extensive borders was too monumental a task for the Israelis to complete successfully. The *fedayeen* infiltrations were only too blatant a reminder of Israel's precarious security situation. The Israel National Police Border Guards patrolled along the borders, but their small numbers proved ineffective. Although they were highly professional, the Border Guards (MISHMAR HAGVUL) had to be reinforced by regular IDF units, in what became known as BITAHON SHUTAF, or 'collective security'. No matter how potent a defence the 'collective security' arrangement provided, the military threat which the infiltrator posed on either side of the Israeli border remained of paramount concern. A force was needed with intelligence and tracking capabilities to deal with the infiltrator either before he attempted his entry into Israel, or once successfully across.

As Egypt was the main sponsor of *fedayeen* as well as espionage activity against Israel, Southern Command was responsible for what surely was Israel's most vulnerable frontier. The short-lived 'UNIT 30' was a crude though important experiment in the use of small, highly mobile units to interdict and pursue guerrillas. The responsibilities of 'UNIT 101' and the Paratroops prevented them from being used for the dispersed and fragmented task of chasing guerrillas. Southern Command as a result formed their own unique response to the threat of the uncontrolled infiltration of guerrillas and Egyptian Military Intelligence agents. Its name was SAYERET SHAKED, or 'Almond Recon' (whose Hebrew acronym also stood for 'Southern Frontier Guardians', or 'Southern Commando Service').

SAYERET SHAKED was probably the most neglected of all IDF front-line combat units. From the end of the fighting in 1949, until 1955, 'UNIT SHAKED', as it was known, was a small entity within Southern Command, without any independent form of command. In 1957 Major David Ben-Hor (a veteran PAL'MACHNIK who had fought under Yigal Allon) was assigned the task of organizing a mixed task force of trackers and fighters to seal the border tight. SAYERET SHAKED's first years were directed towards filling its ranks, as it deployed only a dozen or so men, and two antiquated Command Cars. SAYERET SHAKED was the first IDF unit successfully to integrate Jew and Arab fighter on equal terms. These 'minority' soldiers were needed for their inherent tracking ability as well as their ability to blend into the landscape. They were the only ones capable of achieving the trust of the local Bedouins, who provided the unit with most of the intelligence information. The recon fighters patrolled silently along the border area, a foot patrol supported by a Command Car filled with men. The operations were nerve-racking. Men would sit in ambushes for days on end without any sign of activity, until the spotting of an infiltrator signalled the commencement of a short though fierce fire-fight. Mobility was a key to success, and everything from heavily armed jeeps to camels were employed. As most of the patrols were conducted in civilian dress, the jeeps were decorated with a large white and blue Star of David on the hood, to ensure that the IAF did not not blast them away!

The man who had the most profound effect on the unit and personified its collective nature best was A'bdul Majid Hadar, known simply as Lieutenant-Colonel Amos Yarkoni: SAYERET SHAKED's commander from 1961–67. Of the Hamazriv Bedouin tribe by birth, Hadar was active in the 1936 guerrilla campaign against the Iraqi Petroleum Pipeline. He was known as a courageous guerrilla, and an excellent shot. He also enjoyed friendly relations with his Jewish neighbours (as had been common with Galilee Bedouins), and as a result was targeted for retribution from more nationalistic minded local Arabs. Captured, he was thrown into a deep pit in preparation for his 'death sentence', but managed to escape to the safety of his good friend, Moshe Dayan. He adopted the Hebrew name of Amos Yarkoni, and in 1948 was formerly drafted into the IDF's minority 'Unit 300'. In 1955, Yarkoni graduated from the officer's course, and ended up with SAYERET SHAKED. Although it would take some time for the IDF to fully realize and admit the potential of their Bedouin fighter's ability to command, Yarkoni was to be SHAKED's most influential factor.

Until the 1956 War, SAYERET SHAKED's non-military appearance and performance made it a unique formation. Its fighters wore civilian clothes, carried rare and exotic weaponry, and operated along their own distinct lines of military law. The most popular items identifying soldiers as belonging to SHAKED were Australian slouch hats, expensive American cowboy boots, and Swedish Carl Gustav 9mm submachine-guns and Russian SKS rifles with which they became legendary marksmen. Needless to say, and like their 'UNIT 101' counterparts, SHAKED fighters often found themselves the target of Military Police justice. Never trained as conventional combatants, SHAKED's men considered theirs a 'guerrilla' force answerable only to the unit commander, and to their operational success record. Following Operation 'KADESH', however, the unit shed its civilian trousers, put on its rarely worn IDF uniforms and at the personal urging of Yarkoni, settled into a purely military framework.

SAYERET SHAKED's manpower was drawn from the outstanding Bedouin, Druze and Circassian soldiers in 'UNIT 300', as well as dropouts, or volunteers from the Paratroops. The unit's small size allowed its closely cohesive nature to flourish. When Captain Yarkoni was finally appointed commander of SAYERET SHAKED in 1961, the unit's informal nature expanded into what many 'formal' IDF commanders labelled a summer's camp! Yarkoni looked after his men, and even made sure that if one of his fighters brought a girl back to the base for the weekend, they were given separate quarters. In what could be a model for the solving of Middle East tensions, relations between the Jewish and Bedouin fighter flourished. The Bedouin fighters adopted many Jewish customs, and the Jews were only too glad to adapt to the Bedouin *hafla*, a vast celebrative feast of delicacies topped off by the inevitable 'Belly Dancer'.

The informal atmosphere at the base, did not interfere with its professional and extremely successful performance in the field. Long and hard patrols were initiated, and SHAKED re-wrote many a manual on the art of the 'desert pursuit'. Employing the services of low-flying Piper Cubs, a team would search vast areas by Command Car, and by foot. They were highly disciplined fighters, who did not return to base until their 'target' (the SHAKED term for infiltrator) was dead or captured. Not only did they hunt the *fedayeen* or Bedouin smugglers, but against heavily armed Egyptian intelligence agents who freely crossed the UN-controlled Sinai Desert unhindered to conduct covert intelligence and sabotage missions. These agents were well trained by Russian KGB and GRU officers, but in most instances, their instructors did not take into consideration the determination and skill of the SHAKED trackers. By 1965, enemy intelligence operations against Southern Command had virtually ceased.

By 1966, SAYERET SHAKED maintained only forty fighters, although it was responsible for hundreds of miles of territory. This taxed the small unit in equipment and manpower, but it still succeeded in securing the southern frontier. Following the murder of bus travellers near Ma'ale A'akravim in the Judean Desert later that year, SAYERET SHAKED deployed for the first time as an airborne force, searching for the murderers in three S-58 helicopters. Under the guidance of IAF Colonel Eliezer 'Chita' Cohen (the IAF's foremost helicopter pilot, and the one entrusted with the developing of helicopter deployment tactics with the Paratroops and other élite units), SAYERET SHAKED had trained with the S-58s, but this was its first true test in the field. Such tactics were new to the IDF, and

as a result the helicopters were used to ferry the fighters *only* to points where foot pursuit commenced.

Also in 1966, Major Binyamin (Fuad) Ben-Eliezer reached SAYERET SHAKED as the unit's deputy commander. While he was presenting his orders to Yarkoni, Ben-Eliezer was nearly killed by a bullet which tore through the office. Shocked, Ben-Eliezer was soon relieved to learn that some of the men had 'innocently' set up a firing range in their barracks! Undaunted, though quite cautious, Ben-Eliezer initiated an intensive upgrading training programme. The men received parachute training, infantry refresher courses, and learned to operate as a conventional force. To complete this process, the fighters were issued with Paratroop Class A uniforms, their own special reconnaissance wings, and their own unit tag which they wore proudly.

By 1967 the unit had grown into a force numbering about 150 men. Ben-Eliezer was named SHAKED commander, and further attempted to upgrade his unit's capabilities. Through both official and unofficial channels, Ben-Eliezer secured the unit new jeeps, an increased arsenal, and advanced communications equipment, as well as SHAKED's first communications officer! In March 1967, OC Southern Command, Major General Yeshayahu Gavish, summoned Ben-Eliezer to his headquarters, where he was ordered to prepare SAYERET SHAKED for war.

In 1955, in the north, OC Northern Command, Major-General Yitzhak Rabin, ordered the formation of a reconnaissance unit to secure the borders with Lebanon and Syria. Rabin's approach was different. Instead of forming a unit to patrol within the confines of the Israeli border, a covert, cross-border raiding force was created. The nucleus of this force were Druze volunteers who would be able to operate freely among the local Druze inhabitants of Lebanon, and along the Syrian Golan Heights. The man assigned the difficult task of forming such a unit was Captain Arik Gardi, an ex-NA'HA'L fighter and company commander in 'UNIT 300', a man who was intimately aware of intricacies of dealing with the minority soldiers. The unit was called SAYERET EGOZ (walnut), on account of the nut's soft interior, and hard, armour-type shell.

Gardi assembled the best Druze fighters he could find, and sent them to the unit's new home, Camp 'Ben-Ami' in Western Galilee. Northern Command dispatched the best martial arts, weapons, and combat instructors they could obtain, and within months, the unit began its long, intensive training routine. The mot important aspect of this training was the familiarization of their area of operation along the sensitive border areas. They were taken on

▶▲ Paratroopers prepare themselves 'emotionally' for a training jump, while waiting for the green light in the belly of a C-130 Hercules. (IDF Spokesman-Herzl Kunesari)

▶ The aftermath. One paratrooper hits the dirt hard; a comrade offers assistance. (IDF Spokesman)

forced marches to every unique landmark, and trained to live off the land. As had been the case with the other regional SAYERET, however, SAYERET EGOZ was neglected and was considered a 'bastard' unit. One instance which typified this was on a cold winter's night in 1957 when a SAYERET EGOZ patrol inadvertently walked into a Border Guard ambush near the village of Um el-Faham. No one bothered to inform EGOZ as to the friendly force activity in the area, and in the ensuing chaos, one of the unit's best Druze fighters, Hasan Abu Nijam was killed. The tragic incident resulted in numerous military investigations, and led to the shelving of SAYERET EGOZ operations for seven years.

In 1964, Northern Command rediscovered the need for its élite unit. Following the creation of the Palestine Liberation Organization in 1964, repeated guerrilla and conventional Syrian attacks were conducted against Israel's National Water Carrier apparatus originating at the Sea of Galilee. OC Northern Command, Major-General Avraham Yaffe, decided to reinstate SAYERET EGOZ with the express objective of protecting the National Water Carrier, and he named Colonel Yehoshua 'Shaika' Erez as its new commander. Erez was a veteran of SAYERET GOLANI and SAYERET SHAKED and knew what standards EGOZ had to reach.

The new SAYERET EGOZ began with only eight men, named the 'guerrilla band', who immediately attached themselves as spearheads for Border Guard patrols ambushing el-Fatah guerrillas. The unit slowly grew, attracting men from the local KIBBUTZIM and MOSHAVIM who otherwise would have volunteered into the Paratroops or Naval Commandos. A sniper force was organized, equipped with antiquated Czech K98 Mausers, as was a sapper force, and a special intelligence gathering unit which ventured frequently across the border into Lebanon, Syria, and Jordan. Responsible for securing SAYERET EGOZ with its logistical and operational needs was Emmanuel 'Manno' Shaked, the Operations Officer at Northern Command, and eventual Chief Paratroop and Infantry Officer. With increased pressure from el-Fatah infiltrators operating from Lebanon, Syria, and Jordan, Shaked tansformed SAYERET EGOZ into an operational force on alert and in the field 24 hours a day, seven days a week, 365 days a year.

SAYERET EGOZ's élite reputation slowly spread, and Paratroop and GOLANI officers soon flocked to her ranks. One such volunteer was Captain Haim Sela, who was appointed SAYERET EGOZ commander in June 1965. There were only twenty fighters and three Bedouin trackers in the unit, but Sela pressed for greater support from Northern Command

▼ Who says parachuting is a man's job? Female soldiers serving the Paratroop Brigade undergo their initial indoctrination at Tel Nof. (IDF Archives)

Himself an ex-élite unit commander, Defence Minister Yitzhak Rabin reviews the next generation of paratroop, GOLANI and reconnaissance officers during ceremonies held at the IDF Officer's School, 'BA'HAD I'. (IDF Spokesman-Yoni Reif)

nd within a short period EGOZ boasted its first fully-ledged company. OC Northern Command, Major-General David 'Dado' Elazar (an ex-PAL'MACHNIK and the DF's 9th Chief of Staff) personally saw to it that SAYERET GOZ was issued with top line communications gear and weaponry. The high technology weapons system manu-acturer RAFAEL developed a special relationship with AYERET EGOZ, and new and experimental night vision devices were conceived and issued.

Sela took EGOZ out of the confines and security of northern Israel, and personally led ambushes deep into enemy territory to interdict guerrilla forces before they could close in on the border. From 1966 to 1967, guerrilla activity increased two-fold. SAYERET EGOZ was the only mobilized unit on alert in the command, and it was called on to control what had developed into a chaotic situation. The Lebanese Border alone stretched for 120 kilometres from Rosh Hanikra along the Mediterranean to the foothills of Mt Hermon, and patrolling the area required a tireless effort and a unique type of soldier. To reward the unit for the monotony and tension of the patrols and ambushes, Sela provided his fighters with parachutist training, special recon wings and unit tag, as well as a strong unit pride uncharacteristic even of the TZANHANIM.

In 1966, Chief of Staff Lieutenant-General Yitzhak Rabin ordered the creation of a Central Command reconnaissance force. Known as SAYERET HARUV (carob), the unit was made up originally of Paratroop veterans who provided the command cadre of the unit, until its conscript volunteers had been selected and trained. SAYERET HARUV's zone of operation was the precarious frontier with Jordan, though it was only manned by 90 men supported by a few jeeps and only *two* Command Cars. It nevertheless found an innovative approach to attract the guerrillas. Dressed in civilian clothing, SAYERET EGOZ fighters walked 'innocently' as bait, near sensitive border areas known for guerrilla activity, while a strong back-up force complete with sniper rifles secured their safety. Luckless guerrillas who thought they had found easy prey, soon ended up in body-bags, or in IDF detention.

Insuring the success of SAYERET HARUV was the young and capable Operations Officer at Central Command, Lieutenant-Colonel Arik Regev. A veteran of the 890th Battalion who had served as 'Raful's deputy, Regev was a brilliant tactician, who had a keen sense for the potential of the special talents of small reconnaissance units. Little could he know that the unit he would eventually control, the 'baby' of the territorial force, would develop into the most battle tested and brutalized SAYERET of all.

4
THE SIX DAYS OF JUNE 1967
Operations during the
Six Day War

FROM GAZA TO ALEXANDRIA: THE SOUTHERN FRONT

WAR in 1967 was inevitable as Syrian support for *el-Fatah* attacks against Israel continued. In what was to be the *casus belli*, IAF Mirage IIICs engaged Syrian MiGs in a major dog-fight on 7 April 1967. It resulted in the downing of seven MiGs with no Israeli losses, following which the triumphant Israeli pilots buzzed Damascus in a defiant show of invincibility. Nasser was outraged by such Arab impotence, and as the undisputed leader of the dispute-ridden Arab world he felt compelled to act. He blockaded the strategic Straits of Tiran against Israeli shipping, ordered the UNEF out of the 'demilitarized' Sinai Desert, and mobilized his vast armed forces for war. Arab frenzy soon began to surpass reality as the talk in Cairo, Damascus, and Baghdad centred on pushing the *infidel* Jews into the sea! Even the cautious King Hussein of Jordan agreed to placed his élite Arab Legion under Egyptian command. The hour of truth was at hand.

In Israel, the Arab threats were not taken lightly. Although Arab military might was quantitatively superior to that of the Israelis, the IDF was confident in the quality of its men, and the righteousness of her cause. Israeli intelligence efforts had been supreme, and afforded the IDF an accurate and intimate picture of Arab capabilities. Before his execution, the legendary MOSSAD agent Eli Cohen provided precise tactical maps of the Syrian fortifications on the Golan Heights, while an A'MAN operative posing as a high-ranking Egyptian staff officer provided up-to-date troop, equipment, and strategic insight to his controllers in Tel Aviv.* As tension grew, and May swept into June, the IDF mobilized its civilian army. A war on three fronts was militarily unadvisable, yet the General Staff delegated the most crucial tasks to her élite units. In six days, *they* changed the face of the Middle East.

Colonel 'Raful' Eitan's HATIVAT HATZANHANIM had been on full alert since Israel's 19th Independence Day on 15 May. They had been positioned in the 'anxious' confines of their makeshift camps poised for battle, and ordered to sit tight with an uncharacteristic degree of Israeli patience. 'Raful' was not a patient man, and waiting for the politicians displeased him greatly. Morale in the paratroops' camp was high, however, as the young conscripts were confident in their capabilities and resolve.

HATIVAT HATZANHANIM was part of 'Steel Division', better known as UGDAT TAL, a combined infantry and armour task force commanded by Armoured Corps Commander, Major General Yisrael Tal, future father of the famous MERKAVA MBT. UGDAT TAL'S primary objective was the elimination of the Egyptian northern line of defence, securing an unhindered advance into Sinai by the IDF's two other task forces attacking Sinai (UGDAT SHARON, an armoured division commanded by Major General 'Arik' Sharon complete with the 80th Reserve Paratroop Brigade, and UGDAT YAFFE, an armoured division commanded by Major General Avraham Yaffe). While the armoured forces in Tal's command (including the élite 7th Armoured Brigade commanded by Colonel Shmuel 'Gorodish' Gonen) were to deal with Egyptian armour, the paratroops were to dislodge the heavily fortified Egyptian infantry and artillery positions at Rafah, and seize the towns of Khan Yunis and Gaza. This was all to be completed within two days, following which HATIVAT HATZANHANIM would head towards the Canal, in what was

---

*This nameless agent was tragically killed by an IAF strafing run of his unit's HQ near Bir Gafgafa. The supreme secrecy surrounding his activities forbade even informing the IAF, and although a special GHQ commando team was sent in to save him, they came too late!

▲ Target Rafah! HATIVAT HATZANHANIM Commander, Colonel 'Raful' Eitan, directs the paratroops' battle for the Egyptian stronghold on 6 June 1967. (IGPO)

hoped to be Israel's second smashing Sinai victory in eleven years.

'Raful' commanded three battalions: the NA'HA'L Paratroop Battalion commanded by Major Tibi Shapira; the 202nd Bn. commanded by Major Yair Tel-Tzur, and a third, battalion-sized force led by Lieutenant-Colonel Tzvi Barzani, which would head straight for Gaza and the entrenched Egyptian positions at Tel Eli Montar. Each paratroop battalion was fully mechanized and supported by a company of M-48 Pattons. Leading the paratroops' advance was SAYERET TZANHANIM commanded by Major Dan Shomron, assigned an anti-tank role, and equipped with jeep-mounted 106mm recoilless rifles. There was also an improvised reconnaissance formation of paratroop reservists commanded by Major Danni Wolf, and a scout force from SAYERET SHAKED.

Leading the armour columns was SAYERET SHIRION ('Armoured Recon') a mobile force, based on jeeps fitted with 106mm recoilless rifles and tanks equipped with special communications gear. It was made up of the most promising fighters in the Armoured Corps, all of whom were officer material, volunteers, and graduates of paratroop basic training. SAYERET SHIRION operated in a dual intelligence-gathering and anti-tank role. They were to determine enemy dispositions, and then punch a hole through the defences. Their success and survival depended on speed and accuracy. Following the 1973 War,

the IDF's anti-tank duties were transferred to the paratroops.

At 08.55 hours on 6 June, a smiling 'Raful', wearing an Australian Army slouch hat, led his brigade across the border into Egypt just as the last flights of IAF Fouga and Ouragan attack aircraft were returning from their bombing runs. Their primary objective, the fortifications at Rafah, was a series of well-concealed tank and gun positions defended by deep trenches dug into high and impassable banks of sand. Clearing the trenches proved a most difficult task for the paratroops, who were forced to disembark from the safety of their vehicles and engage the tenacious Egyptian defenders in close-quarter combat. The NA'HA'L Battalion led the assault without armoured support, and immediately bogged down in heavy fighting while the 202nd entered the fray, attacking from the east.

Amid the flying lead, debris, sand and smoke, a well-concealed and extensive mine-field added to the confusion. 'Raful' ordered heavier armour and infantry fire into the area, a tactic which eventually broke the Egyptian's will to fight. Many Egyptian soldiers fled, though most were captured. In all, three Egyptian brigades were destroyed in the sands at Rafah. By nightfall the fighting was over. Rafah Junction was secure, and 'Raful' assembled what remained of his original force and proceeded towards the next task to hand – Gaza. The battle for Rafah had been costly, and dozens of paratroopers were killed or wounded. For the first time in IDF history helicopters were extensively used in a medical evacuation role. Wounded TZANHANIM were heli-lifted from forward battalion aid stations to military hospitals in as little as fifteen minutes!

The battle for Rafah Junction was a true indicator as to the battle-readiness of the paratroops. They had faced a numerically superior enemy with superior firepower, and had triumphed. The Egyptian senior and junior officers fled at the sight of the Israeli onslaught, leaving their men leaderless, confused, and helpless. The paratroop junior officers and NCOs on the other hand displayed impressive signs of innovation and initiative. As always, it was the officers who were cut down first, including NA'HA'L battalion commander Shapria, seriously wounded in the close-quarter fighting.

As opposed to the vast desert emptiness of Rafah, Gaza was a sprawling urban quagmire. Shamefully neglected by the Egyptians, Gaza and its surrounding villages were inhabited by hundreds of thousands of Palestinian refugees. It was defended by the Palestine Liberation Army (part of the Egyptian Army), as well a reinforced company of Egyptian Special Forces. Almost every Gazan possessed a weapon of some sort, and the local Palestinian leaders had raised the Gazans to a battle frenzy. In addition, a heavily fortified Egyptian gun position existed at Tel Eli Montar, a natural obstacle in Gaza which had been encountered by Alexander the Great in 312 BC, Napoleon in 1799, and General Allenby in 1917. It was now HATIVAT HATZANHANIM's turn.

Gaza's capture was assigned to a reserve tank formation

commanded by Lieutenant-Colonel Yehuda Reshef, and 'Force Bar' (Lieutenant Colonel Barzani's paratroopers). At 10.00 hours on 5 June, 'Force Bar' crossed the border, as the paratroopers poked their way gingerly through the maze of mines with bayonets and sticks. Barzani had read his history well, and remembered that the British had lost almost 5,000 men at Gaza. Vowing not to have history repeat itself, he attacked Gaza in a wide-flanking move from the south, going through the abandoned village of Beni Suheila. They proceeded north towards the southern approach to the city, where the battalion split into three spearheads: two companies supported by armour headed towards the city centre, while a mechanized paratroop company was sent in to take Eli Montar, which would fall after hours of bitter fighting.

Egyptian and Palestinian resistance at Gaza was stiff, and Barzani's men encountered murderous sniper fire. Just outside the city, the Egyptians had set up an elaborate system of ambush defenses, and their initial bursts of anti-tank fire transformed dozens of Barzani's M3s into flaming hulks of twisted metal. The paratroops were forced to attack on foot in what amounted to a bayonet charge with their folding-stock UZI submachine-guns! Man was pitted against machine, as the the TZANHANIM, armed only with

personal weapons, charged and defeated the Egyptian armour. The Egyptians were impressed by the courage of the Israelis and frightened by their speed and firepower. In what could very well epitomize the Egyptian fighting spirit in this war, a JSIII 'STALIN' tank crew abandoned their vehicle after a 3.5-inch bazooka shell hit the turret. The shell did not penetrate the 'STALIN's thick armour, but the impact noise was enough to cause the Egyptian crew to flee in panic!

The conquest of the city required great skill and patience, and the paratroops had not been trained adequately in urban combat. The ethic of TOHAR HANESHEK forbad the use of heavy fire power amid Gaza's dense civilian population, and the tedious process of clearing each street, block, and house had to be undertaken. Egyptian determination was limited, and the TZANHANIM were able to seize the city (though not able to secure it) in a matter of hours. In a display of visionary insight, paratroopers, overjoyed in their moment of victory, flocked to the city's

▼ Following a successful battle against numerically superior Egyptian armour forces, a SAYERET SHIRION platoon stands to attention in a ceremony marking the end of the fighting in Sinai. (IDF Archives)

MEA Lebanese Airlines ticket office for a souvenir photograph. Little could they have known that eighteen months later, many of these same fighters would destroy thirteen Lebanese civilian aircraft in one of the paratroops' most spectacular retaliatory raids.

While 'Raful' regrouped his forces near Rafah for the next day's fight, the 80th Reserve Paratroop Brigade commanded by Colonel Danni Matt attached to UGDAT SHARON prepared for one of the most spectacular assaults of the Sinai campaign. Sharon entrusted the 80th with the capture of the best defended of all Egyptian positions at Um Katef. Lying east of Abu Agheila, the positions at Um Katef were built along the Soviet pattern, consisting of three lines of trenches, parallel and supporting one another in a zigzag formation. Defending the trenches were a system of anti-tank and heavy machine-guns which turned any point on the approach into a field of dense fire. Complementing the position were fifty 122mm artillery pieces, and more than eighty tanks. The Egyptians considered it impregnable.

The 80th Brigade was the eldest of the paratroop reserve formations. It was mobilized on 23 May when Nasser closed the Straits of Tiran, and was on full alert at its home base. The General Staff did not know where to station the brigade, and for a while it appeared to Matt that the 80th would take part in Operation 'HAGOR', the breakthrough into Mount Scopus and Jordanian-held Jerusalem. In the end, the brigade was sent to Sinai to prepare for Um Katef. Sharon took personal responsibility for the planning of the assault, and saw a heli-borne assault from the rear, as the only possible means of attack. The man responsible for bringing the paratroops to their target was Colonel Eliezer 'Chita' Cohen who had familiarized the Paratroops, the GOLANI Brigade, and the various SAYEROT with the art of heli-borne warfare.

At 18.50 hours on 6 June, the S-58 helicopter carrying 'Chita' and a 12-man pathfinder unit headed out towards the black vastness of Sinai. One hour later, the 'airborne train' of helicopters ferrying the entire brigade reached the landing zone, four kilometres south of their target. Although asembling the forces in the pitch-dark emptiness was a monumental logistical task, the paratroops force-marched the two kilometres towards Um Katef. At 23.00 hours contact was made with an Egyptian ambush. Artillery from the fort soon rained down on the paratroopers, who made monumental efforts to retrieve their wounded comrades. A battalion commanded by Lieutenant-Colonel Levi Hofesh of Mitla fame proceeded under heavy fire to attack the artillery positions, and silence them after engaging the Egyptian defenders in their trenches. While the 122mm guns were silenced, the armoured columns of UGDAT SHARON led by SAYERET SHIRION attacked and seized Um Katef in a frontal assault.

On 7 June, 'Raful' led his brigade on their journey towards the Suez Canal. Having made a wager of honour with 7th Armoured Brigade's Commander, Colonel Gonen, as to which unit would reach the Canal first,

'Raful' pushed his young conscripts to their limits. As the convoys of M3s, trucks, and jeeps advanced, they passed through a jungle of destroyed Egyptian armour. Some tanks had been destroyed in the deadly accurate IAF bombing runs, others by Major Shomron's SAYERET TZANHANIM. The charred hulks of Russian-made machinery left a lasting impression with the 18-year-old paratroops. Twenty-five kilometres before the Canal, HATIVAT HATZANHANIM encountered a fortified Egyptian position near Kantara. While directing his troops under fire, 'Raful' took a 7.62mm bullet in the forehead which almost knocked him out of his command M3. Only the skill and dedication of Dr Assa, the brigade's medical officer, saved 'Raful's life. He was evacuated to a military hospital, and Chief Paratroop and Infantry Officer Colonel Aharon Davidi arrived at Kantara by Piper Cub to assume command of the brigade. A platoon of paratroops encountered 100 Egyptian paratroopers dressed in leopard pattern camouflage fatigues and armed with AK-47s. The Egyptians immediately surrendered, but the advancing TZANHANIM could not 'maintain' POWs, and allowed them to cross the Canal back home, after their weapons had been confiscated!

With Kantara secure, all that remained for the paratroops were the remnants of Egyptian might at the Firdan Bridge by the Suez Canal. As the paratroops inched closer to the Canal, the three SAYERET formations leading their assault swept into action. In what resembled an Indian attack on a wagon train in the American 'Wild West', the mobile jeeps inflicted havoc among the Egyptian forces desperately attempting to group for a coordinated defence. Dozens of T-55s were destroyed by the combined efforts of the reconnaissance gunners. After the war, Major Shomron would be awarded the I'TUR HAMOFET decoration for exemplary service for his decisive and brilliant command, while his deputy, Captain Tali Fisher, 'made IDF history' by destroying a moving T-55 at more than 1,500 metres (Fisher was killed moments later). After a brief battle, the Firdan Bridge was under paratroop control, and the triumphant TZANHANIM washed their feet in the Canal's blue water. The war in Sinai was over.

In a hospital bed in Beer Sheva, the paratroops' beloved war horse received a bottle of whisky with a small ribbon and note attached. The note simply read: 'After the Paratroops – Gonen'. Victory had been complete.

No examination of élite force operations in 1967 can be complete without a look at the Naval Commandos, or KOMMANDO YAMI. From 1948 until 1967, Naval Commando operations were considered state secrets of the highest order. Although the existence of such a unit in the IDF order of battle was common knowledge, they received no mention in Press dispatches. In fact, the General Staff did not even know what to do with its force of élite frogmen, but The IDF retained control of the unit, however, and the training of the force was split among the Navy and the Paratroops (in fact, many of those who jumped at the Mitla Pass in 1956 with the 890th Paratroop

Battalion were Naval Commandos undergoing squad leader's course with the TZANHANIM).

The lack of public knowledge about the unit was by no means an indicator of their lack of activity. Theirs was a close-knit force of professionals, 'in for the duration', who perfected the art of hit and run warfare together with unique operations for Israel's intelligence agencies. To enhance their élite capabilities, the KOMMANDO YAMI were sent to train in England with the SBS and Royal Marines, and spent time with the French and Italian Marines.

On 10 April, three days after the IAF downed the seven Syrian MiGs, the KOMMANDO YAMI were placed on full alert, and dispatched on numerous intelligence gathering forays.

On 5 June at 19.00 hours, the INS *Tanin* (an obsolete, Second World War British submarine) reached its observation point a few kilometres due north of the Mediterranean port of Alexandria. Minutes later, six frogmen dressed in their protective black neoprene rubber wet suits left the safety of the *Tanin*, and in three groups of two set out on their missions. Their objective was to attach limpet mines to Egyptian naval vessels anchored in the port. They had only six hours to complete their tasks, as *Tanin* had strict orders to clear the area at 03.00 hours on 6 June.

From the outset, the operation encountered unexpected difficulties. The teams were incessantly hounded by Egyptian Coast Guard craft, depth-charges, and hundreds of hand-grenades being tossed into the sea. Clearly the Egyptians were expecting frogmen activity (some reports indicate that successful covert Israeli raids earlier had alerted the Egyptians), and their efforts made a stealthy approach to the harbor virtually impossible. The teams were forced along the coastline, where they found shelter in an underwater cave. Already they were three hours late for their rendezvous with the submarine. At dawn they tried to get away, but they were cornered by a group of spear waving fishermen, and although they tried bluff (they claimed to be British commercial divers, and had been washed ashore), they were hauled off to detention by Egyptian Police and Naval forces. The six, Eitan Lifshitz, Zeev Ben-Yosef, Gad Patish, Eilan Egozi, and Gilad Shnei were interrogated and brutally tortured, although they kept their sense of military discipline and unit dignity. During their weeks of imprisonment, they disclosed only their names, ranks and serial numbers.

Hours later, a KOMMANDO YAMI force was deployed from the INS *Eilat*, eight nautical miles from Port Said, at the Suez Canal's Mediterranean opening. Ferried to the their target by three Zodiac rubber dinghies, the force, commanded by Major Zeev Almog, entered Egyptian waters at 20.45 hours. They proceeded to search for vessels to mine, and set up a temporary CP along the rocky wave breakers. They found nothing of military value to attack, and headed back towards the safety of the *Eilat*.

Similar unsuccessful raids were carried out against the Syrian ports of Latakia and Tartus. Although KOMMANDO YAMI operations were on the whole unsuccessful during the war, they did conduct numerous intelligence gathering operations which were highly successful, and remain classified to this day. More than anything, the 1967 War taught the KOMMANDO YAMI the importance of refining its operational capabilities to perform in all theatres and in all

▲ On the first day of the 1967 War, reservists from Colonel 'Motta' Gur's 55th Paratroop Brigade are briefed prior to their aborted parachute jump on Sharm es-Sheikh. (IDF Archives)

types of combat. For the KOMMANDO YAMI, 1967 was a beginning, which would enable them to put aside their traditional veil of secrecy.

JERUSALEM OF GOLD, TRENCHES AND BLOOD

IN 1967 Jerusalem was a contradiction in reality. It had been Israel's national capital ever since independence was declared in May 1948, yet it was a divided city. Although one of the holiest cities on earth, it was a fortress surrounded by barbed wire, mine-fields, and snipers. A far cry from the international city proposed by the United Nations in 1947, Jerusalem's situation was a direct result of the bitter fighting between the PAL'MACH's HAREL Brigade and the Arab Legion in 1948. Israel had managed to hold on the the western sector of the city, while the Jordanians seized most of the eastern sector, including the walled Old City. The front-line status of Israel's capital and holiest city in Judaism was a painful affront for even the most secular of Israelis. The Jordanians denied Jews access to holy places, and desecration of holy sites, including the Wailing Wall was a blatant provocation which had been left unanswered for too long.

Surprisingly enough, the Israelis had scornfully accepted Jerusalem's divided status. There were no military moves to seize the city, and hostilities were restricted to limited sniper fire along the dreaded 'no man's land'. When war seemed inevitable in May 1967, Israel urged Jordan not to take part in the hostilities. Through the offices of the UN observers in Jerusalem and their Commander, General Odd Bull, IDF Chief of Staff Lieutenant-General Yitzhak Rabin pleaded with King Hussein to keep the long border with Israel quiet. But Hussein was a pariah in the Arab world, and military action was the only way for him to display his 'Arab solidarity'. His armed forces were placed under Egyptian command, and when Israel attacked the Egyptian Air Force in a pre-emptive strike on the morning of 5 June, Hussein responded with force, having been led to believe that it was the Israelis who had been hard hit. Royal Jordanian Air Force (RJAF) Hawker Hunters bombed the Israeli cities of Netanya and Kfar Saba, and Jordanian artillery began to shell Israeli cities, including Tel Aviv and Jerusalem. It was a move the nation of Jordan would forever regret, providing as it did a *casus* belli for the Israelis once and for all to reunite its 'City of Gold' after nineteen years of partition.

Colonel Mordechai 'Motta' Gur was the man destiny chose to lead the historic recapture of Jerusalem. As GOLANI Commander in 1962, his brigade was placed on full alert awaiting the order to seize the city following Jordanian attacks against the Israeli enclave on Mt Scopus. In 1967, his 55th Reserve Paratroop Brigade was originally slated to jump into and seize El Arish or Sharm es-Sheikh in Sinai. Last-minute developments along the Jordanian frontier caused OC Central Command, Major-General Uzi Narkiss, to summon the 55th to his direct command. The 55th Brigade was the youngest of the paratroop reserve forces, and although its fighters were those recently

released from active duty, with little combat experience, the brigade was considered a crack unit. Only two of its officers however were 'regular' army; deputy brigade commander Lieutenant-Colonel Moshe Stampel of 890th Battalion fame, and brigade operations officer Captain Amos Yaron (Chief Paratroop and Infantry Officer during the 1982 invasion of Lebanon).

On the morning of 5 June, the brigade was transferred to Jerusalem by bus. Their objective was the capture of eastern Jerusalem to link up with the Mt Scopus enclave, and then liberate the Old City. The 66th Battalion commanded by Major Yossi Yaffe would attack from the northern approach to the city through the Jordanian Police School and the monstrous fortress atop 'Ammunition Hill'. The 71st Battalion commanded by Major Uzi Ilam would breakthrough at Sheik Jarakh, and Major Yossi Friedkin's 28th Battalion together with the the famed Lieutenant-Colonel Micha Kapusta's 80th Reserve Paratroop Brigade's SAYERET HATIVATIT ('Brigade Recon') would seize the Rockefeller Museum and the Old City, supported by the remainder of the brigade. Since its mobilization on 23 May, the men had prepared themselves mentally for a parachute jump and desert warfare, but they were not at all disappointed with the opportunity of becoming modern-day Maccabees, and hopefully the final conquerors of a much conquered city.

The 66th Battalion was assigned three most difficult positions to capture: the Police School Building, defended by a company of infantrymen from the Jordanian 27th Infantry Brigade; a heavily fortified hill known as the 'Yellow Rag', south of the school; and 'Ammunition Hill', a monstrous complex of trenches and bunkers sealed by a ring of barbed wire which would soon be known as 'Blood Hill'. 'Ammunition Hill' was defended by a company of Jordanian soldiers supported by heavy machine-guns, mortars, and recoilless rifles. The hill commanded the Jerusalem-Ramallah road, as well as access to the Sheik Jarakh section, and Mt Scopus. To capture Jerusalem, 'Ammunition Hill' had to be silenced quickly!

Major Yaffe realized that any assault on the 'monster' had to be done quickly and at night. He knew the determination and capabilities of the Jordanian soldiers, the best in the Arab world, and a daylight attack would cost him his entire battalion. At 02.15 hours on 6 June the first round in the liberation of Jerusalem was fired.

The 66th Battalion's ALEPH ('1st') Company attacked the Police School in a frontal assault. Led by its sapper contingent, ALEPH Company negotiated the dense row of barbed wire and land-mines under heavy Jordanian small arms and 25-pounder artillery fire. The paratroopers were undaunted by the Jordanian's determined defence, and continued their advance all the way to the building's entrance. By now, most of the Jordanian soldiers had fled

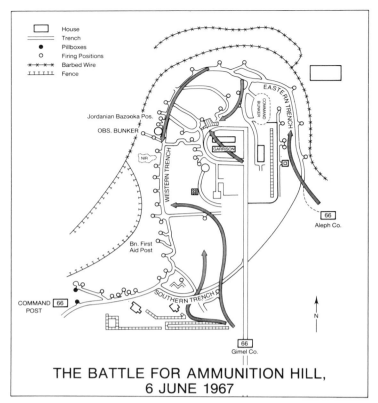

THE BATTLE FOR AMMUNITION HILL,
6 JUNE 1967

Legend:
- House
- Trench
- Pillboxes
- Firing Positions
- Barbed Wire
- Fence

EASTERN TRENCH
COMMAND BUNKER
Jordanian Bazooka Pos.
OBS. BUNKER
NIR
GARRISON
WESTERN TRENCH
88
Bn. First Aid Post
66 Aleph Co.
COMMAND POST 66
SOUTHERN TRENCH
N
66 Gimel Co.

'Ammunition Hill', and clearing the school was assigned to a few 7.62mm FN MAG light machine-gun squads. They cleared the first floor firing hundreds of rounds of ammunition, while the upper floors received a more practised approach. Teams of two would throw a grenade into each room, and then rake it with a magazine emptying burst of fire from their UZIS and FN assault rifles. A final 'flashlight' check of the building by company commander Captain Gabi Magel confirmed the building secure. A platoon was left behind to guard the heavily battered Police School, while the remainder of the company headed out towards the Ambassador Hotel and the Sheik Jarakh section.

For the assault on 'Ammunition Hill', the talents of the 83rd Combat Engineering Company were required. An elaborate, mine-field preceded the thick rows of barbed wire surrounding the numerous bunkers and trenches. The Jordanian defenders had already trained their .50 calibre machine-guns and MI carbines on the valley below, awaiting the sight of the paratroop's lizard pattern camouflage fatigues, and the order to fire. The Jordanians expected a bitter fight, and each firing position had been issued extra supplies of grenades and ammunition. Recal-

◄◄ ▲ Two views of the 'monster', 'Ammunition Hill', a bunker complex overlooking the northern approaches to Jerusalem. The Jordanians tenaciously defended the position, and in three hours of battle the 66th Battalion suffered 38 dead. (Sigalit Katz)

ling the past battles with the Israelis for Jerusalem, bayonets too were at the ready!

By 02.45, the engineers had blasted a hole through a section of the barbed wire with Bangalore torpedoes, allowing the 66th Battalion's GIMEL ('3rd') Company and its supporting six M50 Sherman tanks from the 16th 'Jerusalem' Armoured Brigade to mount its attack. This was conducted in a wide-flanking pincer movement, allowing the trenches to be systematically cleared towards the command bunker and barracks, which would be neutralized in the final assault. GIMEL Company had expected to face only a single company of Jordanian infantrymen, not realizing that 'Ammunition Hill' had now been complemented by the surviving defenders of the Police School. To make the situation more difficult for GIMEL Company, only one hour of total darkness remained.

The narrow confines of 'Ammunition Hill's trenches slowed the paratroopers' advance to a painstaking crawl. The heavily laden men carried extra rucksacks of ammunition and grenades, which were too bulky to afford quick passage through the trenches. Some men were unable to get up after hitting the ground to take cover, while others

◄ Heading towards the battle's cloud of death, paratroopers from the 55th Reserve Paratroop Brigade's 66th Battalion make for 'Ammunition Hill', scene of the fiercest fighting of the campaign on 6 June 1967. (IDF Archives)

acted as giant corks, stopping up movement entirely. It was difficult to identify friend from foe, as the well-concealed bunkers muffled the flash of fired weapons, while hidden snipers took their toll of the beleaguered paratroops. Bazooka fire did not penetrate the thick concrete bunkers, and the battle was fought at too close a proximity to call in artillery, air strikes, or even maximize the M50 Shermans' firepower. Paratroopers soon ran out of ammunition, and so fierce was the fighting that rifles taken from dead Jordanian soldiers were used as clubs. Throughout the battle, the only men who moved about freely were the medics, who saved countless lives under murderous fire.

The task of clearing the trenches required bravery and luck. Officers and NCOs, were the first to be hit; the paratroopers climbing over the bodies of their friends. Volunteers would climb out of the trenches and provide covering fire, but they usually ended up dead or seriously wounded. An hour into the battle, the battalion aid station was flooded with more seriously wounded than it could handle. With little choice, GIMEL's Commander, Captain Oved 'Dadi' Ya'akobi, requested reinforcements from BET ('2nd') Company.

The battle for the western bunker was particularly desperate, as a platoon commanded by Captain Nir Nitzan was pinned down by heavy and accurate Jordanian fire from three sides. His men had been mauled, and wounded soldiers lay atop dead comrades, whose bodies provided cover for the platoon's gunners and riflemen. Realizing that the Jordanian positions had to be pinpointed and dealt with, Nitzan had to send a paratrooper out of the trench to provide covering fire from above. With no time to ask for volunteers, Nitzan assigned the job to one of the unit's FN MAG gunners, Private Eitan Nava, a 23-year-old reservist from MOSHAV Moledet. Nava instinctively jumped out of the 5-foot-high trench, charging and firing in a deliberate though frenzied manner. While Nava fired his FN MAG from above, his besieged comrades broke out and attacked the trench's inner bunker positions. Within a matter of seconds, Nava had advanced thirty metres and had killed twenty Jordanians, until he was hit in the head, by a sniper's bullet and fell back into the trench. Nava's charge rallied the platoon, whose fervour soon spread to other squads and platoons. It was the turning-point in a battle which had desperately needed one. For his courage, Nava was posthumously awarded the IDF's highest decoration for supreme valour, the I'TUR HAGVURA.

By 05.00 hours, the paratroopers had seized the initiative atop 'Ammunition Hill', but Jordanian fire though decreased in intensity, had increased in accuracy. Dawn had broken and the advancing Israelis were now clearly visible. Spotters with a good view from the hill's commanding bunker directed precise and deadly 120mm mortar fire into the trenches, where the Jordanians and Israelis were still engaged in close-quarter combat. The Israelis were impressed and concerned with the tenacity and heroism of the Jordanians' stand. It was known that the

▲ Chief Paratroop and Infantry Officer, Colonel Aharon Davidi interviews the survivors of the 66th Battalion following the battle of 'Ammunition Hill'. Note the bitterness and fatigue apparent on the paratroopers' faces. (IDF Archives)

British-trained Royal Jordanian Army was the finest of all Arab armies, but these men were fighting so fanatically simply because they were trapped in 'Ammunition Hill'. The barbed wire and mined defensive perimeter was so complete that the Jordanian defenders were literally trapped inside. Unable to escape, they fought to the last man!

The capture of 'Ammunition Hill' was of paramount concern to the General Staff, and Central Command Operations Officer Lieutenant-Colonel Arik Regev urged Colonel Gur to get the job done with. There was little that Gur could do, except wait patiently for his men to finish the business. With the combined efforts of the GIMEL Company survivors, and BET Company, the only Jordanian position remaining was the 'big bunker', which overlooked the Jerusalem-Ramallah road. A coordinated effort with bazookas and grenades did little to damage the huge concrete block, and in fact resulted in numerous paratroop casualties from flying concrete fragments. The only option remaining was to use explosives, and satchel charges were quickly prepared. To keep the Israelis at bay, the Jordanians would fire a burst from their .30 calibre machine-guns, throw grenades, and then wait. Each time after the last Jordanian grenade had exploded, four paratroopers hurriedly placed sacks of TNT near the bunker's entrance. Upon receiving the signal from platoon commander Lieutenant Yoram Elyishav, the explosives were activated

The entire hill trembled in a tremendous explosion and a cloud of encompassing smoke. When the dust and debris cleared, the paratroopers threw in a last volley of grenade and machine-gun fire. At 06.15 hours, the Israeli flag was hoisted above 'Ammunition Hill'.

The battle had been one of the epic struggles in Israel's history. In three hours, 38 paratroopers had died, with almost 100 seriously wounded. The Jordanians suffered more than seventy dead, with only the wounded taken prisoner. After the battle, Chief Paratroop and Infantry Officer Colonel Aharon Davidi visited the survivors of BET and GIMEL Companies, and discussed the battle with these seasoned veterans who only hours earlier had been simple reservists untested in battle. In the three hours of fighting, one soldier (Nava) was posthumously awarded the I'TUR HAGVURA, comparable to the British Victoria Cross or US Congressional Medal of Honor, three soldiers were awarded the I'TUR HA'OZ decoration for courage, and nine received the I'TUR HAMOFET decoration for exemplary service. It was a truly remarkable battle which forever changed IDF tactics for attacking fortified positions. Following the war, a song entitled 'Ammunition Hill' sung by the Central Command Choir became a national sensation. It meticulously described the battle to the Israeli public, who until then had been ignorant of the details of their countrymen's heroic self-sacrifice.

As the 66th Battalion's ALEPH and DALED Companies continued their advance, seizing the Ambassador Hotel and breaking through the Sheik Jarakh section, the 71st and 28th Battalions went on the offensive. Their tasks were to storm through the no man's land frontier separating old and new Jerusalem, and to seize control of the strategic Nablus Road. The Jordanians threw up an equally tenacious defence, and each block and house had to be fought for. M50 Shermans from the 16th Armoured Brigade were brought in for added fire power, as both battalions inched their way closer towards the Old City, the ultimate objective in the battle for Jerusalem. The paratroops' lack of urban combat training was clearly obvious, as no strategy existed for clearing the countless alleys turned into fortresses. Both battalions suffered heavy casualties in the fierce fighting, exacerbated by accurate Jordanian artillery and mortar fire into the battalion's staging area.

The seizure of the Rockefeller Museum, overlooking the paratroops' advance path into the Old City as well as to Mt Scopus, was one of the most important objectives of the campaign. Its capture fell to Major Yossi Friedkin's 28th Battalion and Kapusta's reconnaissance force. The Museum was but twenty yards away from the gates of the Old City, and was a stone's throw from the Damascus and Lion Gates. Attempts to reach the Museum were almost as

▼ M50 Sherman tanks are called in to support the 55th Reserve Paratroop Brigade's 71st Battalion's attempt to seize the Sheikh Jarakh section of Jerusalem. The Jordanians proved themselves to be highly skilled defenders, giving little quarter in their determined efforts to stop the paratroopers' advance. (IDF Archives)

difficult as the battle itself, as Jordanian artillery, mortar, and sniper fire took a heavy toll of the battalion. It was in fact the 120mm mortar fire which inflicted the greatest casualties, as a well-directed round into the confines of the narrow streets could wipe out an entire platoon.

The race towards the Rockefeller Museum (known as the 'Rock') produced a flurry of grenade and sniper fire from the parapets along the Old City walls. Many of the Jordanians had M1 carbines fitted with sniper 'scopes, which made the Israeli advance route into a death trap. The paratroops responded by showering the walls with phosphorus grenades, mortar, and recoilless rifle fire. In the end, however, it was the UZI which would determine the course of battle, as well-placed bursts of fire allowed the companies of the 28th Battalion and Kapusta's SAYERET to enter the Museum, and eventually raise a hastily drawn Star of David flag atop the roof. This act provoked a vicious Jordanian mortar barrage, but signified to the entire brigade that the 'Rock' was in Israeli hands. Although suffering the heaviest casualties of the battle, Kapusta's élite SAYARIM (recon fighters) begged Gur for a new assignment.

When night fell, Colonel Gur summoned his battalion commanders for a briefing. Wednesday, 7 June would be the day that the Old City was attacked, and its capture was crucial, especially considering that an expected UN Security Council sponsored ceasefire was to go into effect the next day, and there was still much to be done! As Gur discussed strategy with his battalion commanders that night amid the shelling and machine-gun fire, the men of the 55th Brigade eagerly awaited the order to go into the Old City.

Colonel Gur chose the following attack plan for the assault on the Old City of Jerusalem and its surrounding areas. The 66th Battalion would set out from their rest area at the Ambassador Hotel towards Mt Scopus and attack the 'Augusta Victoria' enclave from the north. The 71st Battalion was to climb Wadi Joz (near the American Colony) towards 'Augusta Victoria' from the west. Micha Kapusta's SAYERET would attack the crossroads at Abu Tor with an armoured force over the Kidron Valley Bridge, and prepare an ambush against a possible Jordanian counter-attack from Jericho. Waiting in the wings was the 28th Battalion, given the historic task of breaking through the Old City at the Lion Gate, the only one wide enough to take armoured vehicles.

On the morning of 7 June, the offensive to secure Jerusalem before the ceasefire commenced. As the 'Augusta Victoria' complex towered above the entire para-

troop route of advance, silencing it was a primary objective. Besides calling in heavy artillery fire, Gur ordered the IAF to make an appearance. At 08.32 hours, a flight of four Mystère IV fighter-bombers appeared over the horizon. Their screaming approach brought wild cheers from the paratroopers, but when they unleashed their deadly loads of napalm, the men looked on in awe. The napalm attack continued for twenty minutes. Clearly Central Command did not want a repeat of 'Ammunition Hill' on their hands. Jordanian resistance in fact had weakened since the first day of combat. The 27th Brigade's commander, Brigadier Ata had organized a slow and calm withdrawal from the city during the night of 6/7 June. So complete had been the Israeli attack, and so devastating the IAF ground support against reinforcements coming from the West Bank, that Ata realized his predicament. His well-trained and loyal Bedouin fighters refused to surrender, however, and the 55th Brigade was to pay dearly for each inch of territory.

Early in the morning, Colonel Gur perched his Brigade CP atop the roof of the Intercontinental Hotel on the Mount of Olives, which afforded him a view of the Old City second to none. All that was needed was permission to enter it! General Narkiss issued the awaited order at 08.04 hours. As Gur and his command echelon descended towards the Lion Gate for the breakthrough, he came over the brigade's communication frequency and announced: 'To all paratroop commanders. We are ascending into the Old City. We are ascending to the Temple Mount and the Wailing Wall. The Jewish nation awaits our victory. Israel awaits this historic moment. Ascend and be victorious!'

For hours before this moment in history, the 28th Battalion's heavy mortar squad had sniped at known Jordanian positions within the Old City, most notably in the Muslim Quarter. The use of heavier fire power was strictly prohibited, as the Old City and its holy sites were to be protected from destruction at all costs. Jordanian defences had already crumbled as most soldiers quickly changed into civilian clothing to blend into the local population. The paratroopers led by Gur searched for a single wall which would signify the end of their quest. At 10.00 hours, a clearly moved Gur went on the brigade's communications frequency once again to announce to his fighters and the entire nation of Israel, 'The Temple Mount is in our hands. Repeat. The Temple Mount is in our hands!' Tears began to roll down the cheeks of the exhausted fighters, as they embraced the Western Wall of their holy temple in an emotionally filled trance of silent prayer. Even secular Jews who never went to Synagogue donned head covering, and began the customary slipping of hand-scribbled notes of prayer into the wall's cracks.

Quickly the dignitaries and generals flocked to the Wailing Wall to partake in the national celebration. When KOL YISRAEL (Israel Radio) announced the liberation of Jerusalem on the air, soldiers in Sinai, near the Syrian border, and those in hospital began cheering and embracing in a wild frenzy. In historical tradition, Defence Minister Moshe Dayan, Chief of Staff Rabin, and Major

▲ Advancing gingerly through the Old City's *suq* (market-place), a squad from the 28th Battalion searches for Jordanian snipers. (IGPO)

▲▶ 'The Temple Mount is in our hands. Repeat. The Temple Mount is in our hands!' Colonel Gur relaxes with his battalion and company commanders at the gates of the Al-Aksa Mosque on the Temple Mount (IGPO)

General Narkiss *walked* victoriously into the Old City. Led by Major-General Shlomoh Goren, the IDF's Chief Rabbi, traditional SHOFAR ram's-horn trumpets were brought out, and sounded in a religious frenzy of relief. As the IDF's top brass touched the wall for the first time in nineteen years, the paratroopers began singing what became the anthem of the campaign, the song 'Jerusalem of Gold', knowing all too well the stiff price in blood they had paid for their country's glory. The liberation of Jerusalem had cost the 55th Brigade and its supporting forces 195 dead, and 1,131 wounded. Israel's most important victory had been one of its bloodiest.

The liberation of Jerusalem was a historic moment which the paratroops shared with the entire nation of Israel. Their participation in the war, however, was not finished, and they were dispatched north to the Golan Heights. The paratroops had not been the only élite unit to operate with Central Command in the campaign against Jordan. SAYERET HARUV was active from day one of war with Jordan, particularly in leading the HAREL Brigade in the capture of the city of Ramallah, north of Jerusalem.

When war erupted along the Jordanian frontier on 6 June, one of the most pressing military threats facing Central Command was the reported presence of an Egyptian commando force operating near Latrun, the scene of such fierce fighting nineteen years earlier. To counter this new development, Central Command Operations Commander Lieutenant-Colonel Arik Regev ordered the company-sized SAYERET HARUV to lead a long-range reconnaissance into Latrun, supported by an AML armoured car unit, and a company of officer cadets. Crossing the border into Latrun, HARUV Commander Major Arieh 'Tzimel' Tzidon reported to Lieutenant-Colonel Regev that the Jordanians had abandoned their positions. HARUV continued its advance until it encountered heavy fire from well-concealed firing positions in the towering hills above. The HARUV fighters jumped out of their jeeps, and attacked. In a brief though decisive battle, the HARUV fighters killed almost a dozen Egyptian commandos, identifiable by their leopard pattern camouflage fatigues, and Russian-supplied mortars and AK-47s.

Although HARUV's push towards Ramallah would bring it into contact with remnants of the destroyed Royal Jordanian Army, including a pitched battle against a Jordanian jeep-mounted 106mm recoilless rifle force, it would be their last conventional form of combat for six years. Immediately following the ceasefire of 10 June, SAYERET HARUV was summoned to Jerusalem to lead Israeli efforts against Jordanian intelligence officers who had remained behind the conquering IDF, masquerading as civilians. In July SAYERET HARUV was sent into the desert wilderness of the Jordan Valley to interdict guerrilla and intelligence infiltration. It would be one of the bloodiest campaigns in IDF history, and would earn HARUV its rightful place in the history books.

TWO FLAGS ON THE GOLAN HEIGHTS:
THE GOLANI BRIGADE, 9–10 JUNE 1967

SINCE 1948, the Golan Heights had been a symbol of Syrian dominance over northern Israel. From its towering vantage-points, Syrian artillery spotters controlled the numerous Israeli agricultural settlements below in the Hula Valley and near the Sea of Galilee. The Syrians took full advantage of their geographic mastery, and harassed the KIBBUTZIM and MOSHAVIM with incessant artillery barrages, turning the civilians into hostages of their own bomb shelters. To secure the heights from Israeli attack, the Syrians established thirteen heavily fortified positions throughout the Golan's 480 square miles of territory. They were impervious to air and artillery attack, as many were embedded in the mountainous hills and volcanic cones known as TELS. Any ground attack against the heights would have to go up a steep rise under the watchful eyes of the Syrian gunners. Needless to say, the Syrians considered the Golan Heights their 'Rock of Gibraltar'.

To Israel, the Golan Heights was a symbol of impotence. Although numerous GOLANI and paratroop retaliatory raids had attacked Syrian artillery positions, the shellings continued unhindered. Even the highly successful GOLANI raids against Tewfiq and Nuqieb in the early 1960s had only temporarily silenced the Syrian guns. To the men of the GOLANI Brigade, many of whom were from northern Israel, the Golan Heights was a matter of honour. Their hard-fought actions had earned them the reputation as guardians of Israel's northern frontier, and as long as civilians were being killed by Syrian artillery, they were failing in their task. When the Middle East once again came close to the brink in the spring of 1967, there was no doubt in anyone's mind on the IDF General Staff as to which unit would be 'responsible' for Syria.

The Golan Heights was not the IDF's primary concern in the opening days of the fighting in June 1967. Although the IAF paid its due to the Syrian Air Force and 'necessary' ground targets, the GOLANI Brigade was forced to wait patiently for the green light to assault the heights. The participation of the brigade's ARAYOT HAGOLAN Battalion of squad leader cadets in the capture of the Jordanian West Bank city of Nablus on 6 June hinted to many that a UN-sanctioned ceasefire might be imposed before GOLANI had the chance to 'deal with Syria'. As each day of inactivity passed, tensions and tempers mounted in the GOLANI camp.

On the morning of Friday 9 June, GOLANI Commander Colonel Yonah Efrat received the go-ahead for the attack on the Golan Heights from OC Northern Command, Major General David 'Dado' Elazar. As Colonel Efrat relayed the eagerly awaited orders to his men, officers and conscripts alike embraced in joy. Some wept with happiness, while others began dancing the HORA (an Israeli folk-step). Although such displays might seem baffling, it is typical for GOLANI, whose trademark of unit cohesion and comradeship is such few other IDF units could boast. GOLANI was a family in every sense of the word. Officers acted as proud and doting fathers in the way they looked after their men, while soldiers enjoyed an open and frank dialogue with their officers about professional and personal problems.

Paradoxically, discipline in the brigade was strict. Although officers distributed food and sweets from home to their men, infractions of military discipline received severe, though sometimes non-conventional forms of punishment. By far the most extraordinary example of this was the punishment BARAK Battalion Commander Lieutenant-Colonel Moshe 'Musa' Klein chose for a young sergeant accused of a minor disciplinary infraction. Klein denied the sergeant the right to go into combat with his comrades, confining him to his quarters. Although to many the opportunity to evade combat might seem a gift, such a prospect was the ultimate in humiliation in the GOLANI Brigade. The sergeant cried and pleaded with his battalion commander, informing him in the most 'respectful of tones' that nothing, including military prison would keep him from the fight. So important was participation in battle with the HEVRA (friends), that soldiers left military hospital beds to join their companies, and soldiers just recently released from active duty though not yet assigned to their reserve unit, returned to their old base of their own accord in inspiring numbers.

Of all the Syrian fortresses on the Golan Heights, Tel Fahar was the largest and most strongly fortified. Positioned on two hills running north to south (the northern peak controlling the entire complex), Tel Fahar was protected by three rows of thick barbed wire each of which surrounded an elaborate mine-field. Its capture fell to Lieutenant-Colonel Klein's BARAK Battalion, one of the brigade's finest. The battalion's three companies were fully mechanized, mounted on M3 halftracks, and supported by a company of M50 Shermans and AMX-13s for their frontal assault on Tel Fahar and the adjacent fortress at Bourj a-Bawil. One of BARAK's secondary objectives was to provide covering fire (if needed) for the HABOKIM HARISHONIM Battalion's assault on the Syrian fortress at Tel Azzaziat, defended by seventy Syrian soldiers, and situated 1,500 metres west of Tel Fahar. The GIDEON Battalion would act as a reserve force, waiting for a situation to develop which required their assistance.

On 9 June at 13.00 hours, GOLANI crossed the border near KIBBUTZ Kfar Szold. The columns of halftracks and tanks was immediately subjected to a murderous barrage of Syrian anti-tank and artillery fire. Tel Azzaziat was closest to the frontier, and HABOKIM HARISHONIM went into action first. Battalion Commander Lieutenant-Colonel Beni Enbar (commander of the ARAYOT HAGOLAN Battalion during the Nuqieb raid, and recipient of the I'TUR HA'OZ) ordered his tanks and halftracks to break through the camp in a frontal assault, while the battalion's sappers removed land-mines in a hurried and unsafe fashion. Enbar's battle plan called for the halftracks and tanks to provide covering fire while the riflemen stormed the already battered trenches. Tel Azzaziat's extensive mine network made that plan impossible, and in the end, the attackers went in alone on foot.

Tel Azzaziat was neutralized in two hours, and according to the book! Covered by accurate fire from machine-gunners, riflemen, and grenadiers, officers and NCOs threw grenades towards the concrete pillboxes, rooting out the Syrian defenders. Such systematic tactics were time-consuming, but allowed for maximum fire support and, most importantly, prevented unnecessary casualties. After two hours of exhaustive combat, the only remnant of Syrian resistance, a well-concealed sniper, was permanently silenced by a well-aimed anti-tank grenade. The Syrians lost more then thirty dead at Tel Azzaziat, while HABOKIM HARISHONIM had only one man killed. In keeping with GOLANI tradition, the brigade's flag was hoisted together with the Israeli flag over Tel Azzaziat's command pillbox.

At 13.30 hours the BARAK Battalion deployed into attack formation for the assault on Tel Fahar. As murderous Syrian tank and anti-tank fire began to rain upon their columns of halftracks and tanks, Lieutenant-Colonel Klein realized that a tragic mistake had been made. Instead of descending on Tel Fahar in an outflanking attack at its unprotected rear, the BARAK Battalion was ascending straight towards the front and centre of the fortress where the Syrians (faithful to Soviet defensive doctrines) had positioned their arsenal of M43 57mm anti-tank guns, B-10 82mm recoilless rifles, and heavy machine-guns.

During the ascent of the slope, one of the three tanks protecting Klein's command halftrack was hit by accurate anti-tank fire and destroyed. Other vehicles began to slacken in pace, as gunfire, land-mines, and the rocky terrain took their toll. With a chaotic situation on his hands, and his vehicle the target of the Syrian gunners, Klein undauntedly continued his push towards the fortress. Command and control soon became impossible; all the tanks had been hit, and the vehicles of Lieutenant Aharon Vardi's ALEPH (1st) Company and GIMEL (3rd) Company bogged down. Already the battalion had suffered serious casualties, and penetration of the fortress had not even begun. Lieutenant-Colonel Klein regrouped and ordered the remnants of the battalion to attack from west to east, but soon more tanks and vehicles became casualties. The situation became more desperate when the battalion's artillery, halftracks fitted with 90mm mortars, were all hit and destroyed.

Even before the bitter fighting inside Tel Fahar began, BARAK's soldiers performed acts of untold heroism. When a M3 Halftrack from ALEPH Company took a direct 57mm hit, one of the vehicle's gunners, Private Moshe Draimer,

ordered 'his' men out of the burning halftrack, while he provided cover with his .30 calibre machine-gun. Draimer fired in a wild though accurate manner; a remarkable feat considering he was badly burned and screaming with pain. Corporal Yisrael Huberman ran towards the engulfed vehicle to rescue the wounded driver, and Private Draimer who were both trapped in the driver's compartment. Moments later the vehicle took one *final* 57mm round near the fuel tank, and exploded in a ball of fire. Although severely burned, Corporal Huberman lived to be awarded the I'TUR HA'OZ decoration for courage, while Private Draimer was posthumously awarded the I'TUR HAGVURA decoration for supreme valour.

Lieutenant-Colonel Klein's CP halftrack was also hit by an anti-tank round, and communications and control between battalion and commander ceased. Klein sent Captain Alex Krinski, the battalion's artillery support officer, to rally the remnants of ALEPH Company for the assault, even though four of its seven halftracks had been destroyed, and 35 of its fighters (of a total of 60) had been killed or wounded. Krinski and Vardi split the survivors between them, and raced towards Tel Fahar's southern approach, defended by two 10-metre-wide barbed wire concertinas which hemmed in Tel Fahar's mine-field. Five metres beyond the barbed wire were the Syrian trenches and the true battle for Tel Fahar.

Attempts to breach the three rows of barbed wire failed. At first Sergeant Dov Rosenblum attempted to cut his way through, but the wiring was too dense, and Syrian fire too deadly. Bangalore torpedoes were also attempted, but they too failed, and the 25 attackers soon found themselves the target of a determined Syrian effort. Instinctively, and without receiving the order, Private David Shirazi jumped on to the wire, and signalled to his comrades to follow across on his back. Private Shirazi's human bridge allowed ALEPH Company to enter Tel Fahar and begin the difficult task of clearing the Syrians from their well-fortified positions. Shirazi then straightened himself, and crawled along the wire to join his comrades. His bleeding body did not hinder his efforts, and Private Shirazi fought like a man possessed. He led 'his' squad of soldiers, firing his FN MAG light machine-gun at any target that moved, neutralizing numerous Syrian positions in his wake. Toward the end of the battle, Private Shirazi was hit in the head by a sniper's bullet, and killed. After the war, he was posthumously awarded the I'TUR HAGVURA.

The brutal battle for the trenches lasted two hours. The GOLANI infantrymen had to fight their way uphill through twisting trenches and concrete bunkers, to reach the northern bunker, and seize Tel Fahar in its entirety. The Syrians fought tenaciously, giving no quarter. Heavy Syrian fire from the first bunker slowed down ALEPH

▶ SAYERET GOLANI Commander, Major Reuven 'Reuvke' Eliaz briefs his recon infantrymen prior to the GOLANI Brigade's rite of passage; the battle for Tel Fahar, 9 June 1967. (IDF Archives)

Company's advance, while the Syrians began to engage the Israelis in hand-to-hand fighting. The men of ALEPH Company used everything in their possession to beat off the Syrians, including small arms, knives, rocks, and fists. During this close-quarter mêlée, Major Krinski was hit by enemy fire and killed.

Lieutenant-Colonel Klein rushed towards Major Krinski's dwindling force which was courageously fighting its way towards the northern bunker. Klein had to race through the trenches, avoiding enemy fire, and stepping on the dead and wounded. By the time he caught up with the main battle, Krinski's force had but one soldier, Corporal Yitzhak Hamui, not killed or wounded. Klein ordered Hamui to follow him and attempt to link up with the other forces in the trenches to coordinate a unit effort. Klein raced out of the bunker first, apparently not hearing Hamui's warning of Syrian snipers. Klein was hit in the head by a sniper's bullet, and killed.

Leaderless, and with dwindling supplies of ammunition, ALEPH and GIMEL Companies were in a precarious situation. They split into small groups of two or three and engaged the Syrians in small though brutal skirmishes. The IAF and artillery bombardments had only scratched the enormous concrete bunkers and pillboxes, and the beleaguered GOLANI riflemen found it virtually impossible to root the Syrian defenders from their 'nests'. Each communications trench was complemented by Goryunov heavy machine-gun positions, which poured murderous

fire on to the GOLANI fighters. The most amazing feats of heroism were made to save the lives of wounded comrades. Soldiers, themselves hurt and bleeding, bandaged their own wounds, and proceeded to take care of and evacuate comrades wounded more seriously. The increasing number of seriously wounded limited the chances for ALEPH and GIMEL Companies to survive.

At this time, however, the BARAK Battalion's BET Company commanded by Captain Avraham Solovitz and SAYERET GOLANI entered the fray. BET Company had completed the capture of the adjacent Bourj a-Bawil fortress without incident, and it was ordered into Tel Fahar. SAYERET GOLANI had been inactive up to this point, much to the chagrin of its commander, Major Reuven 'Ruvka' Eliaz. It had been delegated the capture of Na'amush, but when the 8th Armoured Brigade reached it with little difficulty, Colonel Efrat ordered the SAYERET to wait near Tel Hai for further orders. Major Eliaz was scouting the area in search of Syrian stragglers, when the dire situation at Tel Fahar became known to him. He immediately informed Colonel Efrat who ordered the SAYERET into battle. At 17.00 hours, BET Company and the SAYERET linked up, and entered the battle. BET Company provided fire support with 90mm mortar and bazooka fire, while Major Eliaz led the SAYERET into the trenches. Fierce hand-to-hand fighting ensued. Soldiers running out of ammunition picked up the weapons of fallen comrades or enemy soldiers, until their magazines too were empty, and then

used their bayonets and fists. In one of the most dramatic fisticuff struggles of the battle, a badly wounded Major Eliaz was almost killed by a determined Syrian officer, who was cut down by a burst of UZI fire. The Syrians fought to the last man, but at 18.00 hours, the two flags were hoisted atop the command bunker indicating GOLANI's victory.

Of all the thirteen Syrian positions which the GOLANI Brigade captured on the Golan Heights, Tel Fahar was the hardest fought and bloodiest of all. The BARAK Battalion left behind nineteen dead, including the battalion commander, the operations commander, and three company commanders. Three members of Major Eliaz's SAYERET were killed and in all more 100 GOLANI fighters were seriously wounded. When Colonel Efrat was asked which soldiers should be cited for bravery, he answered 'the entire battalion'. In all, twelve GOLANI fighters were awarded bravery citations, including Lieutenant-Colonel Klein, Captain Krinski, and Major Eliaz.

Hours after the last shots were heard at Tel Fahar, the battalion continued its advance towards Kuneitra, the capital of the Golan Heights. During the remaining 36 hours of hostillities, HABOKIM HARISHONIM captured Banias, and Masada, which was seized in coordination with the 45th Armoured Brigade. Led by SAYERET EGOZ, GIDEON Battalion together with the 8th Armoured Brigade captured Kuneitra. The following day the GIDEON Battalion was heli-lifted to the summit of Mt Hermon.

With the GOLANI Brigade in firm control of the northern sector of the Golan Heights, Northern Command dispatched Colonel Danni Matt's 80th Reserve Paratroop Brigade in a heli-borne assault to seize the southern heights. Led by Micha Kapusta's brigade SAYERET, and including a company of Naval Commandos who had requested to see 'action', the 80th Brigade was heli-lifted to the southern Golan Heights by Colonel Eliezer 'Chita' Cohen's élite S-58 helicopter squadron. They captured Tewfiq, El-Hama, Skufia, El-Al, and Butmia in lightning assaults. It had been a long road for the 80th Reserve Paratroop Brigade: from the desert fortress of Um Katef to the Old City of Jerusalem, to the rocky terrain of the Golan.

Although many different branches of the IDF were represented in the fight for the Golan Heights, the victory belonged to the men of the GOLANI Brigade. One week after the war, the survivors of the BARAK Battalion returned to Tel Fahar for a memorial ceremony honouring their fallen. It was an emotional gathering, as each soldier was able to offer his personal accounts of the chaotic epic battle. Many of the soldiers still wore bandages, while others had 'escaped' hospital beds to rejoin their battalion. At the ceremony, Chief of Staff Lieutenant-General Yitzhak Rabin, himself a veteran of bloody fighting in Jerusalem with the HAREL Brigade in 1948, proudly concluded that the brigade had brought 'honour to the entire IDF'.

The bloodletting at Tel Fahar was the culmination of GOLANI's promise one day to avenge the Syrian harassment of northern Israel. The brigade had earned the right to protect the northern frontier with the blood of its fallen, although little could it realize that its true operational responsibilities in the area had only just begun.

5

THE 1000-AND-MORE DAYS WAR

Operations during the War of Attrition, 1967–70

FIRE IN THE DESERT: OPERATIONS AGAINST EGYPT, 1967–70

THE 1967 War did not bring peace to the Middle East. As Israel basked in her victory, the Arab nations vowed revenge. Israel's leadership believed it would be able to trade off some of her vast new territory in exchange for peace, but the 'three no' resolution from the Arab Summit meeting at Khartoum in Setpember 1967 (no peace with Israel, no negotiations with her, and no recognition of her territorial claims) ensured that hostilities would continue.

Victory brought Israel security problems it had never had to face before as the IDF was forced to defend territory five times the size of the state of Israel; something its economic and manpower capabilities could hardly accommodate. Although Egypt had been crushed in June 1967, she still possessed an enormous standing army, one now motivated by the thirst for revenge. President Nasser was still the undisputed leader in the Arab world, and his victim's image made him more defiant than ever. With confidence induced by massive supplies of Soviet armaments and advisors, Egypt initiated a war of attrition. Nasser knew it would take Egypt years until it could hope to retrieve the Sinai by force from the powerful IDF. But Nasser also knew that Egypt still possessed the capability to shell IDF positions, raid her forces, and make the price of occupying Egyptian land an unbearable one.

On 1 July 1967, an Egytian commando force crossed the Suez Canal and mined a road used by IDF patrols. An IDF tank force was deployed and in the ensuing mêlée, heavy artillery fire was called in by both sides. From that day on, sniping, kidnappings, intermittent shellings, and commando raids became the norm along the Canal's front line. The attempts to outdo each other's provocation reached its peak on 21 October 1967, when the IDF/Navy flagship, the destroyer *Eilat* was sunk by STYX sea-to-sea missiles fired by four Egyptian Navy Komar missile boats. It was the first missile engagement in military history, and forever raised the level of violence in the region.

With increasing casualties in a seemingly winless confrontation, the IDF decided to maximize the defensive potential of her élite forces. SAYERET SHAKED was the first unit dispatched to the Canal, and was ordered to open desert routes, and establish communication lines between the lightly fortified IDF positions. Their most important tasks, however, were search and destroy operations against Egyptian commandos in pursuits similar to their legendary exploits against Egyptian military intelligence agents infiltrated into the Negev Desert in the 1950s. They were equipped with state of the art technological innovations specifically designed for their use, including the DAGAN, an automatic firing device activated by photo-electric rays fitted to machine-guns, and the 'KESHET' portable ground radar. SAYERET SHAKED's most lethal weapon remained her skill and experienced Bedouin trackers!

SAYERET SHAKED was on full alert 24 hours a day, its small size taxing its fighters to the limits of their endurance. Engagements ranged from platoon size pursuits to large-scale battles. The largest involving SAYERET SHAKED occurred early in 1968 when Bedouin trackers supported by a SHAKED squad encountered a 150-man Egyptian force, acting as a diversion for a platoon of commandos which had infiltrated deep into Sinal. While IDF artillery and armour formations dealt with the diversion, SAYERET SHAKED mounted its heavily armed jeeps and headed out for the kill. In a fierce fire-fight, the Egyptian commando force was eliminated!

Speed, intelligence and firepower were SAYERET SHAKED's three-fold arsenal of victory. Within a short time, they became intimate with the area they patrolled, and initiated numerous ambushes on both sides of the Canal. SAYERET SHAKED's tactics were so successful that the unit became a role model for paratroop and GOLANI formations, which were brought in to the front-line positions to study from the masters.

The IDF's defensive responses of artillery bombardments, and long-range air strikes failed to provide a deterrent to Egyptian hostilities. Indeed, the installation of new and deadly Soviet-made surface-to-air missiles (most notably the SAM-3, and SAM-4) made the use of IAF airpower, even with the new American A-4 and F4 aircraft, a costly undertaking. The man who changed IDF policy was Colonel Rafael 'Raful' Eitan, who in 1968 replaced Colonel Aharon Davidi as the IDF's Chief Paratroop and Infantry Officer. After concluding a highly successful tour of duty as commander of HATIVAT HABIKA'A, a paratroop and reconnaissance brigade fighting guerrillas in the Jordan Valley, 'Raful' was ripe to inform the General Staff of his dissatisfaction with IDF strategy in the south. 'Raful' knew the capabilities of the élite units under his command and urged ('ordered') an increased role for them!

The introduction of commando raids altered the balance of power in the region to Israel's favour. It allowed the IDF to operate with the upper hand and to determine under what circumstances engagements would occur. It forced the Egyptians to position hundreds of thousands of troops on routine sentry duties throughout Egypt, when their presence was needed along the Canal facing Israel. For 'Raful', the augmentation of commando operations once and for all established the 'special operations' capability of the élite units, something which had been desperately absent since the 1950s. The War of Attrition was the opportunity for the next generation of 'UNIT 101' disciples to prove their worth.

The target chosen for the first IDF commando operation against Egypt during the War of Attrition was the electricity power plant at Naja'a-Hamadi deep inside the Nile Delta. The plant provided Cairo and much of Egypt with its electrical supply, and it was correctly deduced that its destruction would minimize Egyptian self-confidence, hindering its offensive military capabilities.

The man 'Raful' chose to lead the raid against Naja'a-Hamadi was Major Matan Vilnai, a veteran reconnaissance officer, and deputy commander of the 202nd Paratroop Battalion. Realizing special talents were needed in the campaigns ahead, 'Raful' made him SAYERET TZANHANIM's commanding officer, giving him a free hand with manpower and equipment. To carry out the raid, Major Vilnai chose fourteen men, the very best reconnaissance fighters the IDF possessed. They were to be transported to a landing zone five kilometres east of Naja'a-Hamadi by two Sud Aviation SA 321K Super-Frelons. The raid was codenamed Operation 'HELEM' (shock), and would bring IDF forces the farthest from its borders in the twenty years of its existence.

On the night of 1 November 1968, the two Super-Frelons ferrying the fourteen men (with Major Vilnai) landed at the appointed place. Navigation towards Naja'a-Hamadi posed few problems for the experienced helicopter pilots, and the paratroopers encountered no enemy resistance upon landing. The '14', faces blackened, carried UZI submachine-guns fitted with silencers as well as rucksack loads of high-explosives. They marched the five kilometres to the power plant in haste, but encountered no enemy forces. To Major Vilnai's delight, the plant was poorly defended, and the '14' climbed the outer walls undetected: an Egyptian guard, wearing a traditional white Galabiya robe, escaped in fright; Major Vilnai choosing not to kill the hapless sentry. The '14' hurriedly prepared the explosives around the plant's two main transformers when, moments later, five armed Egyptians appeared. In a brief exchange of gun-fire, they were quickly disposed of. During their withdrawal to the rendezvous point, the plant's explosion produced a blinding light and a horrific recoil which threw the paratroopers on to the desert sand. One hour later, the '14' were back in Sinai, celebrating with 'Raful' over the traditional bottle of whisky.

Operation 'HELEM' shocked the Egyptian High Command into silence. The raid indicated Egyptian vulnerability in light of determined and innovative Israeli efforts. To ensure that the Egyptians comprehended the significance of Operation 'HELEM', 'Raful' sent SAYERET TZANHANIM back to Egypt days later. In similar heli-borne raids which followed, a SAYERET TZANHANIM contingent blew up a power-station and high-tension cables along the Aswan-Cairo road, while a major bridge was destroyed over the Nile near Qina. In Operation 'BUSTAN 37', a paratroop force destroyed high-tension cables south of Suhaj. The Egyptians were traumatized by their inability to predict or stem the attacks. Nasser authorized the creation of a 'Peoples Militia', but the 'real' security details fell to crack Egyptian troops who were pulled off the front line. For months following the raids, Egyptian guns along the Canal were silent. While Egypt revised her strategy, the Israelis consolidated their front-line positions, and work began on the series of heavily fortified defensive outposts known as the 'Bar-Lev Line' (named after the 8th IDF Chief of Staff, Lieutenant-General Haim Bar-Lev).

To 'Raful' and the paratroopers, GOLANI infantrymen, and reconnaissance 'commandos' under his command, the raids represented 'one long celebration', as each raid had been a smashing military success, achieved with no casualties. They were truly classic commando operations featuring speed, stealth, and decisive action. Such spectacular operations had been the focus of IDF planning and training for many years but for political reasons, they had never been implemented. The War of Attrition was such that innovation was required to achieve the initiative, something the IDF was vehemently dedicated to maintaining!

The guns along the Canal remained silent until 8 March 1969, when the Egyptians shelled IDF positions along the Canal in a day-long barrage. The IDF responded with artillery and air strikes, although a strengthened Egyptian anti-aircraft radar and surface-to-air missile screen soon took its toll of the IAF. The most threatening 'string' of radar emplacements was along the Red Sea coastal area, an area which the IAF had fondly referred to as 'their backyard of manoeuvrability'. The decision was reached once again to demonstrate Egyptian vulnerability to commando raids, although this time military positions would be targeted, with the Naval Commandos commanded by Lieutenant-Colonel Zeev Almog in the forefront.

Born in 1935, Almog was a 17-year veteran of the Naval Commandos, and was considered by many to be one of the finest officers in the IDF. He had long favoured a re-evaluation of Naval Commando tactics, and disdained their traditional role as an underwater unit. Although Naval Commandos were subjected to an intense regime of infantry assault training, includng airborne infiltration, cold-killing, and weapons proficiency, they had never been called upon to attack a 'hot target' in an amphibious assault. The KOMMANDO YAMI needed a boost in morale following their poor performance in the 1967 War. Lieutenant-Colonel Almog found in 'Raful' a sympathetic ear, and a special relationship developed between the two. The KOMMANDO YAMI's baptism of *fire* was Operation 'BULMUS 5', the raid on the Egyptian coastal radar facility at Ras al-Adabia.

Originally, the paratroopers were entrusted with the silencing of Ras al-Adabia, but Almog intervened, and proposed using a smaller attack force of Naval Commandos only. A model of the installation at Ras al-Adabia was built in the Negev Desert, and the Naval Commandos trained twenty hours a day on perfecting their assault tactics. Every soldier knew his mission as well as the other nineteen of his comrades, and they had perfected their assault to split-second precision. As 'Raful' gazed upon the young soldiers rehearsing the raid, he was amazed at the skilfull and accurate manner in which the men had been trained to use their UZIS and AK-47s by Major Shaul Ziv, a native Ukranian and Holocaust survivor who was Lieutenant-Colonel Almog's deputy. 'Raful' was in fact so impressed by the Naval Command's display, that he attached himself to the operation as an observer, although Chief of Staff Bar-Lev forbad him to leave the safety of the Zodiac craft in order to *enjoy* the battle personally!

Reports indicated that between 30-50 Egyptian soldiers were stationed at Ras al-Adabia, including ten technicians operating the Soviet-built naval radar. Complementing Ras al-Adabia's defences were a battery of 130mm artillery and AA guns just south at Ras Mahagra.

On 21 June at 20.59 hours, seven Zodiacs set out for sea from their home port of Ras Masala in Sinai. The force consisted of fourteen craft handlers, twenty commandos divided into four four-man teams and a five-man support force equipped with FN MAGs and 52mm mortars. A further force of divers was on full alert, as was a squadron of IAF helicopters, nothing being left to chance. Sitting in the command Zodiac which led the flotilla were Major Ziv,

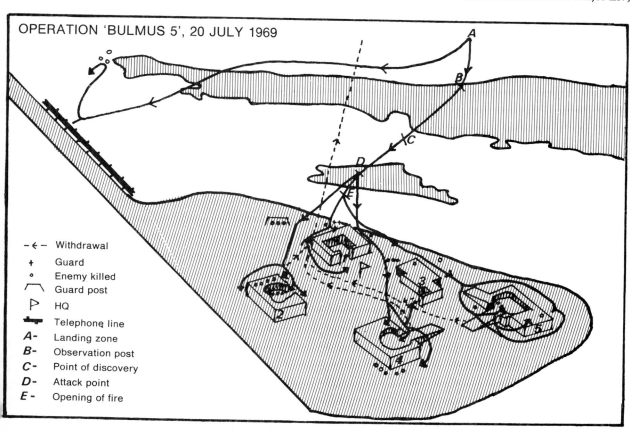

OPERATION 'BULMUS 5', 20 JULY 1969

- ←- Withdrawal
+ Guard
∘ Enemy killed
⌐ Guard post
P HQ
⊨ Telephone line
A- Landing zone
B- Observation post
C- Point of discovery
D- Attack point
E- Opening of fire

Lieutenant-Colonel Almog, and an eager 'Raful'. They silently approached Ras al-Adabia, the electronic sensors judging whether or not the base's radar was operational. As they reached shallow water just off the coast, the crews cut their engines, and the naval commandos, wearing a combination of fatigues, black neoprene diving vests, and civilian swim-suits, began their 30-minute crawl towards shore.

The lead force immediately cut telephone lines along the shoreline, and placed explosive charges along possible routes of an Egyptian counter-attack, while the others landed. Led by Major Ziv, the raiders attacked the camp from the north. They all carried explosives, communications gear, and their favourite weapon, the Russian AK-47. Major Ziv noticed two Egyptian sentries enjoying a smoke, and carefully examined the possibilities of attacking from a different angle. This led to a delay in the assault, causing Chief of Staff Bar-Lev to lose patience. He ordered the attack to "commence or abort, causing Major Ziv to turn off his radio, and disobey an order for the first time in his military career.

The attack caught the Egyptian sentries by surprise, and they ran off into the desert darkness in panic. Other Egyptian defenders followed suit. The guns of the twenty naval commandos opened up simultaneously, and in a matter of seconds, the surprised defenders had been neutralized. Within minutes it was all over. The radar, transformer, signal equipment, and positions were destroyed. As Major Ziv's men prepared their withdrawal, the covering force poured fire into the area. During the twelve minutes that the KOMMANDO YAMI force was at Ras al-Adabia, 32 Egyptians were killed, and twelve wounded. The only Israeli casualties were three lightly wounded. When the force returned to the safety of Sinai at 04.30 hours, 'Raful' ordered IDF artillery batteries to shell the Egyptian coast.

The success of Operation 'BULMUS 5' ensured future 'work' for the KOMMANDO YAMI. On 10 July 1969, an Egyptian commando force attacked a tank refuelling depot south of Port Tewfiq. Seven IDF soldiers were killed, and five seriously wounded. The target chosen for retaliation was Al-Ah'dar, better known as Green Island, a fortified Egyptian position lying at the southern mouth of the Suez Canal, three kilometres south of Port Tewfiq. Although such an attack suited the IDF's policy of hitting Egyptian air defensive positions, the main objective of the raid was to 'kill as many of the enemy as possible'. Green Island was not Ras al-Adabia, however. Defended by a garrison of more than 100 Egyptian infantrymen, including a dozen or so élite *Sa'iqa* ('lightning') commandos, Green Island boasted four 85mm anti-aircraft gun positions, two 37mm anti-aircraft guns, fourteen 14.5mm machine-guns and 20mm gun nests, and was surrounded by three rows of barbed wire concertinas and 8-foot-high walls. Both 'Raful' and Lieutenant-Colonel Almog knew it would be a tough nut to crack. The raid was code-named Operation 'BULMUS ('obsession') 6'.

Also taking part in Operation 'BULMUS 6' was SAYERET MAT'KAL, General Staff Reconnaissance: the IDF's most elite and secretive unit. Little is known about SAYERET MAT'KAL; it was often referred to as the 'Chief of Staff's Boys', or the 'Elite Unit'. Shrouded in a mysterious aura of self-imposed secrecy, all that was known or was rumoured about SAYERET MAT'KAL was that it was a small force made up of the best soldiers the IDF possessed. It conducted missions of the highest national importance in the Middle East. Their role in the attack on Green Island was in fact the first official mention of the unit's existence.

At 22.00 hours on 19 July, the task force set out by Zodiac craft towards Green Island, after training for days without respite. At 23.00 hours, the lead contingent of twenty divers commanded by Captain Dov descended into the chilly water to begin their swim towards Green Island. Their mission was to break through the defences and engage the Egyptian forces, while the reserve force commanded by Lieutenant-Colonel Almog, consisting of the SAYERET, would race towards the target aboard Zodiac craft. Waiting 200 yards south of Green Island were two Zodiacs commanded by Captain Amnon with eight commandos to provide covering and diversionary fire with light machine-guns, mortars, and RPGs. At 01.30 hours, Captain Dov and his men had reached the water level base of the radar station tower after an exhausting swim in which the currents had pushed them off course several times.

As Captain Dov and his men began cutting the wires, two Egyptian sentries suddenly appeared overhead, shouting in heated discussion. The force was still undetected, and Captain Dov took full advantage of this to find a breach in the lower defences, where the Egyptians dumped their rubbish. At 01.38 hours (eight minutes behind schedule) the commandos, led by Lieutenant Eilan Egozzi, shed their Scuba gear, and broke through the gap, firing at the Egyptian sentries. Egozzi ordered the other teams (who were looking for gaps of their own) to 'break through from the right'. Egyptian machine-gun and rifle fire was inaccurate, although they threw dozens of grenades at the commandos, one of which seriously wounded, though did not stop Egozzi. Accurate bursts of UZI and AK-47 fire killed dozens of the Egyptian defenders.

Systematically, the commandos neutralized the Egyptian positions, while a command post was set up. Almog and the SAYERET arrived behind schedule, forcing Captain Dov to delegate their fire support and demolitions tasks to his men, many of whom were already wounded. In heroic fashion, a group of commandos cleared machine-gun nest '5', while Captain Amichai Ayalon, himself wounded, led a squad which 'purified' an Egyptian 37mm gun emplacement. SAYERET commander Menachem Digli and the remainder of the Naval Commando force reached Green Island at 02.00, followed by the command Zodiac with Almog. The reinforcements began their work immediately, while a heavy battle raged in which Captain Ayalon was wounded a second time by grenade fragments. The

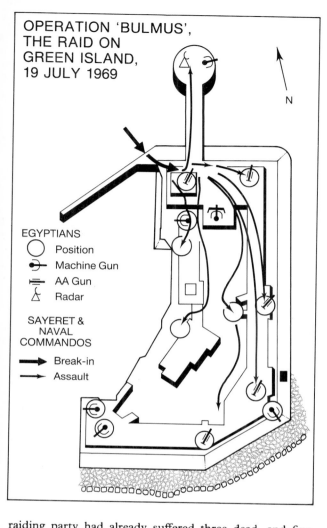

OPERATION 'BULMUS', THE RAID ON GREEN ISLAND, 19 JULY 1969

N

EGYPTIANS
- ◯ Position
- ⊕ Machine Gun
- ⊨ AA Gun
- ⋏ Radar

SAYERET & NAVAL COMMANDOS
- ➡ Break-in
- → Assault

of all IDF commando operations, creating waves of in-fighting supressed from the public for many years. Many had been critical of Lieutenant-Colonel Almog's lack of command during the operation, while others argued the futility of using the IDF's top fighters to attack Green Island, a secondary target at best. Numerous studies and commissions examined the conduct at Green Island, although the findings reinstated the fact that under such murderous enemy fire, lesser units would have crumbled. Studies later commended the naval commandos for their calm under fire, and their weapons proficiency.

Following Green Island, the KOMMANDO YAMI returned to covert intelligence gathering and sabotage operations. Their last support role for a 'conventional' operation was the sinking of two Egyptian P.183 torpedo-boats near Ras Sadat on 8 September 1969 in preparation for Operation 'RAVIV' (9 september), a large-scale armoured strike across the Canal. Operation 'RAVIV' was the brainchild of Major Shlomoh Baum, the one-time deputy commander of 'UNIT 101', who commanded the 7th Armoured Brigade's reconnaissance company. The armoured task force commanded by Lieutenant-Colonel Baruch 'Pinko' Harel and led by Baum masqueraded as an Egyptian force with captured Russian T-55s and PT-76s. In ten hours, the force raced throughout Egyptian radar and military installations, bringing destruction to the enemy's rear. The spectacular success of the raid was made possible by Lieutenant-Colonel Almog's KOMMANDO YAMI, who secured the waters, prepared the landing site, and secured the force's withdrawal.

Although the attack on Egyptian air defence positions was an IDF priority, they usually waited for the Egyptians to provoke a response. Provocation came on 14 December 1969, when Egyptian commandos crossed the Canal and kidnapped Captain Dan Avidan. Outraged, the IDF General staff vowed revenge. Through intensive intelligence efforts, they located an Egyptian Russian-made P-12 radar base near Ras A'rab, cleverly concealed in desert tents. Its destruction was entrusted to the IAF, though a sergeant at the air base suggested the practical notion of 'just stealing' the radar. His suggestion was raised with senior IAF officers, who in turn contacted 'Raful'. Operation 'TAR-NEGOL (chicken) 53' was born.

The General Staff dragged its heels, and authorized the raid only on 23 December, later ordering it to be carried out four days later. 'Raful' summoned Lieutenant-Colonel Arieh 'Tzimel' Tzidon, Commander of the NA'HA'L's 50th Paratroop Battalion (SAYERET HARUV commander during the 1967 War), who was honoured that his unit should be offered the opportunity to enter the history books. SAYERET TZANHANIM was attached to Lieutenant-Colonel Tzidon's command, although precious little time remained for pre-operation preparations.

Aerial reconnaissance photographs provided an accurate picture of the Ras A'rab base. The radar installation itself was divided in two, attached on two Russian ZIL trucks. The paratroopers were sent to an IDF base to practise

raiding party had already suffered three dead, and five wounded, and still the demolitions had not begun. Egyptian 130mm shore batteries had been alerted and they began to shell the island, adding to the confusion, and the body count.

Sitting helpless in the choppy waters, 'Raful' ordered the raiders to demolish only the northern part of the fortifications, and to withdraw. The fighters headed quickly towards their Zodiacs while Major Ziv, and the wounded Lieutenant Egozzi prepared the demolition charges. The voyage back to Sinal was hampered by Egyptian artillery fire. One Zodiac was hit by fragments, forcing its human cargo to float for hours awaiting the rescue helicopters of the IAF's élite Aeromedical Evacuation Unit. Six Israelis died at Green Island, three naval commandos, and three SAYERET fighters. Eleven were seriously wounded. Six naval commandos were cited for bravery, including Captain Ayalon, awarded the I'TUR HAGVURA, while five others, including Lieutenant Egozzi, received the I'TUR HAMOFET.

Operation 'BULMUS 6' was one of the most controversial

disassembly procedure on captured Russian trucks, while the helicopter pilots practised low-level flying manoeuvres carrying heavy loads. After watching the force conduct a dry run, 'Raful' reported to Chief of Staff Bar-Lev that the radar was ready to fly! The task force was made up of seventy fighters, and split into four groups: 'Force 1' consisted of the SAYERET, assigned the task of setting up road-blocks; 'Force 2' was to seize control of the generator and radar; 'Force 3' would attack the command bunkers; while 'Force 4' took care of the tent living quarters. On Friday 26 December, after four days of brutal training, four sleepless nights and disconnected telephones (for security reasons) the force flew over Sinai towards Egypt.

The three Super-Frelons flew at low level to avoid enemy radar, and reached the LZ with little difficulty. The force deployed immediately for action, and within minutes headed out towards Ras A'rab. The SAYERET had farthest to go, and the heaviest loads to carry, as each soldier carried land-mines and extra ammunition. The full moon had assisted navigation, but presented the danger of the force being discovered, especially since they all wore olive

▲ A mechanized force from SAYERET SHAKED searches for Egyptian commandos along the Suez Canal, December, 1969. (IDF Archives)

fatigues bleached khaki in order to 'impersonate' Egyptian soldiers!

At 300 metres from Ras A'rab, Lieutenant-Colonel Tzidon ordered his men to crawl towards the perimeter; their cumbersome movement was well camouflaged by the grumbling noise of the radar's generator, which was on full power in search of the IAF. The force then split into its teams, and commenced the attack. The Egyptians put up little resistance, and within minutes work on the radar began. The paratroopers were surprised to find no Russian advisors, nor any officers present, only simple conscripts not at all eager to die.

The disassembly of the radar was attended to at frantic speed. It took longer than planned to remove the radar from the truck, as rust made the disconnecting of the metal attachments a difficult task. Nevertheless, the force persevered, and twenty minutes later, the 2.5-ton radar was

January 1970. The three years of costly fighting had been characterized by the use of commando forces in spectacular raids, even though the majority of the paratroop and reconnaissance forces spent most of their operational time sitting out bombardments in the Bar-Lev Line, and patrolling lines of communication. Such tedious duty was also costly, and in one day's bloodletting, fourteen paratroopers were killed on 'Black Sabbath', Saturday 30 May 1970. Calm descended on the line in 1971, however, and it lasted until 6 October 1973.

One of the most overlooked, yet most significant campaigns of Southern Command's War of Attrition was SAYERET SHAKED's brutal fighting against Palestinian terrorist cells in Gaza, a hotbed of resistance to Israeli presence. Ordered into the strip by OC Southern Command, Major-General 'Arik' Sharon, SAYERET SHAKED initiated an unrelenting campaign to destroy the uncontrollable terrorist activity originating from Gaza. SAYERET SHAKED's Commander, Lieutenant-Colonel Danni Rahav, divided the area into quadrants, each of which was combed and 'purified' in a meticulous fashion by teams of heavily armed troops. The lower branches of trees were cut down, improving the soldiers' field of vision as well as diminishing potential guerrilla hiding-places, while caves and bunkers were sealed tight. Arabic-speaking SHAKED soldiers, including the Bedouin trackers who traditionally loathed the 'urban' Palestinians, disguised themselves as locals to conduct surveillance. It was a campaign of nerves, where the SHAKED men rarely took their fingers off the triggers during patrols through Gaza's casbah.

During the day, the fighters enjoyed the serenity of the local beaches, though at night they returned to the squalor of the camps for the searches, round-ups, and fire-fights. Sharon personally led many of the missions, AK-47 and flashlight in land; and was accused by many of ordering the

airborne; even though a hydraulic malfunction in one of the helicopters made the trip quite 'eventful'. What could not be carried back was destroyed, and the paratroopers returned to Sinal unmolested and without incident.

Operation 'TARNEGOL 53' was one of the most innovative and spectacular raids in modern military history, and it secured a 'James Bond' image for the IDF's élite forces. More than anything, the raid was an intelligence coup for the West. Analysts were given the rare opportunity to examine the inner workings of a Russian radar, and to develop the means to counter it. For Egypt, the raid had fatal conclusions. In a rare show of disgust, Egyptian conscripts and officers were executed, and the Russians refused to supply the Arabs with any more state of the art military hardware. The effect of the raid can best be summarized by cartoons with appeared throughout the world's Press days later showing Israeli helicopters stealing the pyramids!

The paratroops' last major commando raid of the War of Attrition was the heli-borne assault on Shedwan Island at the mouth of the Gulf of Suez (Operation 'RODOS') on 22

▲ Dressed in their khaki-dyed field jackets, paratroopers from the NA'HA'L's Battalion prepare to dismantle an Egyptian Russian-made P-12 radar for its flight back to Israel, 26 December 1969. (IDF Archives)

'executions' of many terrorists captured alive. SAYERET SHAKED literally intimidated terrorist activity out of the strip, as intimidated civilians refused to provide the terrorists with popular support, logistics and shelter. The figures indicate the extent and success of the campaign. From June to December 1971, 742 terrorists were killed or captured, following which, only a single act of terror was recorded. Once again, SAYERET SHAKED had proved their

▲ Recon paratroopers from SAYERET TZANHANIM deploy for the final assault against Egyptian defenders on Shedwan Island during Operation 'RHODOS', 22 January 1970. (IGPO)

importance and innovation in defending Israel's southern frontier.

INTO THE LAND OF THE PURSUITS: THE JORDAN VALLEY, 1967–70

FOLLOWING the 1967 War, Israel's border with Jordan was reduced to a single geographic barrier – the shallow River Jordan. From the River Yarmouk in the north by Syria, to the Dead Sea, to Aqaba, the River Jordan was all that separated the two warring nations. The new frontiers also brought Israel control of the West Bank and its 550,000 hostile Palestinians who, although they had lived under Jordanian occupation for nineteen years, saw this as their opportunity for military action to achieve a national homeland. Palestinian nationalistic activity was forbad by the Jordanians, whose security and intelligence services kept repressive control over the West Bank's inhabitants. The IDF had captured Jordanian Police files on the Palestinian movements, and within a short period, their infrastructure and arsenals were crushed. To re-establish their military and political presence on the West Bank, the Jordanian-based *el-Fatah* faction of the Palestine Liberation Organization (PLO) sent armed infiltrators across the Jordan on intelligence missions, and terrorist assignments. Central Command's War of Attrition had begun.

The IDF knew it faced a precarious security situation on the Jordanian frontier, and immediately sent in engineers to establish physical obstacles, and mine-fields along the border. IDF and National Police Border Guard observation posts and patrols secured a portion of the frontier by day, but the night belonged to the infiltrator. They crossed freely under the cover of darkness, hiding in caves and ravines until reaching Hebron, Nablus, Jenin, Kilkilya, and East Jerusalem to establish terrorist cells. On 1 October 1967, a terrorist band crossed the Jordan and attacked KIBBUTZ Hamadia in the Beit Shean Valley, killing one of its residents. Two weeks later, terrorists from Jordan attacked KIBBUTZ Maoz-Haim, and on 5 November Palestinian terrorists were infiltrated into Israel under Jordanian artillery cover. The IDF response was slow and reluctant. Conscripts and reservists alike disliked serving in the Jordan Valley's brutal 40° (C) plus heat. Operations under such climactic hardships proved difficult, and the IDF had little time to establish a tactical response.

The IDF General Staff concluded that the only man capable of bringing order to the Jordan Valley was Colonel Rafael 'Raful' Eitan; who was recovering from his serious head wound in hospital. 'Raful' was quick to respond to the task. He ordered the withdrawal of all 'regular' forces from the valley, and formed a unit of conscript and reservist paratroop units and SAYERET HARUV called HATIVAT HABIKA'A, 'Valley Brigade'. For subordinates 'Raful' summoned the best paratroop officers he could find, including HATIVAT HABIKA'A'S deputy commander, Lieutenant-Colonel Arik Regev, and its young operations officer, Lieutenant Gad Menale. Menale was a strict disciplinarian who had been profoundly affected by the

legendary exploits of Meir Har-Zion. He made a point of visiting the recluse Har-Zion, learning from the master as much as he would disclose.

'Raful' established certain rules of engagement he thought necessary for securing the Jordan Valley. Knowing that lying in ambush on a cold desert night could unnerve even the best trained conscript, 'Raful' ordered that senior officers lead every ambush and pursuit personally. Not only would the presence of an experienced officer instil confidence in the ranks, but it would ensure quick and decisive battlefield decisions in the face of a determined and highly capable enemy. As always it would be the officers who died first.

Of the units that participated in the Jordan Valley campaign, SAYERET HARUV was always in the vanguard. Until then, SAYERET HARUV had been operational in the West Bank, in a secret campaign against Jordanian and Palestinian intelligence agents. It had no experience in the art of 'pursuit warfare', and was forced to learn it through bitter experience. SAYERET HARUV suffered heavy casualties in the early pursuits; a price its small size and family atmosphere could hardly accept. Morale did not diminish however; the loss of a comrade was mourned and avenged. in addition, SAYERET HARUV was the first territorial reconnaissance unit to accept women soldiers. The women made life in the desert bearable, and one of the first to volunteer was Zohar Bar-Lev, the 18-year-old daughter of the Chief of Staff. Within months, SAYERET HARUV acquired an élite status unrivalled by other similar units; and many eager 18-year-old conscripts soon volunteered for service in her ranks.

Lieutenant-Colonel Arik Regev invested heavily in SAYERET HARUV, and upgraded it to battalion strength. he provided jeeps, command cars, halftracks, electronic sensing devices, and unlimited helicopter reconnaissance and attack support. SAYERET HARUV's responsibilities were four-fold: training and tactical development, ambushes, pursuits and the difficult task of interdicting terrorist activities in the West Bank cities. Their limited manpower was divided into three primary companies: a 'surveillance force', an 'ambush force', and the ever beleaguered 'pursuit force'. Little respite was offered the men, all volunteers, and leaves were few and far between. Results were impressive, however, and by the end of November 1967 the IDF had killed 63 infiltrators, captured 350, and arrested 54 West Bank *el-Fatah* commanders.

SAYERET HARUV's commander during this difficult period was Lieutenant-Colonel Amos Ne'eman, an experienced paratroop officer, known for his innovative approach to military problems. As early detection capabilities in 1967 were primitive, Ne'eman concentrated SAYERET HARUV's best fighters into the ambush force. The ambushes were demanding, and deadly. Each man lay in ambush an average of twenty days a month, in brutal heat by day, bitter cold by night. Anxiety became as dangerous a factor as the terrorists, only exacerbated by the brutal climate, inhospitable terrain and permanent feeling of isolation.

The MIRDAFIM or pursuits were equally difficult. The primary objective of SAYERET HARUV and the paratroops was to prevent the infiltrators from reaching urban areas, where the chances were that they would blend in with the local population undetected, and be able to ferment their intended revolution. The HARUV fighters knew only too well that each terrorist slipping through their clutches would result in the deaths of innocent civilians. There was no room for failure, and each terrorist had to be stopped. To achieve this task, pursuits commenced with the

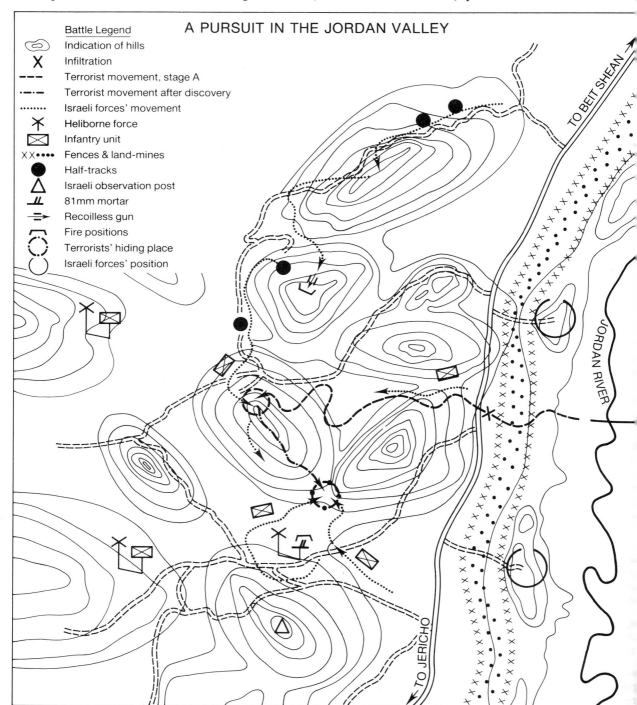

A PURSUIT IN THE JORDAN VALLEY

Battle Legend
- Indication of hills
- X Infiltration
- − − − Terrorist movement, stage A
- −·−· Terrorist movement after discovery
- ········· Israeli forces' movement
- Heliborne force
- Infantry unit
- X X •••• Fences & land-mines
- ● Half-tracks
- △ Israeli observation post
- 81mm mortar
- Recoilless gun
- Fire positions
- Terrorists' hiding place
- Israeli forces' position

TO BEIT SHEAN

JORDAN RIVER

TO JERICHO

Bedouin and Druze trackers' dawn patrol which determined if infiltration had occurred. If the skilled trackers spotted a footprint, a Jordanian cigarette butt, or drop of grease a HARUV or paratroop platoon was ordered in for the chase. The pursuit was a classic example of élite force capabilities used to their maximum potential. To survive, a soldier's speed, strength, training and courage were tested to the limits.

Most terrorist infiltration and Katyusha attacks against central Israel (Jerusalem, Petach Tikvah, and Netanya) and the lower Beit Shean Valley originated at the Jordanian town of Karameh, an extensive *el-Fatah* base two miles from the Israeli border. Karameh became *el-Fatah*'s strongest base in the region, and *fedayeen* 'men of sacrifice' volunteers throughout the Middle East flocked to its training facilities which maintained 2,000 fighters. On 21 March 1968, the IDF brought the war into Jordanian territory, in Operation 'TOFET' (hell!).

OC Central Command, Major-General Uzi Narkiss, commanded the assault on Karameh which was carried out by three forces. The lead force was HATIVAT HATZAN-HANIM, commanded by Colonel Danni Matt, and consisted of 800 paratroopers from the 202nd Battalion commanded by Major Dan Shomron, and the 50th NA'HA'L Paratroop Battalion commanded by Lieutenant-Colonel Tibi Shapira. Attached to Colonel Matt's paratroopers were seventy halftracks, and seven Centurion tanks commanded by Lieutenant-Colonel Avraham Bar-Am. In addition, three other forces were sent in to isolate Karameh from all sides, and included a tank force from the élite 7th Armoured Brigade commanded by Colonel Shmuel 'Gorodish' Gonen from the south, a contingent of HATIVAT HABIKA'A's mechanized paratroopers from the north, and a heli-borne force from SAYERET TZANHANIM commanded by Major Matan Vilnai from the east. SAYERET TZANHANIM had the most important objective of the operation, to block terrorist commanders intending to escape to Amman. Their assault was to be preceded by the IAF dropping pamphlets ordering the Palestinians to surrender, and the Jordanian Army not to intervene!

At 05.35 hours on 21 March, 'Raful's paratroopers seized the Allenby and Damia Bridges over the River Jordan, while Centurions from the 7th Armoured Brigade crossed the Jordan on Bailey Bridges hastily prepared by

▲▲ A recon paratrooper from SAYERET HARUV 'assumes the position' after spotting a squad of Palestinian terrorists who have infiltrated into the Jordan Valley. (IDF Archives)

▲▶ Contact! A SAYERET HARUV squad joins battle with dug-in Palestinian *fedayeen* in the Jordan Valley, February 1968. (IDF Archives)

▶ After tracking a *fedayeen* squad to a desert hut, the paratroopers attack! Three minutes later, eight Palestinian terrorists would lie dead. (IDF Archives)

▲ A SAYERET HARUV squad take up firing positions in a deserted cave near Jericho, March 1968. (IDF Archives)

Combat Engineers, followed by Colonel Matt's mechanized paratroopers. At a staging-point in the Jordan Valley, SAYERET TZANHANIM underwent its final debriefing and weapons check, before heading out towards the waiting Super-Frelon helicopters for the quick jump into Jordan. Technical difficulties delayed their departure by thirty minutes, although the IAF Ouragan fighter (observing radio silence) with the 'surrender' pamphlets departed on schedule. The Jordanians and the Palestinians had been forewarned about possible Israeli intentions by CIA reports to King Hussein, although the arrival of the pamplets confirmed the time and location of the IDF attack. Three guests of the terrorists, British Labour Party Members of Parliament, were whisked away quickly, while Yasir Arafat (who happened to be at Karameh at the time), commandeered a motorcycle, and fled in haste.

Unlike their courageous commanders, the majority of the Palestinian fighters stood fast, and headed towards their fortified positions to prepare Karameh's defence. A force of Palestinians fired on Major Vilnal's helicopters which landed on one of the towering hills east of Karameh, but no casualties were incurred. They did not engage the paratroopers, and Major Vilnal was forced to order a frontal attack on their positions. The paratroopers raced down the slopes firing. The battle with the terrorists was fierce and hard fought. The terrorists mistakenly hid in underground bunkers, which were quickly neutralized by fragmentation grenades. For five hours, a brutal close-quarter battled raged. Casualties were heavy on both sides, and by 10.00 hours Major Vilnal had four dead, and a

dozen wounded. The terrorists lost more than twenty killed, and countless more hurt.

At 07.00 hours, Lieutenant-Colonel Bar-Am's tanks entered Karameh. They fired in a 360 degree radius, and were targeted by heavy anti-tank fire. The tanks advanced three kilometres through Karameh's main street, and softened up the defensive positions for Colonel Matt's mechanized paratroopers following close behind. The 50th Battalion spread out to the west, while the 202nd went east. The paratroopers engaged the terrorists at close range, throwing dozens of grenades and pouring heavy machine-gun fire into the sandbagged firing positions. Their decisive and quick breakout secured Karameh quickly, and dozens of terrorists were killed and wounded. Many were captured, and swiftly interrogated by paratroop intelligence officers.

After four hours of brutal fighting, battalion commanders Lieutenant-Colonel Shapira and Major Shomron reported to Colonel Matt that their missions were completed. Matt ordered a thorough search of the town, and each house, office, and filing cabinet was searched and seized. The intelligence rewards were astounding. Files revealed numerous plans of imminent Palestinian terrorist attacks inside Israel, including the planned bombings of cinemas, supermarkets, and nursery schools.

All was not well at Karameh, however. Colonel Matt received reports that the 7th Armoured Brigade task force had engaged Jordanian tank forces. The Jordanian tanks, sniping from the towering hills above, surprised Colonel Gonen's forces, which began to take heavy casualties. IDF artillery batteries opened up, while the IAF provided close ground support. 'Raful's HATIVAT HABIKA'A was sent in to rescue the besieged tank force, and an AML90 Armoured Car paratroop reconnaissance company named SAYERET DUCHIFAT ('Hoopoe Recon') commanded by Captain Amnon Shahak (Lipkin) was sent into the fray. Captain Shahak raced under murderous fire to rescue the wounded tankers, while HATIVAT HABIKA'A's Operations Officer Lieutenant Manela ran out in to the open, drawing enemy fire on himself so that others could be rescued. Both Captain Shahak and Lieutenant Manela were awarded the I'TUR HA'OZ for their bravery under fire.

At 15.00 hours, after Colonel Matt's and Major Vilnai's forces had completed their tasks, Major General Narkiss ordered the town razed. In all, 175 houses were destroyed, the subsequent explosions creating a cloud of choking dust which concealed the paratroops' withdrawal, which lasted well into the night. Hundreds of files, and thousands of tons of weaponry were brought back with the paratroopers, as were 141 prisoners. In all, 150 terrorists were killed at Karameh, and 61 Jordanian soldiers. Israeli casualties were heavy as well; 28 killed, three missing in action, and more than 90 wounded.

As the battle at Karameh raged, a diversionary armour and paratroop raid was directed against el-Fatah bases south of the Dead Sea in Operation 'ASUTA' (remedy). A mixed armoured and heli-borne paratroop force attacked he bases in the harsh desert terrain, and in the day-long battle 74 terrorists and Jordanian soldiers were killed. The Israelis suffered no casualties.

The IDF's costly victory at Karameh severely hampered terrorist capabilities to mount attacks into Israel, and brought Israel the much needed time to consolidate its forces and defences in the Jordan Valley. To the Arabs Karameh was a victory of historic proportions. For the first time the Palestinians had fought the mighty IDF on equal terms, and inflicted impressive casualties on the hated enemy. The Jordanians had also made an impressive showing and the sight of King Hussein inspecting destroyed and abandoned Israeli vehicles brought prestige back to the Arab world. Karameh soon became the battle cry for numerous 'new' Palestinian terrorist movements which sprang up following the battle, including Dr George Habash's Marxist Popular Front for the Liberation of Palestine. Karameh marked the beginning of the end of an armed Palestinian presence in Jordan.

Following Karameh, HATIVAT HABIKA'A prepared for the inevitable increase in hostilities. 'Raful', who was appointed Chief Paratroop and Infantry Officer, was replaced by Lieutenant-Colonel Regev, and the reins of Central Command were turned over to Major-General Rechavam 'Gandhi' Zeevi, a hard-line and experienced paratroop officer who vowed a non-relenting approach to the infiltrators. In a monumental logistical task, HATIVAT HABIKA'A built a defensive fence along the River Jordan, similar to the French Morice Line in Algeria (many IDF officers had been invited to Algeria by the French to observe counter-guerrilla tactics in the late 1950s). It consisted of three rows of barbed wire obstacles, followed by physical barriers hemmed in by extensive mine-fields. Its most important element was a 3-metre-wide path of lightly sanded turf which would betray the slightest sign of trespass. It was affectionately called the 'indistinct road', and was patrolled regularly by trackers who could differentiate between the signs produced by man and animal. The terrorists tried to deceive the trackers by wrapping their Khaki commando boots in sheep-skin, and by using 10-metre ladders to cross the obstacle. Their attempts were futile in light of the Bedouin and Druze trained eyes, superhuman senses, and determination.

Increased infiltration attempts and improved methods of detection signalled the beginning of the end of the Jordan Valley campaign. While IDF, Border Guard, and SHIN BET (Hebrew abbreviation for SHERUT BITAHON, Israel's internal security and counter-intelligence force) efforts made sanctuary in the West Bank towns precarious, paratroop and SAYERET HARUV pursuits engaged the terrorists in open combat. They proved to be resourceful opponents and gave as good as they got. They maximized the geographic conditions of the desert, and were impervious to the harsh climate.

The men of HATIVAT HABIKA'A also developed certain invaluable senses in detecting, pursuing and fighting the infiltrators. After days in the desert, they became intimate with the areas patrolled, and increasingly confident. Lieutenant Manela became the IDF's most accomplished 'desert warrior', achieving the status-grabbing nickname of 'terrorist hunter'. He led or accompanied almost every desert pursuit, and developed a sixth sense for finding terrorist hideouts. One mistake in the desert was one's last however, and Lieutenant Manela's luck would soon run out.

On Friday, 26 July 1968, a Bedouin tracker team discovered footprints of eight infiltrators on the 'indistinct road', and summoned headquarters. The trackers followed the prints to the Jericho road, five kilometres from the point of detection, and a company of paratroopers was

▼ Heavily armed paratroopers prepare to assault a Palestinian stronghold during Operation 'TOFET', the combined armour and paratroop raid on the Jordanian town of Karameh, 21 March 1968. (IDF Archives)

▼▼ Mechanized reinforcements from Major Dan Shomron's command reinforce a beleaguered paratroop position at Karameh. (IDF Archives)

called in for the pursuit. A heli-borne force commanded by a Sergeant Lufo encountered part of the infiltration team and a fire-fight broke out in which two paratroopers were wounded, and two terrorists were killed. A 'medevac' Bell-205 helicopter was called in to remove the casualties, while the remainder of the squad continued the chase.

Joining the pursuit by helicopter was HATIVAT HABIKA'A's Commander, Lieutenant-Colonel Arik Regev, and its Operations Officer, Lieutenant Gad Menale. The terrorists' tracks were followed to a cave embedded deep in a desert mountain, from where automatic fire was directed on to the paratroopers, two of whom were hit immediately. Throwing grenades in with one hand, and firing his AK-47 with the other, Lieutenant-Colonel Regev instinctively led the assault into the cave. Following a moment of reassuring silence, Regev entered the cave, only to be hit in the head by machine-gun fire. Manela raced into the cave after the killers of his beloved commander, only to be hit in the chest by a burst of automatic fire. Another band of terrorists entered the fray from a neighbouring hilltop, which lasted until an armour force was called in to destroy the Palestinian firing positions.

The loss of both Lieutenant-Colonel Regev and Lieutenant Manela was a grievous shock to the IDF. The 'follow me' ethic of the commander at the helm had exacted a high price, and one not easily accepted. The two had been close friends, who invested much of themselves in the war against terrorism. They rarely ventured home

on leave, and were known to do everything humanl possible for their men. Their funerals were attended by th top IDF brass, and grieving friends and comrades. Con dolences for Regev were also received from Kurdish leade Mullah Mustafa Barzani. Regev had been covertly des patched into Kurdistan to help in the rebellion agains Iraq, and a close friendship had developed between th two warriors. Near the site where the two fell, an agricul tural settlement was established, named after the two falle heroes. It is called MOSHAV Argeman, and it thrives toda in a safe and secure Jordan Valley.

For HATIVAT HABIKA'A, the deaths of Regev and Manel was only a tragic beginning for officers in the Jorda Valley. On 19 September, a pursuit conducted by youn NA'HA'L paratroopers, cornered a band of terrorists in stone hut. 50th NA'HA'L Paratroop Battalion Commande Lieutenant-Colonel Moshe Stampel (the 890th Battalio veteran, and first Israeli soldier to reach the Wailing Wa in 1967), led the charge, and was killed by a fragmentatio grenade. Stampel was replaced by his deputy commande Major Doron Manor, who also was hit, and later died fro loss of blood in the medevac en route to hospital.

In late November 1968, Lieutenant-Colonel Tzvi Ofe was appointed commander of SAYERET HARUV. One-tim commander of SAYERET GOLANI, and a veteran paratroo officer, Ofer had extensive experience in dealing with th Arabs of the West Bank. Following the 1967 War, h served as the military commander of Nablus and Hebro

and was intimate with the terrorists' infrastructure and methods. He knew that the HARUV was a young unit, lacking in many vital characteristics to enable it to lead the fight against infiltration. He took personal charge of developing an NCO cadre into HARUV, effectively to lead 'small' unit ambushes and pursuits, and also attempted to transform HARUV into a commando force. Unfortunately, Lieutenant-Colonel Ofer was SAYERET HARUV's commander for only twenty days.

On 12 December 1968, HARUV's overworked trackers discovered signs of infiltration along the 'indistinct road' between the Allenby and Abdullah Bridges. Led by Major Salah Al-Haib, SAYERET HARUV's chief tracker officer, the force joined with a paratroop force nearby led by Major Dan Shomron, and gave chase. Heli-borne forces were called in to assist in the search operations which centred on Wadi Kelet, near Jericho. The descent into the wadi was made with great caution, as the numerous caves and boulders provided too many possible terrorist firing positions. The pursuit was joined by Lieutenant-Colonel Ofer, HATIVAT HABIKA'A commander Lieutenant-Colonel Yehuda Reshef, and OC Central Command Major General Zeevi. Ofer took immediate control of his HARUV fighters, and led them in the assault on a cave sheltering the terrorists. He was hit by enemy fire, and killed.

The deaths of so many senior officers sent shock waves throughout Israel, and paratroop sapper squads were ordered to demolish caves throughout the Jordan Valley. During 1969, the men of HATIVAT HABIKA'A patrolled the Jordan valley, carrying heavy loads of explosives with them on each assignment. Searches into the caves were made with great caution, and entering each cave was preceded by a heavy barrage of small arms fire and grenades. Many caves were used by the terrorists as arms caches, while others were communications bases, their transmitters hidden deep within extensive labyrinths. During one such operation, a paratroop patrol led by Major Yossi Kaplan (a 'UNIT 101' veteran), brought into a deep wadi by helicopter, spotted an Arab woman nursing her child. Major Kaplan approached the seemingly innocent women, and asked her if there were any terrorists in the area, only to receive a negative response. The force headed out, and were attacked by a force of heavily armed terrorists dressed in khaki fatigues. Major Kaplan and his deputy Major Hanan Samson shouted 'Follow me!' and were dead moments later.

In mid-1969, the 55th Reserve Paratroop Brigade was sent into the Jordan Valley attached to HATIVAT HABIKA'A. The reservists dug in along the front line in fortified outposts, exposing themselves to endless Katyusha barrages, but also forcing the terrorists to pass their positions en route to the West Bank towns. The open confrontations allowed the reservists to display their conventional combat expertise, while the terrorists soon found themselves outgunned, and outfought. They responded by attacking Israel by boat across the Dead Sea, and through the lightly defended Arava Desert in the south. HATIVAT HABIKA'A replied in turn, and resumed its policy of cross-border raids. From 1969 to 1970, seventeen large-scale paratroop raids were conducted against Palestinian bases in Jordan with astounding effects.

The infiltrations presented both sides with a war of nerves, and clearly the IDF was winning. Intelligence reports indicated that the Palestinian terror groups were planning large-scale raids to 'celebrate' Israel's 21st Independence Day in May 1969, and SAYERET HARUV was placed on full alert. When the infiltration occurred days later, SAYERET HARUV was ready and waiting. In an hour-long fire-fight, 21 terrorists were killed, dozens wounded, and five were taken prisoner. During the following weeks, more than twenty attempts to cross the Jordan were attempted and all were unsuccessful. SAYERET HARUV responded by raiding terrorist bases and laying mines in what was known as the 'Yasir Arafat Trail', the PLO's supply and attack route. Lieutenant-Colonel Yossi Koller,

◄ Defence Minister Moshe Dayan and Chief Paratroop and Infantry Officer Colonel 'Raful' Eitan share a joke with paratroopers on manoeuvres in the Jordan Valley, 1969. (IDF Archives)

► The successful end result of the paratroop and SAYERET HARUV pursuit campaign in the Jordan Valley. Captured Palestinian weapons on display at Paratroop HQ, Jordan Valley. (IDF Archives)

SAYERET HARUV's commander exacted high standards from his fighters. In the IDF, each soldier serving along border or frontier positions is automatically awarded the 'Operation Service Pin'. Koller issued the Pin to a HARUV fighter only after his third raid into Jordan!

The pursuits soon became something of national sport. Celebrities, and political figures managed to attach themselves to HATIVAT HABIKA'A units in the field, hoping for a bit of extra-curricular excitement. Opposition leader Menachem Begin was even invited on an eventful 10-hour pursuit in which a platoon of paratroopers cornered a band of terrorists in a cave. After tense negotiations, all the terrorists surrendered, except for their commander who commited suicide. Mr Begin received the dead terrorist's Tokarov pistol as a souvenir for a 'successful day's hunting'.

Ironically it was not the Israelis but the Jordanians who brought about the demise of the infiltrators. Since the battle at Karamah, the various left-wing and Marxist Palestinian terror factions devloped a Palestinian state-within-a-state in Jordan, ignoring Jordanian law and sovereignty. Following 'Skyjack Sunday' of 6 September 1970, Jordan responded in force. In the ensuing civil war known throughout the world as 'Black September', little quarter was given in fighting fiercer than anything seen in the Arab-Israeli conflict, and in which thousands were killed indiscriminately. King Hussein's Bedouin Army was not as merciful as the 'hated' IDF, and few live Palestinian prisoners were taken. Many in fact 'infiltrated' into Israel in order to surrender to the merciful Israelis, but many too surrendered to HATIVAT HABIKA'A's Bedouin trackers, who offered less than kind terms of surrender!

Beaten and in disarray, the terrorists moved their infrastructure to Lebanon, whence they initiated a war against Israel along the northern border, and throughout the world. The Jordan Valley however remained secure!

THE THREE-BORDER WAR: OPERATIONS
ALONG THE NORTHERN FRONTIER

THE 1967 War was supposed to have brought peace to Israel's northern frontier. Syrian artillery no longer threatened the northern settlements, and for a brief period it appeared as if the Golan Heights would not follow the path of the Egyptian and Jordanian fronts. Syria was not Northern Command's only concern however. The inability of Palestinian terrorists to achieve a military and political initiative through the Jordan Valley forced its leadership to look elsewhere for venues of operations. Attacks soon commenced against Israeli civilian and military targets throughout the Beit Shean, and northern Jordan Valley. In 1969 alone, terrorist attacks from northern Jordan across the River Yarmouk resulted in eight deaths, and 59 wounded, and the town of Beit Shean was transformed into a battlefield. IDF and Border Guard morning patrols were often shelled, and the local agricultural settlements were forced to exist as fortresses under siege. Fortunately, IDF Northern Command had had time to study Central Command's campaign in the Jordan Valley, and it responded to the challenge by entrusting security operations to the two élite units under its command: the GOLANI Infantry Brigade and its territorial reconnaissance battalion, SAYERET EGOZ.

These were two formidable military formations, although quite different in role and capabilities. Even though EGOZ fighters underwent the rigorous 6-month basic training to qualify as paratroops, they resembled a guerrilla army more than a conventional airborne infantry battalion. Commanded by Lieutenant-Colonel Uri Elchanani (a veteran GLOANI officer no less), SAYERET EGOZ's four reconnaissance companies were thinly stretched along a lengthy frontier, beginning at the Lebanese border on the Mediterranean, and stretching through Rosh Hanikra, to the Golan Heights, to the tributaries of the River Yarmouk in north-west Jordan. Forced to operate in small 'guerrilla bands', the battalion relied on its heavily armed jeeps for mobility, and fire-power. Its speciality was the ambush, and it was common for an EGOZ fighter to participate in as many as 300 night ambushes during his thirty months of operational duty.

The GOLANI Brigade, on the other hand, had become national heroes following the 1967 victory. The unit's legend, 'My GOLANI', became something of a national slogan, and for the first time in its history, conscripts

▼ SAYERET HARUV commanders discuss pursuit tactics, before coordinating a heliborne search for Palestinian infiltrators, 8 May 1969. The use of helicopters gave HATIVAT HABIKA'A's élite forces the edge in the fierce Jordan Valley compaign. (IDF Archives)

volunteered in large numbers. Commanded by the experienced Colonel Yekutiel 'Kuti' Adam (killed during the 1982 invasion of Lebanon), the brigade's five condensed infantry battalions and reconnaissance company boasted impressive offensive capabilities. The men were experienced, well-equipped and eager for activity beyond routine and hapless patrols along the never-ending border fences. After years of casual military response to terrorist provocation, OC Northern Command, Major-General David 'Dado' Elazar, was given the green light to strike hard at terrorist installations in north-west Jordan. In May 1969 he placed GOLANI on the offensive!

The first target entrusted to GOLANI was the Jordanian village of Wadi al-Yabas, a major terrorist base. Assigned to the best fighters from the BARAK Battalion and SAYERET GOLANI, the raid was code-named Operation 'ASUTA 12'. On the night of 8 May, the attack force crossed the Jordan in three Zodiacs. While the BARAK contingent prepared ambushes along the village road, the SAYERET searched Wadi al-Yabas for an enemy presence. Preliminary IAF and artillery attacks, prompted most of the inhabitants to flee, and the houses were found empty. While one squad cleared the homes of documents, another force set the explosive charges in place. A minor fire-fight erupted, in which three terrorists were killed, including their regional commander, after which all twelve buildings were destroyed.

In July 1969, SAYERET GOLANI was ordered to attack and destroy the *Hacharut*, a Jordanian Army fortress across

▲ Always preferring action and observation to subord nates' reports, Chief Paratroop and Infantry Office Colonel 'Raful' Eitan prepares *his* FN MAG 7.62mm ligh machine-gun prior to a heliborne patrol into Jorda September 1969. (IDF Archives)

from KIBBUTZ Ashdot Ya'akov parallel to the River Ya mouk. *Hacharut* had regularly harassed morning ID patrols, as well as providing *el-Fatah* with intelligence an an observation post from which Katyusha rocket fire w directed against Israeli targets. The SAYERET crossed t Yarmouk through a thick row of banana fields, an engaged the target, which was busy directing artillery fi against pre-positioned 'dummy' Israeli targets. Th SAYERET split into two spearheads, and simultaneousl attacked the position from opposite directions. It w quickly seized in a lightning assault, as most of th Jordanians and terrorists fled. Those remaining offere only a token resistance. Two central bunkers were d stroyed, causing the collapse of the entire fortress. Th raid cost the SAYERET one dead and three wounded.

Jordan's collusion with the terrorists continued, an further action was required. In August 1969, after caref political consideration, Northern Command was final allowed to attack the O'r Canal, the principal water carri from the River Yarmouk to the Jordanian agricultur settlements of the Jordan Valley, which needed the wat in order to survive. Code-named Operation 'AMAH', th aid was carried out by lead units from SAYERET GOLANI (entrusted with destroying the canal's underground facilities), and two naval commando officers, attached to the raiding party to destroy the underwater canal. A direct military confrontation with the Jordanian Army was not desired, and the small force crossed the Yarmouk in Zodiacs, carrying hundreds of kilograms of high-explosives, at night, and without covering fire. It took the combined SAYERET and KOMMANDO YAMI force forty minutes of feverish labour to set the charges in place; the satisfying explosion was heard during their withdrawal across the Israeli border. Although numerous GOLANI and SAYERET EGOZ raids followed, the attack on the O'r Canal marked the virtual cessation of terrorist activity in the area. With one frontier secure, Northern Command was able to concentrate its resources on Lebanon.

Although sharing a common frontier with Israel, the Lebanese abandoned military action following their poor showing in the 1948 War. Lebanon maintained a small, insignificant standing army of 11,000, and preferred to concentrate its national energies on anything but military matters, but there were hundreds of thousands of Palestinian refugees living in the squalor of refugee camps in Tyre, Sidon, Beirut, and Tripoli. They had been segregated from much of Lebanese life, and left to their own devices. Although they refrained from overt military activity, the post-1967 Palestinian revolution changed everything. With Syria unwilling to risk Israeli reprisals for terrorist attacks originating from her territory, and the Jordanian front quiet, terrorist attacks across the Lebanese border into Israel began.

Israel's border with Lebanon was not the Jordan Valley. Instead of hundreds of square miles protecting the Israeli populace from terrorist infiltration, Israel's northern frontier was a mere defensive barrier. Well-fortified, the fence was patrolled 24 hours a day by Border Guard and SAYERET EGOZ units, although breaches were always being found and exploited. To make the security problem more complex and immediate, dozens of KIBBUTZIM and MOSHAVIM flourished only a stone's throw from the border. They had all the trappings of many Israeli border settlements, including bomb shelters, barbed wire defences, and round the clock military protection. The introduction, however, of a determined terrorist presence within their gates troubled everyone.

Only one SAYERET EGOZ company was responsible for the Lebanese border, and the demanding though routine patrolling of the agricultural settlements took its toll of the small force. Lieutenant-Colonel Elchanani requested that his men be relieved from routine patrols, and used only for cross-border ambushes and raids. His request was accepted by Northern Command, and EGOZ soon found itself operating entirely on Lebanese soil. Ambushes ranged from 3-man squads equipped with FN MAGs, to platoon-sized forces supported by halftracks and jeeps seeking large-scale engagements.

EGOZ was not alone in the Lebanon campaign. The terrorists had established a vast staging-area along the southern slopes of Mt Hermon between the Syrian and Lebanese borders. It was nicknamed 'Fatahland', and was a constant thorn in Northern Command's side. On the night of 4 October 1969, a task force from SAYERET GOLANI, SAYERET EGOZ and the ARAYOT HAGOLAN Battalion raided Lebanese villages in 'Fatahland'. The operation was a success, and resulted in the destruction of 24 buildings in three villages. Dozens of similar raids were executed, primarily in retaliation for acts of terror committed inside Israel, although pre-emptive strikes were also conducted.

The terrorists enlarged the sphere of violence on 22 May 1970 when a school bus transporting children from MOSHAV Avivim was attacked near the Lebanese border. A total of seven 82mm rockets were fired, resulting in twelve killed and nineteen wounded. The blood-chilling carnage warranted swift Israeli measures, and the IAF bombed numerous Lebanese villages that supported terrorist activity. The attack signified an end to Israel's respect for Lebanese sovereignty, and GOLANI and SAYERET EGOZ were ordered to seize the initiative *inside* Lebanon. The true war up north had begun.

The task of purifying 'Fatahland' was entrusted to a large IDF task force, consisting of the 188th BARAK Armoured Brigade, with SAYERET EGOZ responsible for clearing the terrorist camp at Kfar Hamam. It was code-named KALAHAT (turmoil) 1, and was the first battalion-sized raid carried out by EGOZ. Kfar Hamam was seized after a lightning assault in which terrorist opposition was quickly silenced. Houses were searched and destroyed. Dozens of terrorists were killed, and eight captured. Some 150 rifles and 200 land-mines were seized, as were numerous documents of great intelligence value. In all fourteen buildings used by the terrorists as communications and operations centres were demolished.

In 1970, Lieutenant-Colonel Uri Simchoni was appointed SAYERET EGOZ commander. A veteran paratrooper who had jumped with the 890th Battalion at Mitla, Simchoni had served in a wide variety of postings in the GOLANI Brigade and Northern Command. He was intimate with the security problems in Northern Command, and provided an immediate response. SAYERET EGOZ was dispatched into the heartland of southern Lebanon, and organized dozens of week-long forays to interdict enemy capabilities. Simchoni commanded most operations personally, and enjoyed an irreproachable reputation with his men. The ambushes were difficult, and entailed patience, disregard of the bitter winter climate, and the ability to destroy enemy forces with decisive fire-power. The campaign cost the small unit a heavy price in dead and wounded, and would mark the peak of SAYERET EGOZ operations.

In December 1970, OC Northern Command, Major-General Mordechai 'Motta' Gur, rewarded SAYERET EGOZ for its brilliant success rate with ambushes, by ordering it to raid the Lebanese village I'nta, a major terrorist staging-base in 'Fatahland'. Dozens more raids soon followed. The terrorists that had fled 'Black September' in Jordan

soon entrenched themselves in 'Fatahland', and SAYERET EGOZ was determined to make their tenure a brief one as the paratroops and SAYERET HARUV had succeeded in doing in the Jordan Valley.

During December 1970, seventeen acts of Palestinian terrorism were directed from 'Fatahland' into northern Israel. Northern Command's response was decisive. It ordered the destruction of the village of Ya'atur, thirteen kilometres north of the Israeli border. More than thirty hard-core PFLP terrorists were positioned at Ya'atur, and their facilities included barracks, an armoury, an operations room, and a communications centre. The village was defended by Goryunov machine-guns and was patrolled regularly by sentries toting AK-47s and RPGs.

On 27 December 1970, a mixed company from SAYERET GOLANI and HABOK'IM HARISHONIM, burdened with automatic rifles, anti-tank weapons and explosives, crossed the border and proceeded towards Ya'atur. They marched at a fast pace along a rocky route, their passage made more difficult by their heavy loads. Just outside the village, SAYERET GOLANI Commander Major Yudke addressed the PFLP sentry in Arabic. The guard instinctively fired into the air, but his warning was too late. The 2 – 4-man squads neutralized their assigned targets, and although heavy resistance was encountered, the facilities were destroyed.

▲ A SAYERET COLANI fighter roots out a Palestinian terrorist from a bunker in 'FATAHLAND', January 1969 (IDF Archives)

The GOLANI withdrawal was difficult. Each man was carrying his personal weapons plus at least two captured weapons, and the use of stretchers to carry the wounded was impossible due to the narrow rocky terrain. The withdrawal was also followed closely by Palestinian mortar harassment, and a medevac was finally ordered in to clear the wounded (one died en route to hospital). The remainder of the force made it back to Israel on foot.

On 6 September 1972, the civilized world was horrified by the massacre of eleven Israeli athletes at the Munich Summer Olympics. Ten days later, the IDF responded with a four-day invasion of southern Lebanon in which 22 villages were targeted. Operation 'KALAHAT 4' was carried out by a task force from the 188th BARAK Armoured Brigade together with the GOLANI Brigade and SAYERET EGOZ in the vanguard. The task force consisted of 1,350 men, 45 Centurion tanks, 133 halftracks and M113 APCs supported by four batteries of self-propelled artillery, and three squadrons of IAF A-4, and F-4 fighter bombers. Israel's first true invasion of Lebanon netted eighteen Lebanese soldiers and forty terrorists killed, twenty prisoers, tons of captured equipment, 70 facilities destroyed, 6 bunkers, and seventeen tents burnt.

During Northern Command's War of Attrition, Syria ad been spared the fate of Egypt, Jordan, and Lebanon. Although thought to be the main enemy threat following the 1967 War, the Golan Heights remained relatively quiet until 1973. Nevertheless, the threat led to constant vigilance and innovation. One of the most interesting developments stemming from the fear of a widening conflict against Damascus was the creation of SAYERET HADRUZIM, the IDF's Druze Muslim reconnaissance force. The brainchild of Major Muhamad Mullah, the idea of a uniquely Druze reconnaissance force sprang from the desire for an expanded and more direct role for the Druze conscripts in the IDF, otherwise serving in the minorities 'UNIT 300'. In 1968, Major Mullah had come up with the novel idea that if hostilities against Syria escalated, a parachute-qualified force of Druze commandos able to infiltrate into the Syrian Druze mountains could be of military value! Chief of Staff Bar-Lev eagerly accepted the idea, and SAYERET HADRUZIM was born. In addition to SAYERET HADRUZIM operations in the north during the War of Attrition, the paratroops also conducted several deep penetration raids into Syria, including Operation 'Princess Marylin' (16 March 1970), the destruction of high-tension cables along the Damascus-Homs road, and Operation 'SHAFAT' (17 June 1970), a commando raid against Syrian military installations and the destruction of a bridge along the Damascus-Suida road.

The most significant, audacious and yet most secret operations against Syria were the two ARGAZ (basket)

operations in June 1972. The Syrians were still holding three IAF pilots shot down over Damascus two years before. Although the IDF held 45 Syrian, and 60 Egyptian POWs, the Syrian Government refused to negotiate the pilots' release. In June 1972 A'MAN received word that senior officers from Syrian Air Force Intelligence (the controlling body of Syrian intelligence and espionage efforts) would be travelling to Lebanon to coordinate a new round of terrorist attacks. This news rang bells at General Staff Headquarters, and it was thought that if the Syrian could be captured it would not only secure the release of the three pilots, but would prove to the world Syrian complicity in terrorism. Only one unit was capable of conducting such an operation, and SAYERET MAT'KAL was summoned immediately.

Commanded by Lieutenant-Colonel Ehud Barak (Israel's most decorated soldier, and at present the IDF Deputy Chief of Staff), SAYERET MAT'KAL crossed into Lebanon on the night of 12/13 June near the town of Zra'ait. They prepared an ambush for the Syrian's entourage, but the presence of Lebanese armoured cars caused 'ARGAZ 1' to be aborted. Eight days later SAYERET MAT'KAL returned to Zra'ait for another try, although this time Barak remained at the CP, while the 'kidnapping' was entrusted with a then unknown Captain Yonatan 'Yoni' Netanyahu, supported by a mechanized force led by

▼ With all fingers on triggers, a mechanized SAYERET EGOZ patrol keeps Israel's northern border with Lebanon secure from Palestinian terrorist infiltrators, March 1970. (IDF Archives)

Captain Muki Botzer. Both soldiers would later receive immortal status for their command of the raid on Entebbe.

After hours of waiting in ambush, Captain Netanyahu spotted the Syrian entourage, consisting of a Lebanese Gendarme jeep, and two unmarked civilian vehicles. A Lebanese family on the road spotted the MAT'KAL ambush and warned the Syrian convoy. Before the Lebanese and Syrians could react the MAT'KAL men leaped out of concealment and captured them. The Syrian officers, a Brigadier-General, two Colonels, and two Lieutenant-Colonels, quickly surrendered their weapons, shouting in English '*Please, without bloodshed!*' While the Syrian officers and Lebanese bodyguards were identified and assembled for their short trip back to Israel, Captain Botzer's mechanized covering force went into action against the village of Ramiah. In the ensuing battle, three Lebanese policeman, and one MAT'KAL fighter were killed.

Operation 'AGAZ BET' (or '2') was a monumental loss for Syrian integrity and intelligence efforts against Israel. The inevitable interrogations produced a mine of information, and the Syrian officers were eventually bargained off for the three Israeli pilots. Syria's obvious insecurity in future Lebanese operations resulted in a temporary quietening of the Lebanese-Israeli border. For Israel, the raid was a covert, though astounding military, political, and intelligence victory. It ensured future large-scale assignments for Major Barak's élite group of fighters, and signalled the IDF's reliance on commando operations in the war against terrorism.

6

FOUR VERY SPECIAL
OPERATIONS, 1972–3

A GIFT FROM THE SKY: OPERATION
'TSHURA', BEIRUT, 28 DECEMBER 1968

BEFORE 1967, Israeli intelligence had suspected an upsurge in Palestinian terrorist activity both inside Israel and abroad. Israel's worldwide diplomatic and economic installations were placed on a high state of alert, but the threat failed to materialize. Then, on 23 July 1968 an EL AL (Israel's national airline) Boeing 707 carrying 35 passengers from Rome to Tel Aviv was hijacked by a heavily armed 3-man PFLP squad, and flown to Dar al-Beida airport near Algiers. Taken by surprise, Israel was offered little room to manoeuvre, and accepted the terrorists' demands that Arab prisoners serving sentences in Israeli prisons be released in exchange for the hostages. In September of that year, the exchange took place, and this set a most dangerous precedent.

Excited by their 'EL AL conquest', and their own independence from mainstream PLO methodology following the victory at Karameh, the PFLP initiated a wave of bloody terror throughout Israel and the world. They set off explosive devices in Tel Aviv, and a car bomb in a Jerusalem market which killed twelve in November 1968. But it was their exploits against EL AL that gained the greatest Press coverage. With a network of sleeper agents in place throughout western Europe, and a force of friendly left-wing European terrorists to assist them the PFLP resumed its 'offensive in the air'. On 26 December 1968 an EL AL Boeing 707 was attacked with grenade and machine-gun fire by two PFLP terrorists as it taxied on the runway at Athens Airport, resulting in the death of one passenger. It soon became apparent that the Palestinians had uncovered Israel's 'soft underbelly'.

Israel had long searched for a military solution to the PFLP's wave of air terror. A national airline symbolized a nation's independence and prestige, and Prime Minister Levi Eshkol ordered preventive measures to ensure the end of attacks against EL AL. While the SHIN BET directed its efforts to initiate dramatic security controls for EL AL, A'MAN searched for a military response to the PFLP challenge. One common factor was obvious in each PFLP attack. The terrorists had all originated from and undergone training and received their orders in the Lebanese capital. All fingers pointed towards Beirut, so Beirut's International Airport was the IDF's only practical choice for military retaliation. On 27 December, Israel's cabinet met to discuss possibilities of retribution. After heated political debate typical of Israeli political life, Prime Minister Eshkol ordered Chief of Staff Bar-Lev to prepare a preliminary plan for an assault on Beirut's International Airport. Chief Paratroop and Infantry Officer Colonel Rafael 'Raful' Eitan was ordered into action.

Beirut International Airport was well known to 'Raful', and the IDF's élite paratroop and infantry forces. Ever since the hijacking of the EL AL flight to Algiers, contingency plans had been filed to deal with a similar situation in Beirut, and other Arab capitals. When Chief of Staff Bar-Lev ordered 'Raful' to carry out the raid the *following* day, it posed little problem. The objective of the raid was to destroy all Arab national airliners on the tarmac at Beirut International Airport on the day of the raid. Strict orders were issued that no civilians or 'innocent' property was to be harmed. The raid was intended to state to the Arab world that Israeli aircraft would not be the only ones hit in this new type of warfare. 'Raful', however, wanted the raid to display to the entire world the unique and far-reaching capabilities of *his* élite forces. He rightly codenamed the raid Operation 'TSHURA' (gift).

Intelligence reviews prior to the raid had been extensive and exhaustive, 'Raful' received the 'green light' only 24 hours prior to the operation's H-Hour. He knew exactly which Arab airliners would be on the tarmac, the type of aircraft and their intended take-off and landing schedules.

▶ Operation 'TSHURAH'; Beirut International Airport, 28 December 1968. By the light of a burning Lebanese MEA airliner, paratroopers dressed in their Class A uniforms and laden with packs of explosives proceed towards their next MEA target in the first of many spectacular IDF commando raids that captured the world's imagination. (IDF Archives)

The assault force was under strict orders not to harm any civilians, and to display maximum restraint against Lebanese forces attempting to intervene. In order to make the paratroopers' appearance in Beirut the more obvious, though less threatening, 'Raful' ordered his men to wear their Class A uniforms; silver metal parachutist wings and bright red TZANHANIM berets. Of course the paratroopers had faces blackened, carried full kit, and sported AK-47 assault rifles with inserted magazines and safeties off!

Most of 28 December was spent at Lod Airport, where EL AL technicians offered their expertise in showing the paratroop sappers the 'proper' locations for explosive charges to be placed on aircraft. Following last-minute meetings of minds between 'Raful', his officers, and the helicopter pilots, the Beirut operation was ready. At 21.00 hours (15 minutes behind schedule due to last-minute word that further flights of airliners were expected in Beirut), the 150 paratroopers from SAYERET TZANHANIM, HA'AN TZANHANIM (the conscript brigade's sapper company), and HATIVAT HATZANHANIM lifted off from an IAF base in northern Israel for their short trip to Beirut. The helicopter armada consisted of three SA 321K Super Frelons ferrying the sapper and attack force, a Bell-205 serving as 'Raful's airborne command post, and another Bell-205 entrusted with stopping Lebanese reinforcements from reaching the airport. As the IDF was relatively inexperienced in the use of helicopters, four IDF/Navy gun boats were stationed off the coast, and three IAF transports were fuelled and airborne awaiting the order to exfiltrate 'Raful' and his men. They were never needed. At 21.15 hours, after only 45 minutes in the air, the 'red berets' reached Beirut.

The identification, sweep for civilians, and placing of the explosive charges was accomplished with impeccable timing. Many of the paratroopers had to convince the Lebanese ground crews that they were not part of a 'Lebanese Army' training exercise, but Israeli commandos! The apron was full of planes sporting the MEA (Middle East Airlines, the Lebanese national carrier) logo, and great care was displayed in setting the detonations. Each plane (mainly Boeings and DC-10s) carried approximately thirty tons of fuel, the simultaneous detonations of which would create a hellish inferno of unimaginable proportions. During the entire operation, great effort was also made to

isolate the aircraft from other properties not slated for destruction, as well as keeping civilians (many of whom gazed in awe from the departure lounge terrace) away.

On the road leading from West Beirut to the airport, a Lebanese Army contingent attempted to engage the Israelis. The Bell-205 went into action immediately, and grenades and nails were thrown on to the roads making them impassable, while machine-gun fire was directed just ahead of the oncoming traffic. Within minutes, a snarling traffic jam was created, bottling up the Lebanese soldiers in a hopeless mêlée of vehicles en route to and escaping from the airport.

The entire operation took the paratroopers only 29 minutes, one less than had been planned. Traffic on the tarmac was even busier than expected. Fourteen Arab aircraft were indentified and explosives were fitted. Thirteen were destroyed (one explosive charge failed to detonate). At 23.00 hours, the paratroopers were back in Israel, enjoying a well-deserved victory celebration, while firefighters in Beirut slaved for hours extinguishing thirteen infernos. Not one civilian or soldier was hurt during the raid, as the principles of TOHAR HANESHEK had been strictly adhered to. Nevertheless, the raids had significant political ramifications. An outraged French President De Gaulle suspended all weapons shipments to Israel, while the Arabs deplored Israel's act of international terrorism in the world community. For Israel, the operation was seen as a milestone, a statement of a national resolve against terrorism voiced louder than the protocols of diplomacy could ever hope to express. Most importantly, Operation 'TSHURA' worked. Not a single EL AL airliner has been hijacked since!

It was a brilliant text-book, 'commando raid', planned, led, and executed by Israel's finest and most innovative combatant, 'Raful' Eitan. Reports were transformed into folklore, following Operation 'TSHURA', of Colonel Eitan's trip to the departure lounge bar, and paying for a cup of Lebanese coffee with an Israeli pound note. Although enjoying the 'James Bond' image, 'Raful' had not been in Beirut long enough to enjoy such a luxury. Operation 'TSURA' would not be 'Raful's last visit to Beirut, however. He would return fourteen years later, once again fighting the terrorist scourge, this time commanding an army in the hell that Lebanon would soon become.

THE DEATH OF CAPTAIN RIFA'AT: OPERATION 'ISOTOPE 1', LOD AIRPORT, 8–9 MAY 1972

THE year 1972 was a banner year for Palestinian terrorism. The various Palestinian factions committed 22 acts of terror ranging from routine sabotage against Israeli targets worldwide, to the blood-chilling massacre of eleven Israeli athletes at the Summer Olympic Games in Munich. In the forefront of the terror campaign against Israel was a sinister organization called 'Black September'. They were an integral element of Yasir Arafat's *el-Fatah*, although the connection remained secret. Although as their title suggests, their initial objective was revenge against Jordan for September 1970, Israel remained the primary target.

On 8 May 1972, four 'Black September' terrorists hijacked Sabena Belgian Air Lines flight 571 (a Boeing 707) flying from Brussels to Israel via Vienna. The terrorists, two women (Rima Aissa Tannous, and Thereseh Halaseh) who boarded the flight at Brussels, and two men (Ali Abu-Snina, and Abdul Aziz al-Atrasi), who boarded the flight at Vienna, had managed to smuggle pistols, grenades and explosives aboard the aircraft through the airport's lax security apparatus. Ali Abu-Snina was no stranger to the art of hijacking, in fact, he was an experienced veteran. In 1968, he commanded the El Al hijacking to Algiers. Fours years later, and as part of 'Black September', Abu-Snina had more ambitious plans. As the flight began its descent above Rhodes, Abu-Snina entered the cockpit, pulled his gun, and announced to the 99 passengers, half of them Israeli nationals, 'that "Captain Rifa'at" was in command!' As his three companions collected passports, and prepared explosive charges throughout the aircraft, 'Captain Rifa'at' ordered the pilot, Captain Reginald Levy (a Belgian Jew who had flown with the RAF in the Second World War), to fly to a most unlikely destination – Lod Airport, Israel!

Word of the hijacking sent shock waves throughout the IDF General Staff. It had long been suspected that both the PFLP and 'Black September' were planning a suicide air-assault into Israel, by either crashing a hijacked airliner into central Tel Aviv, or detonating it on the ground at Lod Airport near the passenger terminal. As the Sabena 707 approached Israeli airspace, a flight of IAF F-4E Phantoms followed close behind in formation, awaiting the order to intercept, and shoot it down. At 19.00 hours, the aircraft was allowed to land, and was diverted to a remote runway. Teams of Border Guard snipers, emergency medical crews, and fire-fighters were ordered into position, awaiting the inevitable. The terrorists were quick with their demands: the immediate release of 370 convicted Palestinian terrorists in exchange for the lives of the hostages. 'Black September' was not known for its flexibility, and time appeared to be a diminishing commodity.

Observing the situation from their command post in the airport control tower were Defence Minister Moshe Dayan; Chief of Staff Lieutenant-General David 'Dado' Elazar; Head of Operations Major-General Yisrael Tal; A'MAN's Chief, Major-General Aharon Yariv; OC Central Command, Major-General Rechavam Zeevi; OC IAF, Major-General Mordechai Hod, General Staff Operations Chief, Colonel Emanuel 'Mano' Shaked; and 'Raful', coming to the end of his tenure as Chief Paratroop and Infantry Officer. Although the convergence of so many officers created a chaotic command and control environment, their first order was clear and direct. Lieutenant-Colonel Ehud Barak's SAYERET MAT'KAL was summoned to the airport immediately.

SAYERET MAT'KAL was the IDF's premier élite unit, but

not the only one capable of freeing hostages from an airliner. Ever since the EL AL hijacking in 1968, SAYERET TZANHANIM, SAYERET HARUV and SAYERET GOLANI units had trained regularly in rescuing passengers from hijacked airliners. Nevertheless, with a precedent to be accomplished, and with the lives of a great number of foreign nationals at stake, the General Staff opted to go with its 'sure thing'.

In keeping with his name, Lieutenant-Colonel Barak (Hebrew for Lighting) went into action in lightning fashion. His primary objective was to immobilize the aircraft, ensuring that the terrorists and their hostages remained within striking reach. Covered by teams of commandos armed with UZIS and AK-47s who fanned out to form a defensive perimeter, Barak and an EL AL technician stealthily proceeded to the plane's undercarriage, and drained the hydraulic fluid from the brakes, as well as gingerly letting the air out of the tyres. The process took four hours to complete, and required three trips to and from the aircraft. 'Captain Rifa'at' only realized what had been done at 01.30 hours on 9 May, and ordered repairs to be effected immediately. His demand initiated a dialogue with Israeli security officials and International Red Cross (IRC) representatives, after which the terrorists agreed to postpone their deadline until 13.00 hours. In fact, Israel started false negotiations with the terrorists, intending to gain their confidence, which bought Barak the upper edge: time!

Throughout the night, the commandos perfected assault techniques on a Boeing 707 at an Israel Aircraft Industries hangar nearby. As negotiations regarding the details of the 'prisoner' exchange continued into the next day, 'Captain Rifa'at' became suspicious, and unpredictable. To let the Israelis know that he meant business, he sent Captain Levy to the control tower with a sample of the explosives with which the aircraft would be destroyed. Levy gave Dayan and Elazar precise details of the aircraft's layout, the positioning of the terrorists, and their state of mind; including the first report that two of the hijackers were females. Levy was told to inform 'Captain Rifa'at' that the Israelis had capitulated, and would agree to their demands. 'Captain 'Rifa'at' obliged by pushing the deadline up a few hours, 'giving the Israelis enough time to arrange the prisoner exchange and their transportation to Cairo'.

Under intense pressure, the commandos perfected their assault to split-second timing. They would be dressed as EL AL technicians, carrying their .22 calibre Beretta automatics beneath their white overalls. Appearing as if preparing the aircraft for take-off, the commandos would split into groups of three, and break through the four emergency exits on top of the wings, the two starboard exits, and an additional exit near the cockpit. A TWA airliner, the aircraft intended to bring the released prisoners to Cairo was brought to a point where the terrorists could see it.

At 16.00 hours, the rescue force headed out towards their target. After being frisked by IRC representatives (the pistols were explained as being for self-defence only), the force produced ladders, and set itself into position, awaiting Lieutenant-Colonel Barak's whistle, signalling the attack. The assault had to be postponed for a few minutes, as a young commando, who hours earlier was on a security detail aboard an EL AL flight, made a mad dash for the lavatory. Although their training and exploits confirmed the commando's extraordinary capabilities, they were after all still human beings, prone to anxiety and fear. His return to formation signalled the go-ahead for the operation.

The whistle sounded at 16.29 hours, and the six teams stormed through their pre-determined exits simultaneously. They fired their Berettas at any standing target. 'Captain Rifa'at' was the first to be hit. Attempting to struggle with one of the commandos, he took a burst of fire in the chest and died immediately. The 'EL AL technicians' were immediately followed by commandos wearing fatigues, whose task it was to clear the passengers out of the aircraft as fast as possible. The entire search and destroy operation took only 90 seconds, in which a total of 60 shots were fired, ten by the terrorists. In the shootout, a 22-year-old woman hostage was killed, and three commandos wounded. The two male terrorists were killed, and the two females captured.

Operation 'Isotope 1' was a great victory for Israel. By responding to terror instead of retaliating against it, Israel exhibited to the world her resolve and capabilities in combating terrorism. For 'Black September', the 'Sabena affair' was a humbling and humiliating defeat. For Lieutenant-Colonel Barak and his commandos, the operation was an emotional triumph. In contrast to their countless covert operations against conventional enemies, the results of 'Isotope 1' were real and tangible. The secretive unit had shed its mask to save human lives, and were duly thanked by the grateful survivors. The commandos became an overnight sensation in Israel, and throughout the world. One of the commandos wounded in the attack, had been ferried to the operation by taxi, the driver of which surprisingly broke through security at the military hospital to return the soldier's cab fare. The protocols of the unit's secretive work had to be maintained however, and moments after the hostages had been secured, the commandos were whisked away before the arrival of the Press. In fact, the name of the unit which carried out the assault was kept secret for many years afterwards, and they were referred to only as the 'angels in white'.

'TO THE SHORES OF TRIPOLI': OPERATION 'BARDAS 54–55', TRIPOLI, 20–1 FEBRUARY 1973

IN June 1972, Chief of Staff David 'Dado' Elazar appointed Brigadier-General Emanuel 'Mano' Shaked to the post of Chief Paratroop and Infantry Officer. A PAL'MACH veteran, and a decorated reconnaissance officer in the GIVA'ATI Brigade, Shaked had served in a wide variety of postings throughout his illustrious military career. Prior to this new appointment, Shaked had been Chief of Operations for the General Staff, a sensitive position which afforded him the opportunity to formulate 'special military' responses to terrorism. Following the Munich Olympics Massacre, the seizure of the Israeli Embassy in Bangkok, and the Palestinians' letter-bomb campaign, the time was ripe for Brigadier-General Shaked's ideas to be put in to practice.

On 16 February 1973, the IDF General Staff met, and in a lengthy deliberation, planned a raid against the northern Lebanese port city of Tripoli, 180 kilometres from the Israeli frontier. Just north of Tripoli were two Palestinian refugee camps, Nahar al-Bard, and al-Badawi, in which were located *seven* major terrorist bases and headquarters.

▼ The Chief Paratroop and Infantry Officer during the paratroops' spectacular era, 1972–73, the PAL'MACH and paratroop veteran, Brigadier-General Emanuel Shaked. (IDF Archives)

These were not only staging-points for terrorist attacks worldwide, but also served as training facilities for terrorists from Europe, Africa, Asia, and South America. Chief of Staff Elazar informed Shaked that the raid had to be carried out within the next four days, and asked if it were possible. Shaked wryly replied, 'Affirmative, but I'll need the entire IDF under my command!' Shaked received all that he required; missile boats, Naval Commandos, and Air Force assistance. Less than 24 hours later, an operational plan was on the Chief of Staff's desk in Tel Aviv.

Because of the distance between the two targets, the operation became in essence two separate, though inseparable raids. The force that would attack the camp at Nahar al-Bard (Operation 'BARDAS 54') was commanded by the deputy commander of HATIVAT HATZANHANIM, Lieutenant-Colonel Amos Yaron, and was split into three spearheads. The first, a paratroop force commanded by Lieutenant-Colonel Yitzhak Mordechai, was assigned GEULAH 1, the PLO (*el-Fatah*) 'FORCE 17' naval commando base where the international contingent of terrorists trained. The second, a force from the paratroop squad leader's battalion commanded by Major Doron Reuven was assigned 'GEULAH 2', the headquarters of the Popular Struggle Front. The third and final assignment, 'GEULAH 3' the headquarters of the Popular Front for the Liberation of Palestine, fell to a force of Naval Commandos commanded by Major G.

The raid on the al-Badawi camp (Operation 'BARDAS 55') which was situated two kilometres north of Tripoli, was under the overall leadership of HATIVAT HATZANHANIM Commander, Colonel Uzi Yairi. 'BARDAS 55' had four objectives: 'AHUVA 1', a series of *el-Fatah* command, control, and communications installations entrusted to Lieutenant-Colonel Amnon Shahak's 50th NA'HA'L Paratroop Battalion; the destruction of 'AHUVA 2', the PFLP prison, and finally 'AHUVAS 3 and 4', the *el-Fatah* local area headquarters in Tripoli, and the main *el-Fatah* armoury in the camp respectively; the heaviest defended targets of the entire operation, assigned to Major Avner Harmoni's SAYERET TZANHANIM. Both camps were heavily fortified, and defended by hundreds of well-trained hard-core, Palestinians equipped with a wide array of weapons, including anti-tank and anti-aircraft guns. A 'footnote objective'; the assassination of PFLP warlord, Dr George Habash, and senior Black September members, rumoured to be in the camps that evening!

Operation 'BARDAS 54-55' was the first large-scale IDF raid in which each three combat arms were represented. Although this was a year before the notion of 'combined arms' would be initiated, the raid on Tripoli was unique in that aerial support, naval transport, and the ground forces were all under one unified command. All commands contributed equally to the logistics, planning and execution of the raid. Time allotted to training for the raid was minimal. The paratroopers trained at a site near Jericho in a brigade-sized exercise followed by amphibious assault training near Haifa. The soldiers had but a few hours to sleep during the three frantic days of preparation, and were forbidden contact with the outside world. Such spartan conditions pointed to the importance of the preparations, and by the morning of 20 February, Brigadier-General Shaked informed Chief of Staff Elazar that his forces were ready.

At 20.15 hours on 20 February the missile boat flotilla ferrying the assault force reached the Lebanese coast just off Tripoli. The seven-hour voyage across heavy winter seas, caused even the most seasoned paratroop veterans to 'race for the buckets', and pray for land, even if it lay deep in enemy territory.

At 21.55 hours Colonel Yairi's task force landed just south of the al-Badawi camp, and proceeded towards the target in a neat and orderly formation. The dozens of drivers of cars on the main road failed to notice the long row of heavily armed paratroopers, and the advance continued smoothly. Colonel Yairi led at a hectic pace through the barely passable rocky terrain, many of even his most experienced officers having difficulty keeping up. Because the attack on Nahar al-Bard and al-Badawi were intended to begin simultaneously, Yairi was ordered on several occasions to halt his attack and wait for Lieutenant-Colonel Yaron's force, which had been delayed by rough seas, to reach their targets. At 01.07 hours, an anxious Brigadier-General Shaked, listening in from his command post aboard an IDF/Navy missile boat, ordered the attack to commence without Yaron.

Because 'AHUVAS 3 and 4' were considered the more problematic of the objectives, the SAYERET went into action first. 'AHUVA 3' was attacked by eleven reconnaissance paratroopers led by SAYERET TZANHANIM Commander Major Harmoni. The force entered the headquarters position raking the building with machine-gun and rifle-grenade fire. Major Harmoni entered the building, and eliminated a uniformed PLO sentry clutching an AK-47, but not before he got off a burst which hit Harmoni's right hand. By now the battle was in full swing. Grenades were thrown from all sides, seriously wounding Major Harmoni, and three of his subordinates. After a heavy fire-fight, Palestinian resistance crumbled, and the SAYERET tended to its wounded, ransacked the building, and prepared its demolition. The attack on 'AHUVA 4' was much easier, as most of the armoury guards retreated at the sound of gun-fire from 'AHUVA 3', and it was destroyed with little difficulty.

Lieutenant-Colonel Mula Shaham's attack on the PFLP prison was conducted in true 'commando' style. The force of paratroopers had silently surrounded 'AHUVA 2', when thirty metres from the gates, they encountered a PFLP patrol, and a fire-fight erupted. Lieutenant-Colonel Shaham shouted a rousing 'Follow me!', and the ring of paratroopers closed in for the kill. Dozens of grenades were thrown at the building's defences, allowing the attackers to enter the building unmolested. Once inside the prison compound, a close-quarters battle developed, in which the combatants literally fought each other eye to eye. In the darkness and confusion, the paratroopers displayed remarkable marksmanship skills. In all eighteen Palestinians were killed in the attack on 'AHUVA 2', and most of the buildings surrounding the base were destroyed in thundering explosions. Lieutenant-Colonel Shaham's force was unscathed.

The attack on 'AHUVA 1' by Lieutenant-Colonel Shahak's NA'HA'L paratroopers was completed without incident. Its defenders had fled at the first sound of gunfire, and Shahak's force was afforded enough time to sift through the files before razing the facilities.

Having encountered heavy seas and difficult terrain, Lieutenant-Colonel Yitzhak Mordechai's attack on the Nahar al-Bard camp did not begin until 01.24 hours. His force entered their target, 'GEULAH 1', after silently eliminating the base's two sentries, and destroying the gate with Bangalore torpedoes. Surprise was total, and the fire-fight was quick and decisive. The élite el-Fatah frogmen chose to flee rather than fight and Mordechai's 24 paratroopers were able to seize the base and destroy it. Dozens of files, maps, plans, and photographs were seized and placed in secure water-proof pouches. After a quick head-count, the force withdrew to its rendezvous point to await their helicopter ride back to Israel.

Major Reuven's mixed force of paratroopers and naval commandos had been lying in wait in a citrus grove near their target, 'GEULAH 2', awaiting the order to attack. When shots rang out from the nearby el-Fatah naval base, they swung into action. The Popular Struggle Front's office building was surrounded by a stone wall, which was dealt with by a satchel charge. The explosion not only breached the wall, but destroyed a heavily armed jeep in the courtyard, and killed three terrorists. As Major Reuven's force cleared the area of terrorists a small naval commando detachment commanded by Major Eilan Egozzi, the hero of Green Island, came under heavy RPK fire from a first-floor window. One of Major Egozzi's men threw a fragmentation grenade at the window, but the grenade hit the window's bars and rolled down back among the naval commandos. Instinctively, Major Egozzi picked up the grenade in an attempt to throw it away from his men but it exploded, resulting in the loss of his right hand and eye. Four others were wounded by the grenade. Although seriously hurt, Major Egozzi continued to give orders, and calmly told the medic tending to his wounds to finish his mission before wasting time on him. After killing a total of seven terrorists, the office was razed.

Major Reuven frantically requested a doctor for Major Egozzi, who was lying in a puddle of mud, losing blood rapidly. A tourniquet was applied, as were massive doses of liquids administered through an intravenous drip. To keep their beloved commander warm, paratroopers and naval commandos alike shed their blouses, draping them over Major Egozzi's shivering body. For his bravery and self-sacrifice, Major Egozzi was awarded the I'TUR HA'OZ, his second decoration in four years.

The final objective of the raid, 'GEULAH 3' was carried out by the Naval Commando contingent commanded by Major G. After silently killing one of the sentries at the PFLP commando base, the commandos entered the compound and quickly seized control following a brief engagement. After a thorough search of the area for anything of intelligence value, the complex was destroyed. No casualties were sustained.

The paratroopers were evacuated by Super Frelon and CH-53 helicopters, while the naval commandos returned to the waiting missile boats for the trip back to Israel. A'MAN estimated that 37 terrorists were killed during Operation 'BARDAS 54–55', and approximately 65 were seriously wounded. Five terrorist bases had been totally destroyed, another two seriously damaged. Of the seven separate IDF attack forces, only eight suffered serious wounds. It was Colonel Yairi's first operation as HATIVAT HATZANHANIM commander, and a striking success. A souvenir which Colonel Yairi carried with him from the battle was an AK-47, taken from a dead terrorist. He would carry that weapon into many a future battle, and to his death two years later, leading the rescue operation against Black September terrorists holding Tel Aviv's Savoy Hotel in March 1975.

'HEARTS AND MINDS': OPERATION 'AVIV NE'URIM', BEIRUT, 9–10 APRIL 1973

THE Munich Olympics Massacre horified the people of Israel. Although a deep penetration air raid against Palestinian training camps in Lebanon and Syria, and Operation 'KALAHAT 4', was Israel's immediate response, the thought of vengeance obsessed even the wisest, political and military leaders, and the biblical 'eye for an eye' code of justice was implemented against Black September. According to foreign Press reports Prime Minister Golda Meir authorized MOSSAD hit teams 'selectively' to assassinate a long list of 'Black September' and PLO officials responsible for the outrage at Munich. In a matter of months, the MOSSAD had killed scores of 'Black September's chief officers in the streets of Europe. The long arm of MOSSAD stretched far and wide, but further pre-emptive and retaliatory action was demanded. The IDF's brilliant execution of the raid on Tripoli in February 1973 convinced even the sceptics that a raid into the heart of Beirut would be a good idea.

Originally, the raid on Beirut had not been intended to be a large-scale selective 'hit', but merely a routine commando assault. As early as January 1973, there were reports of an *el-Fatah* explosives factory in southern Beirut, near the Sabra refugee camp in the el-Ouzai section of the city. The development of an indigenous Palestinian weapons manufacturing capability had ominous significance for the Israelis. Fifty years earlier, it had been the YISHUV's own minuscule weapons producing industry that had been an important stepping-stone on the road towards independence. It was rightly felt that the small factory in Beirut had historical similarities too close to ignore.

The IDF General Staff had originally ordered Lieutenant-Colonel Barak's SAYERET MAT'KAL to carry out the raid, but they soon found themselves in stiff competition with Naval Commando Commander Colonel Shaul Ziv, who urged a central task for his unit. After bitter infighting uncharacteristic of the IDF special operations planning and execution, persistence paid off, and the raid was given to the Naval Commandos. The raid on Beirut obsessed Colonel Ziv, and he initiated a fanatical training routine which occupied his forces almost 24 hours a day, seven days a week. A full-scale model of the target was built at the Naval Commando's home base, which was 'assaulted' every Friday morning before the Sabbath leave. Defence Minister Moshe Dayan cancelled the raid however. Recalling the political backlash of 'Raful's raid on Beirut International Airport in December 1968, Dayan wanted any raid on Beirut to provide decisive and spectacular results which would be felt throughout the Middle East for years to come. Colonel Ziv realized that he would eventually reach Beirut, and preparations continued.

Beirut was the main topic of conversation at the Chief Paratroop and Infantry Officer HQ as well. Brigadier-General Shaked had long urged the General Staff to sanction a policy of hitting the terrorists in their 'hearts and minds', and had spent many a sleepless night conjuring up contingency plans for such an eventuality. The success of the reported MOSSAD hit teams throughout Europe made it inevitable that the IDF's élite units would emulate them. The green light for an IDF 'selective elimination' operation initiated numerous zealous ideas, including one by Deputy Chief Paratroop and Infantry Officer Lieutenant-Colonel Shmuel Pressberger, who had toyed with the idea of once and for all eliminating Yasir Arafat.

While PLO Chairman Arafat and PFLP warlord George Habash remained elusive targets, two 'interesting addresses' in Beirut were discovered. One house, in the Rue Khartoum, was a seven-story headquarters and living facility for 170 terrorists of Nayif Hawatmeh's Democratic Front for the Liberation of Palestine (DFLP). The second address, two adjacent apartment blocks in Rue Verdun in the exclusive Ramlat el-Bida section of Beirut were home to three of 'Black September's top leaders. Muhamed Najer (known by his *nom de guerre* of Abu-Yusef), the *el-Fatah* operations and intelligence chief for worldwide terrorist attacks, as well as one of the leaders of 'Black September' and planner of the September Munich Massacre. Kamal A'dwan, a senior *el-Fatah* officer, who was responsible for running terrorist cells in the West Bank and Gaza Strip, and lastly Kamal Nasser, the PLO Spokesman, and a high-ranking 'Black September' officer. This timely information brought new life to the prospects of a foray into the Lebanese capital. In Israel, three death-warrants had been signed!

Training for the raid into Beirut was attended to in fastidious fashion. This was to be the IDF's largest, and most important commando raid in her 25-year history, and nothing was left to chance. Many officers felt that since the IDF was attacking Beirut anyway, simultaneous attacks against other targets would prove economic as well as militarily necessary. The raid on Beirut expanded into a large, well thought out operation, once again encompassing joint IDF, IAF, and Navy cooperation. In March 1973, the IDF's computer came up with the mission's code-name; Operation 'AVIV NE'URIM', 'Spring of Youth'.

Operation 'AVIV NE'URIM' consisted of four primary and one diversionary objectives. The targets and executors in order of mission importance were:

'AVIVAH', the assassination of Abu Yusef, Kamal A'dwan, and Kamal Nasser by Lieutenant-Colonel Ehud Barak's ubiquitous force of commandos (including Majors Yoni Netanyahu and Muki Botzer).

'GILAH', the destruction of the DFLP's apartment complex in Rue Khartoum by Lieutenant-Colonel Amnon Shahak and a force from SAYERET TZANHANIM.

'VARDAH', the destruction of *el-Fatah*'s headquarters

responsible for the West Bank and Gaza, as well as the explosives factory at el-Ouzai by a Naval Commando force commanded by Colonel Shaul Ziv.

'TZILAH', the destruction of a major el-Fatah ammunition dump located just north of Beirut's port, by a force of Naval Commandos commanded by Major G. (of Tripoli fame), under the overall command of Colonel Shumel Pressberger.

'YEHUDIT', the diversionary raid against an el-Fatah ammunition dump north of Sidon by a force from SAYERET TZHANHANIM led by Lieutenant-Colonel Amos Yaron.

'Operation 'AVIV NE'URIM' was a gamble with fatal consequences. Should anything go wrong, the five separate forces would find themselves alone, far from friendly borders, and with little chance of returning home to Israel alive. In fact, Brigadier-General Shaked was only given authorization for the raid by Prime Minister Golda Meir after he had promised her that 'all the boys would come home'.

Besides the essential pre-operation training, great attention was paid to familiarizing the volunteer force with Beirut's distinct geography. This was three years before Israel's friendship with Lebanon's Christians, and survival depended wholly on the commandos' wits, preparation, and proficiency. Brigadier-General Shaked made it a point personally to quiz his fighters as to street names, intersections, and local landmarks. A wall map of Beirut became the 'Bible' for many soldiers during the month of March, and within a matter of weeks, Beirut became as familiar as downtown Tel Aviv or Jerusalem. Military training was initiated at an intense pace. Models of each objective were constructed, and assault procedures were perfected to split-second timing, as well as the commander's own high standard of perfection.

Lieutenant-Colonel Barak opted to train his unit in more realistic surroundings. In Tel Aviv's upper class Lamed suburbs, Barak found a luxury high-rise apartment complex under construction which closely resembled 'AVIVAH', the houses in Rue Verdun. Without notifying the local police patrols, Barak's force landed on a nearby Tel Aviv beach from Zodiac craft, and proceeded by automobile to their target; exactly as had been planned for the raid. Dressed in civilian clothes, the commandos perfected their assault techniques on the buildings, oblivious to their immediate environs. Many of Lamed's residents became frightened by the sight of armed men doing 'strange things' in their peaceful neighbourhood, and summoned the police. Patrol cars were called in, and the night sergeant on duty was not appeased by Lieutenant-Colonel Barak's tight-lipped refusal to explain the situation. After receiving orders from Headquarters to leave the site immediately, the now curious policemen left frustrated. Barak was then allowed to resume the training unhindered. So important was the 'AVIVAH' objective, that both Chief of Staff Elazar and Brigadier General Shaked took part in the training, in order to familiarize themselves with the intricacies of the operation.

Since the assassinations would entail a covert infiltration into a civilian housing complex, the commandos were ordered to wear civilian clothes; one size too large, in order to accommodate their ammunition belts underneath. During the first days of April 1973, dozens of commandos went on shopping trips throughout Tel Aviv to purchase their Beirut wardrobe. In one trendy Tel Aviv boutique, Lieutenant-Colonels Barak and Shahak had to argue with a salesmen, who insisted that their purchases were the wrong sizes. Undaunted, Barak and Shahak continued their shopping spree, buying women's dresses, impressive size brassieres, and blonde wigs!

Intensive preparations were also under way in SAYERET TZHANHANIM's camp. The most pressing concern appeared to be the 'proper' amount of explosives to use in destroying the DFLP headquarters. One of SAYERET TZHANHANIM's chief sapper officers, Avida Shor, was worried that the planned 200 kilograms was too much, and might result in the destruction of an adjacent complex housing civilians. Shor brought the matter up with Chief of Staff Elazar, and argued that he had no volunteered for SAYERET TZHANHANIM and for Operation 'AVIV NE'URIM' in order to kill innocent women and children. Elazar agreed, and ordered that only 100 kilograms be used. The ever-important 'purity of arms' ethic remained of paramount importance.

On 1 April, a 35-year-old Belgian named Gilbert Rimbaud checked into Beirut's Sands Hotel, 'in need of a few days rest', as did a German tourist, Dieter Altnuder. The two men appeared not to know each other, and proceeded towards their sea view rooms ignorant of the other's existence. Both took separate, long walks into the city, night strolls along the Beirut coastline, and Altnuder enjoyed a particular night-time hobby, fishing off Beirut's isolated Dove Beach. On 6 April, the Sands Hotel received three new guests. Two Englishmen, Andrew Whichelaw, and George Elder, as well as Charles Boussard, a Belgian national. These 'tourists' were also quite interested in the beach, although their mannerisms, habits, and naïveté aroused little suspicion. On that same day, a man named Andrew Macy with a British passport checked into the city's Atlantic Hotel. Uncharacteristic of the British, he was a good tipper, but he fitted back into character when asking about the weather thrice daily. All six men made extensive walking and driving tours throughout the city, although concentrating in and around Rue Verdun and Rue Khartoum. They rented strong and sturdy automobiles (three Buick Skylarks, one Plymouth station wagon, one Valiant, and one Renault 16), and appeared to be enjoying the as yet soft life of spring in Beirut. These tourists, according to foreign press reports, were seasoned MOSSAD agents, sent into the Lebanese capital to make the final preparations for Operation 'AVIV NE'URIM'.

On the morning of 9 April, an armada of nine IDF/Navy missile boats and two DABUR ('Bee') patrol craft, left Haifa harbour bound for Beirut; while two missile boats, the INS *Mivtah* and *Ga'ash*, ferried Lieutenant-Colonel

Amos Yaron's force from SAYERET TZANHANIM, to Sidon. The disposition of forces was as follows: the INS *Herev, Eilat, Misgav* and *Sufah*, brought the Barak's, Shahak's, and Ziv's forces just off the el-Ouzai section. The INS *Miznak*, and *Sa'ar* positioned Brigadier-General Shaked's command group plus a paratroop 'rescue' force off the Beirut coast, while the INS *Akko* brought Lieutenant-Colonel Pressberger, Major G. and the Naval Commandos to Beirut's north. The fleet's radars had been turned off, and strict radio silence was observed. At 21.00 hours, pre-civil war's Beirut skyline became impressively clear. The grey Zodiac craft were lowered into the water, and Brigadier-General Shaked radioed Chief of Staff Elazar on a secure frequency. 'we've arrived!'

The operation was brilliantly coordinated, allowing each objective to be executed separately, and in order of importance. The first to go into action were Lieutenant-Colonel Barak's commandos. A few seconds before midnight, the twelve Zodiac craft ferrying task forces 'AVIVAH', and 'GILAH' (Barak's and Shahak's commandos) landed at Beirut's Dove Beach. Here, foreign journalish believe, they were met by the MOSSAD's six rented cars. Following a brief exchange, the forces split into two, and three cars headed towards Rue Verdun, while the remaining three made their way to Rue Khartoum. It was a fine night, and the streets were alive with activity. The Lebanese Gendarmes were out in force because of a series of student riots which had plagued the city only days earlier. The commandos reached their targets unnoticed.

At 01.29 hours on 10 April, Lieutenant-Colonel Barak's task force left their cars just off Rue Verdun, near the Iraqi Consulate. The commandos carried a wide assortment of silenced weapons, Beretta .22 calibre automatics, 9mm UZI's and the American .45 calibre MAC-10 submachine-gun, all hidden beneath their sweaters, blouses, and blazers. Each hit team also carried suitcases full of explosive charges to be used for destroying the doors to three apartments, and to carry back documents found in the flats. The commandos wore civilian clothes except for their commander. The ever-innovative Barak was dressed in drag, complete with blonde wig and 'impressive' false breasts.* To complete their deception, Lieutenant-Colonel Barak walked 'arm and arm'; romantically enthralled with Major Muki Botzer, both of whom entered the building first to make sure all was clear. While a small force remained outside the apartment block as cover, the hit squads entered the building.

The first slated for execution was 'Abu Yusef'. Majors Muki Botzer, 'Yoni' Netanyahu, D., and L. (names and ranks withheld for security reasons) raced up the six flights of stairs and reached 'Abu Yusef's apartment unnoticed. After breaching the door with an explosive charge, the five-room luxury apartment was searched. In the bedroom, 'Abu Yusef' was found attempting to reach his AK-

47, while his wife Maha tried to shield her husband from the inevitable. A 20-round burst from Major Netanyahu's silenced UZI killed them instantly. Following a thorough search of the flat for documents, the forced headed back down the stairs towards the street.

Seconds later, the other two teams burst into action in the adjacent building. Kamal A'dwan's second-floor apartment was breached by a sharp kick, and he was found hiding behind the window's curtain, firing his AK-47. He managed to wound one of the commandos, but was eventually killed by a burst to his head and chest. His wife and two children, standing terrified in a nearby room were left unharmed. Three suitcases filled with documents were retrieved from his flat.

Kamal Nasser was found sitting at his desk, writing a speech to be given the following day. Although a fully loaded Kalashnikov was against the wall, Nasser made little attempt to resist. Two magazine loads were sprayed into his body, and the PLO's spokesman was silenced permanently. Other team members searched the apartment and took away the papers.

Outside in Rue Verdun, things began to heat up. Lieutenant-Colonel Barak's men were busy engaging a Lebanese Gendarme Land-Rover patrol, and in a quick exchange of fire, its three occupants were killed. A second Land-Rover appeared seconds later, but it too was silenced by heavy machine-gun and grenade fire. Throughout the operation, the commandos' American-made MAC-10 proved a big disappointment. In engaging the Lebanese Gendarmes, the MAC-10s proved inaccurate at ranges as short as fiteen metres, forcing the commandos to allow the Lebanese to get dangerously close.

The entire operation at Rue Verdun lasted 29 minutes. En route to the shore, a mere 200-metre trip, the commandos saw numerous Gendarme Land-Rovers heading towards Rue Verdun, but no attention was paid to their movement. The descent to the beach was made in such haste, that one of the commandos left a suitcase filled with documents in the abandoned car. Lientenant-Colonel Barak did not allow him to retrieve the 'merchandise', concentrating the unit's efforts in reaching the safety of the missile boats off shore. Minutes after Barak signalled the missile boat fleet with his flashlight, six Zodiacs appeared from darkness, and carried the relieved fighters to safety.

Lieutenant-Colonel Shahak and his force reached Target GILAH five minutes before schedule, established a command post in a nearby street, and made last-minute checks on their weapons and explosives. The twelve reconnaissance paratroopers and one naval commando officer under Shahak's command had been dressed in a wide variety of civilian clothing, ranging from well-dressed sophisticates, to casually dressed hippies. The force was split into four teams of two, plus a command force consisting of Shahak, the team's medical officer, and, it is reported, the observing MOSSAD agents. Each team had one Motorola walkie-talkie, and each fighter carried a

*Following the raid, a Rue Verdun resident told the western Press the entire story of how the commandos had been led by a beautiful, voluptuous blonde woman with a body of which 'fantasies are created'.

silenced weapon. At Shahak's signal, the four teams headed for the DFLP Headquarters.

The first team, which consisted of Avida Shor and Hagai Ma'ayan, were dressed as European hippies, and succeeded in approaching the target without arousing the suspicion of its four DFLP defenders. Shor pulled a cigarette out of his pocket, and in English, asked one of the gunmen for a light. Seconds later, the two DFLP gunmen were dead, hit in the head with well-placed .22 calibre bursts. Before dying , one of the gunmen managed to yell '*Wa allah!*' ('Oh God!'), and DFLP guards arrived manning a Degtyarev 12.7mm heavy machine-gun. They opened up on the two Israelis. Avida Shor was killed instantly, and Ma'ayan was seriously wounded. Shahak received word of the operation's bad start, and ordered the force into immediate action.

Within seconds, the house in Rue Khartoum was jumping and exploding to the sounds of automatic rifle fire. The Israelis were at a great fire-power disadvantage, although they succeeded in getting into the building. While the cover force pinned down many of the DFLP gunmen firing from the building's windows, the attackers set off smoke-grenade canisters on the staircases, forcing the defenders to come down to street level by lift. Foolishly many did so only to be met by murderous Israeli fire. Not one DFLP gunmen reached ground level alive by lift. Nevertheless, the Palestinians put up a stiff resistance. They poured heavy and accurate AK-47 fire into the Israeli firing positions, as well as throwing numerous anti-personnel and anti-tank grenades down on to the street. Shahak responded with rifle-grenades fired into the building, causing thunderous explosions. Hundreds of residents in Rue Khartoum watched the fire-fight in awe.

The battle in Rue Khartoum was fierce, and hard fought. After five minutes the Israelis had one dead, and two wounded. One of the wounded, Yigal Pressler, was almost brought to safety by A., the force's naval commando. A DFLP gunman mistook Pressler for a wounded comrade about to be taken prisoner by the Israelis, and whisked him off A's back. A vicious hand-to-hand battle followed, while Pressler tried in vain to summon Shahak with his Motorola, which had taken a 7.62mm round. With two fingers, A. pulled the magazine out of the gunman's AK-47, and managed then to retrieve Pressler's UZI. With the initiative lost, the DFLP gunman ran in panic.

Under heavy fire, the sappers prepared the 100 kilograms of explosives along the support pillars of the DFLP building. Under the cover of grenades and boxes of nails thrown on to the street, the force made its hasty withdrawal. Three minutes later, the DFLP Headquarters existed no longer. The thunderous blast covered the withdrawal, diverting attention from the force assembling at Dove Beach for the short trip back to the missile boats. The entire operation had lasted 30 minutes, and resulted in thirty DFLP killed. The Israelis lost two dead, and three wounded, including Pressler, who was evacuated by helicopter. For his cool, and decisive handling of the operation

Lieutenant-Colonel Shahak* was awarded his second O'T HA'OZ in five years, and two other paratroopers were awarded bravery citations by Chief of Staff Elazar.

While the battle in Rue Khartoum was in full swing, Brigadier General Shaked ordered the naval commandos into action. This was a brilliant stroke, confusing the Lebanese and Palestinian authorities as to where the main burst of the attack lay. At 01.40 hours on 10 April, Colonel Ziv's force reached the explosives factory at el-Ouzai. The operation lasted only five minutes. After killing two sentries, and destroying an indigenous Opel Accord armoured car with a mounted RPG, the naval commandos set their charges in both installations, and withdrew. Colonel Ziv's intensive preparations had been well worth the effort. The naval commandos had been the last force to go into action, and were the first back on board the missile boats.

The attack on the *el-Fatah* ammunition dump north of Beirut harbour was also carried out without incident. Major G.'s force had been ferried to the mouth of the harbour by a *Dabur* patrol craft. While the conscript seamen nervously manned their 20mm Oerlikon cannon, the frogmen slipped into the water, and swam the short distance. Soon a shattering explosion was heard and *all* the frogmen returned to the *Dabur*.

Lieutenant-Colonel Amos Yaron's diversionary attack north of Sidon had also been executed brilliantly. They laid ambush to the Sidon-Beirut highway, poured nails over the road, and prevented any Palestinian reinforcements from reaching the capital. After destroying the ammunition dump, the force received its withdrawal order, and returned to ship. No Israeli casualties were suffered.

Chief of Staff Elazar and Defence Minister Dayan were overcome with joy following the force's return to their home base of Haifa the following morning. Brigadier-General Shaked had been saddened by the loss of two of his men, and refused to partake in the post-mission Press conference. Nevertheless, Lieutenant-Colonel Barak's entire unit was awarded citations by Lieutenant-General Elazar, and the other participants all received honourable mentions. For Israel, Operation 'AVIV NE'URIM' had been a remarkable victory, and one of the IDF's most audacious overt operations.

Operation 'AVIV NE'URIM' was the culmination of Israel's obsessive search for vengeance following the Munich Massacre. For almost a year, the entire Israeli defence and security apparatus had been mobilized for the destruction of the 'Black September' international network. While their efforts had been impressively successful, and 'Black September' had indeed been crippled beyond repair, Israel's immediate security concerns had also been crippled. The quest for revenge had so massively drained her intelligence capabilities, that the threat from conventional enemies had been dangerously overlooked. A

---

*Major-General Amnon Shahak is the current IDF head of military intelligence (A'MAN).

MOSSAD error in Norway in which an innocent waiter had been killed instead of the notorious Ali Hassan Salameh (the infamour 'Red Prince', eventually assassinated in Beirut in 1979), had caused the Defence and Foreign Ministries to lose faith in its reports, while A'MAN had been tapped dry, assisting the special operations capabilities campaign against terrorism. Against this dangerous labyrinth of negligence, the success of the élite units in special operations had peaked in an aura of over-confidence and invincibility, born in the aftermath of the 1967 victory. Israel would pay a dear price for its poor judgement six months later on that day in Judaism when man and Creator settle all scores: *Yom Kippur*.

7

THE EARTHQUAKE
OF OCTOBER
Operations during the
1973 Yom Kippur War

'SEE YOU ON THE MOUNTAIN...':
GOLANI AND PARATROOP OPERATIONS
ON THE GOLAN HEIGHTS

IN late October 1973, the 1st GOLANI Infantry Brigade was supposed to have conducted its 25th anniversary celebrations in Tel Aviv's Hayarkon Park. GOLANI veterans from each of Israel's wars were to gather to pay emotional homage to the fallen, the scarred, and the survivors. Most importantly, the anniversary was to initiate a new age for the GOLANI Brigade. Following four major wars, and countless retaliatory raids and operational forays, the brigade was to enter into its second quarter-century of military responsibility for Israel's northern sector, stronger and better equipped than ever before. On Yom Kippur Day, GOLANI's existence was put to the test.

The Syrian surprise attack against the Golan Heights at 13.40 hours on 6 October was the culmination of what to many seemed utterly inevitable. On 13 September 1973, twelve Syrian MiG-21s had been blown out of the skies above Latakia by an IAF counter-ambush. The Syrians replied by mobilizing her armed forces along the 'Purple Line', the border between Israeli and Syrian forces along the boundaries of the Golan Heights. The failure of A'MAN to monitor the Syrian build-up in coordination with indentical Egyptian moves along the Suez Canal prohibited adequate defensive response from being implemented. The military formation responsible for defending the Golan Heights was UGDAT RAFUL, a mixed armoured and mechanized division task force commanded by Brigadier-General 'Raful' Eitan. UGDAT RAFUL boasted impressive armour capabilities, including the 188th BARAK Battalion under Colonel Yitzhak Ben-Shoham's leadership, as well as Colonel Avigdor 'Yanush' Ben-Gal's élite 7th Armoured Brigade. In fact, the ferocious and epic tank battles which resulted in the destruction of the 188th

Brigade, and the 7th Brigade's legendary defence of the 'Valley of Tears' have come to characterize the war on the Golan Heights in 1973. It is extraordinary to note that every Israeli tank committed to the Golan fighting was hit by enemy fire at least *once* during the war! Yet, UGDAT RAFUL also consisted of the GOLANI Brigade.

On 6 October, the only GOLANI unit positioned on the Golan Heights was the GIDEON Battalion, which was spread out thinly along the series of seventeen fortifications called MUTZAVIM along the 'Purple Line' from Mount Hermon to the Jordanian border (the southern MUTZAVIM were defended by units of Lieutenant-Colonel Yoram 'Ya-Ya' Yair's 50th NA'HA'L Paratroop Battalion). The HABOK'IM HARISHONIM Battalion had just completed a rough anti-terrorist operation in Gaza and was on well-deserved leave; while the BARAK Battalion, SAYERET GOLANI and ARAYOT HAGOLAN, were all on 'pre-anniversary' leaves. Brigade OC, Colonel Amir Drori, faced a monumental task in bringing his forces into battle during the dark hours of the initial Syrian onslaught.

The only position to fall on the Golan Heights was 'MUTZAV 104', the electronic intelligence gathering post on Mount Hermon. Defended by a mere thirteen GIDEON Battalion NCOs (with 41 non-combatant electronics specialists) the position known as the 'eye of the nation' was seized by a determined heliborne force from the Syrian 82nd Paratroop Regiment.* Under cover of a massive Syrian artillery bombardment, four MI-8 helicopters attempted to land on the Israeli peak. One MI-8 was hit by .50 calibre fire and exploded in mid-air, but the others

---

*The seizure of the bunker complex itself was carried out by the regiment's mysterious 'Suicide Company'.

soon landed and quickly disgorged their loads. The Syrian paratroopers quickly seized the initiative against the lightly armed GOLANI garrison and secured the outer perimeter. Forced into the complex's underground bunkers and rooms, the Mount Hermon defenders soon found themselves cut off and desperately short of ammunition.

The beleaguered defenders voiced their opinions, and opted for breakout. Led by the position's commander, Captain Hagai, they raced to safety along various mountain paths, under determined Syrian fire. Only eleven of the twenty who set out survived. On the morning of 7 October, Colonel Drori gazed towards the Mount Hermon position from UGDAT RAFUL's headquarters at Nafakh and vowed revenge. Mount Hermon would be retaken!

During the first days of fighting, the thought of a GOLANI counter-attack was little more than fantasy. The Syrian offensive on 6 October had been fantasic. Syrian war plans called for the entire Golan plateau to be captured in a single 24-hour period, and the Syrians were well prepared for this task. A massive combined artillery and aerial bombardment of the Israeli lines was followed by a massive *five-division* advance by armour and mechanized infantry forces. To stop any Syrian attack, the IDF had established a strong defensive line of barbed wire and mines, supported by the commanding MUTZAVIM along the entire frontier. Each MUTZAV or position was a heavily fortified stone and sand-bagged complex complete with mortar positions, and machine-gun nests, strategically positioned on the volcanic cones or *Tels*. They were each defended by 13–20 GIDEON infantrymen, obviously quite inadequate to repel such a massive Syrian offensive. Under extremely brutal artillery and tank fire bombardments, the GOLANI defenders succeeded in pouring steady and accurate fire into the Syrian charge which had by now bypassed and laid siege to the MUTZAVIM. It was the classic Israeli combat ethic of the outnumbered fighting off the many. As night fell, the GOLANIs' absence of night-fighting equipment was painfully felt, as Syrian infra-red and SLS apparatus turned night into day for unrelenting attacks.

Colonel Drori ordered the GIDEON Battalion to withdraw from the MUTZAVIM, but his order received a resounding negative! The MUTZAVIM commanders argued that the situation was 'under control', and there was no reason to evacuate. With such a strong 'human element', the GIDEON Battalion held its own. One .50 calibre machine-gunner succeeded in downing a strafing Sukhoi-7 fighter-bomber, while riflemen at a nearby bunker fortification seriously damaged a MiG-21. In all, seventeen Syrian aircraft were downed by GOLANI fire – a feat in which even seasoned anti-aircraft units would take pride.

The MUTZAVIM and their beleaguered defenders were not forgotten. Elements from SAYERET GOLANI were infiltrated into their surrounded positions to supply food, ammunition, and of course, medical care. By 7 October, the brigade had been reinforced to strength by the thousands of soldiers who raced up north by all means possible to join their units. The brigade was divided into two primary forces: one under Colonel Drori's command, operating along the Buqata-Masa'da-Tel Shams line; and a multi-battalion task force under deputy brigade commander, Lieutenant-Colonel Reuven 'Ruvka' Eliaz (SAYERET GOLANI commander during the 1967 War) which held the Abu Nitzah-West-Nafakh line, and were responsible for securing supply routes to the battle areas.

Lieutenant-Colonel Yair's NA'HA'L paratroopers also put up a tenacious defence of the southern Golan MUTZAVIM. Overwhelmed by the Syrian juggernaut as had been their GOLANI comrades, the young and inexperienced paratroopers fought fiercely, and exacted a heavy toll on advancing Syrian units. In MUTZAV 116, approximately fifteen paratroopers engaged a force of fanatical Syrian infantrymen on tanks and BMP APCs. As night fell, the Syrians attacked, screaming '*Etbach al-Yahud!*' (slaughter the Jews!) in their gallant charge. They were met by determined and deadly machine-gun fire. Several attempts to take the positions were attempted that night; all failed. At dawn MUTZAV 116's defenders saw hundreds of Syrian bodies sprawled on their position's outer perimeter barbed wire fence. The young and inexperienced conscripts had proven their worth.

The fighting was typical of the Golan front's first days; frantic and desperate. Against tremendous odds, the GOLANI forces struggled desperately against Syrian armour, mechanized, and heliborne commando breakthroughs. One of the fiercest engagements was between BARAK infantrymen and Syrian commandos from the '1st Commando Group' who landed just outside UGDAT RAFUL's HQ at Nafakh. A similar Syrian commando landing was attempted at Buqata, but this too was beaten off after heavy fighting against units of the GIDEON Battalion, and 7th Armoured Brigade's SAYERET mounted on M113 APCs.

GOLANI units were also ordered to assist the armoured forces in the holding action against Syrian armour; a task for which they were poorly trained and equipped. GOLANI bazooka teams did, however, succeed in destroying dozens of Syrian armoured vehicles throughout the northern Golan. The GOLANI units were most notable for their courageous retrieval of wounded 7th Brigade tankers in the midst of some the fiercest armour battles in military history.

When the IDF finally counter-attacked to remove the Syrian military presence from her territory, it was the GOLANI Brigade that was in the forefront. GOLANI's task was to clear the Syrians from the area north-east of Masa'da and Buqata. The BARAK Battalion was entrusted with the seizing of the village of Kfar Jubrana al-Hashav, HABOK'IM HARISHONIM with Tel Dahar, and SAYERET GOLANI with Marnajiya. The battles were fierce, and the Syrians fought impressively well. In one instance, BARAK Battalion Commander Major 'Yankele' Shahar was briefing his officers for the pending offensive when word was received of a Syrian infantry attack against Tel Varda. Immediately, Major Shahar assembled his men and led them to battle. In the ensuing close-quarter mêlée, the Syrian effort was beaten off, though at a stiff price. Six BARAK soldiers were killed, including Major Shahar, only one of the tragically many GOLANI battalion commanders to die in the eighteen days of the war.

The IDF eventually pushed all Syrian forces out of the 'Purple Line', and eventually got to within 22 kilometres of Damascus. Towards the end of the war, GOLANI's infantry efforts were assisted by elements of the 317th Reserve Paratroop Brigade commanded by Colonel Haim Nadel, and the 18th Paratroop Battalion commanded by Lieutenant-Colonel 'Ilan', of which Major 'Yoni' Netanyahu was a senior officer. Attached to UGDAT LANER (a reserve division-sized task force commanded by Major-General Res. Dan Laner), the 317th Brigade was assigned a crucial role in pushing the Syrians out of Kuneitra and into Syria proper. Together with tank formations, the 317th Brigade took part in the capture of Tel Shams, and Tel Kudne. When on the night of 11/12 October, Lieutenant-Colonel Yossi Ben-Hanan, commander of the survivors of the 188th BARAK Brigade, was seriously wounded in the armour attempt to capture Tel Shams,* Major Netanyahu immediately volunteered his company to lead his rescue. In the process he defeated a major Syrian commando force. For his courage and self-sacrifice, 'Yoni' was awarded the I'TUR HAMOFET.

With regard to 'special operations', the Yom Kippur War remains somewhat of an enigma. The immediacy and dire consequences of Syria's Blitz, exacerbated by the proximity of the fighting to major centres of population, inhibited the use of élite forces for anything but conventionally stopping the Syrians cold. It is well documented that Chief Paratroop and Infantry Officer, Brigadier-General Emanuel 'Manno' Shaked had urged the Chief of Staff, Lieutenant-General David 'Dado' Elazar, to authorize special operations against Syria. On 12 October intelligence reports of Iraqi reinforcements moving towards the Golan Heights were received at IDF GHQ. After clear hesitation from 'Dado', Shaked finally received the order to summon SAYERET TZANHANIM. Operation 'KUTONET' (nightdress) was under way!

At 23.00 hours on the foggy night of 12 October, a lone IAF CH-53 helicopter landed near Kasr al-Hayr, on the main Baghdad-Damascus road, approximately 100 kilometres from the Syrian capital. The CH-53 had flown from a base in northern Israel at low-level over the Lebanese border, crossing the Syrian border from the west of Mount Hermon to avoid the deadly ring of surface-to-air missiles. While a small force of reconnaissance paratroopers guarded the CH-53, a force of twelve paratroopers and a jeep fitted with a 106mm recoilless rifle headed out for a bridge along the main Damascus road. Targeted were elements of the Iraqi 8th Mechanized Infantry Brigade from the 3rd Armoured Division, ferried to the Golan fighting on tank transports and 'luxury' Mercedes buses.

As the convoy began to cross the bridge, a squad of

▲ The GOLANI Brigade's deputy commander, Lieutenant-Colonel Eliaz confers with his battalion commanders prior to the first attempt to retake Mount Hermon on 8 October 1973. Days later, Lientenant-Colonel Eliaz was dead! (IDF Archives)

paratroopers with RPGs and anti-tank rifle-grenades attacked the front, while the 106mm rifle caused havoc in the Iraqis' rear. The Iraqis were dumbfounded by their predicament, and failed to respond to the attack. Armed with mines and explosives, the paratroopers destroyed the bridge. With the convoy bottled up in fiery chaos, the paratroopers withdrew; followed by a flight of F-4E Phantoms which destroyed what had been left behind. Operation 'KUTONET' had been a smashing success due to a number of factors, among them accurate intelligence, teamwork and coordination between the paratroopers and IAF. It resulted in the destruction of scores of Iraqi vehicles and troops, and remains the only *publicized* 'special operation' of the war's northern front.

As the war up north had begun with the seizure of Mount Hermon, so there did it end. The Syrian flag on Mount Hermon was a symbol of Israel's unpreparedness for the October 1973 War, and immediate attempts to remedy the situation were ordered. On 8 October, Colonel Drori ordered Mount Hermon to be recaptured. The GOLANI attack force consisted of only two mechanized companies of riflemen from HABOK'IM HARISHONIM, ARAYOT HAGOLAN and SAYERET GOLANI. Shortly before their ascent into the unknown began, a few more straggling GIDEON Battalion survivors managed to elude the Syrian guns and reach Israeli lines. They completed the picture of the Israeli defeat, and provided last-minute intelligence.

*Although the initial armour assault on Tel Shams met with heavy resistance and Israeli casualties, the heavily defended Syrian positions were captured the following day by elements of the 317th Brigade, and SAYERET HADRUZIM.

HABOK'IM HARISHONIM Commander, Major Yudke, assembled his forces and set out to regain the brigade's pride.

On the steep cliffs from Majdel Shams, the attack force with two supporting Centurion tanks began their ascent, keeping to the main road, while SAYERET GOLANI's fighters fanned out along the rocky embankment, providing a tenuous covering force. As the advance continued, dozens of Syrian paratroopers suddenly appeared from behind large boulders and dug-in firing positions. Syrian snipers with Drugenov 7.62mm rifles exacted a heavy toll from the surrounded and cut-off lead GOLANI fighters. While the SAYERET engaged the Syrians in hand-to-hand fighting, the remainder of the force attempted in vain to advance. Syrian fire was murderous, and within an hour, dozens of soldiers were lying dead or wounded. Accurate RPG fire had turned numerous M3 Halftracks in to balls of flame. ARAYOT HAGOLAN Commander, Lieutenant-Colonel Dubi Dror was killed when his command M3 took a direct RPG hit. GOLANI's only response was to continue its attack, but it was met with a fresh force of approximately 100 Syrian paratroopers. Hand-to-hand combat soon followed in some of the fiercest fighting seen during the war. Outnumbered and outgunned, the order was given to withdraw. Twenty-five GOLANI soldiers were killed that day, 57 were wounded. The soldiers who had taken part in the campaign were tired, bitter and thirsting for revenge. A score had to be settled.*

For the next thirteen days, Mount Hermon remained in

▲ GOLANI Brigade OC, Colonel Amir Drori (seated, wearing battledress jacket) confers with paratroop officers prior to the second battle for Mount Hermon, on 21 October 1973. (IDF Archives)

the background of military thought. But by 21 October, with the IDF deep inside Syria, and a United Nations imposed ceasefire imminent, the chance to retake Mount Hermon was at hand. Assisted by heavy air and artillery support, the GOLANI Brigade was to assault the mountain at night, while a two-company sized force of approximately 300 paratroopers from Colonel Nadel's 317th Brigade would land by helicopter on the 'Syrian' peak of Mount Hermon, capture that position and support the GOLANI assault. The operation was code-named 'KINUACH' (gift)!

GOLANI's staging-ground was the outer limits of Masa'da, where only days earlier vicious fighting had taken place between Israeli and Syrian tank forces. GOLANI's order of battle and objectives for Operation 'KINUACH' were: HABOK'IM HARISHONIM was to clear two lower peaks of an enemy presence, later seizing the strategic Hills '16' and '17', as well as the upper cable-car station (where only months earlier happy Israeli tourists had gone skiing); the

*Unofficial reports claim that various SAYERET formations had waged a brutal and unrelenting campaign against the Syrians on Mount Hermon; killing more than 6 enemy troops. Their success had led to SAYERET MAT'KAL being slated for more than Hermon's recapture, but due to obvious unit pride, GOLANI received the mission.

8th Battalion would seize the lower cable-car station and the 'captured' position on Mount Hermon; while SAYERET GOLANI would advance ahead of all forces, and provide cover and assistance to the 8th Battalion's efforts on the mountain. To ensure that the Syrians were dealt a death blow, ARAYOT HAGOLAN would advance from the south-east, destroying any Syrian attempts to escape GOLANI's wrath. In the early evening of 21 October, Colonel Drori addressed his fighters in a moving speech. He told his men, many of whom had seemed youthful novices only three weeks earlier, but were now bloodied veterans, that 'the eyes of the nation were upon them'. He closed on a cheerful note, wishing everyone the best, and that he hoped to see them up above.

At 20.00 hours, the ascent of the mountain began. The GOLANI fighters were equipped with extra loads of ammunition; they all knew that the first battle for Mount Hermon would be but a harbinger of worse to come. The dark night provided ample cover from the Syrian guns, but made the climb a difficult and frightening experience. Undiscovered, HABOK'IM HARISHONIM reached an area south of Hill '16', while the 8th Battalion reached the lower cable-car station. The climb took eight hours. At 02.00 hours on 22 October, the silence was shattered by an explosion of automatic fire. The second battle for Mount Hermon was under way.

Unknown to the men of HABOK'IM HARISHONIM, they had advanced to within metres of Syrian dug-in positions.

Green tracers suddenly filled the sky, as thousands of bullets began to concentrate on the GOLANI fighters racing for cover. Syrian mortar and RPG fire was called in, and casualties soon began to soar. At dawn the Israelis discovered the extent of their plight. They had stumbled into the middle of a major Syrian defensive position! The desperate cries for 'medics' were heard even over the gunfire; the self-sacrificing medical orderlies soon became the brigade's most valued asset.

Because of HABOK'IM HARISHONIM's difficulties, the task of capturing the upper cable-car station (100 metres south of the military fortifications) was given to SAYERET GOLANI. Commanded by Captain Shmaryahu Vinnik, a fine young officer, the SAYERET succeeded in reaching their objective with little incident. Initial patrols discovered a major Syrian military presence, and a pitched battle developed. From the protection of a large boulder, a Syrian para-trooper fired off a burst at Vinnik, before he was in turn cut down by Israeli fire. Bleeding profusely, Captain Vinnik continued to issue orders, directing his men in battle. Attempts to rescue the SAYERET commander met with failure, as medics were cut down by accurate bursts of Syrian automatic fire. The SAYERET managed to secure a

▼ 'The eyes of Israel have returned to their rightful owners.' SAYERET GOLANI units proceed towards the main bunker complex on Mount Hermon, following the bitter battle of 22 October. (IDF Archives)

fire base for themselves, and with the assistance of rifle-grenade fire, and RPGs taken from dead Syrians, managed to quell the Syrian resistance. At 07.30 hours, the Syrians began fleeing their positions, and surrendering to the exhausted men of the SAYERET. Captain Vinnik was brought down the mountain by stretcher, but died hours later. His dying words were: 'We must never descend from the Hermon.' He was given posthumously the rank of Major, and awarded the I'TUR HAMOFET.

Seconds after Captain Vinnik was wounded, Colonel Drori himself suffered a critical chest wound while leading HABOK'IM HARISHONIM's assault on Hill '16'. While being carried off to the battalion aid station, he ordered that not one soldier should leave the mountain until it was back in Israeli hands. Command of the battalion was transferred to Lieutenant-Colonel Yudke, but he too was wounded by sniper fire. The reins of command would switch several times that morning, while ARAYOT HAGOLAN was called in for reinforcements.

With the sun making an uninvited appearance, the battle entered its final stage. The closer the brigade reached GIDEON Battalion's former positions, the fiercer the fighting became. At 09.00 hours, with all enemy opposition neutralized except for the 'Israeli' Hermon, a combined force from ARAYOT HAGOLAN and HABOK'IM HARISHONIM stormed the complex. Its purification lasted almost three hours, with every room, bunker, and trench cleared in meticulous fashion. The GOLANI fighters found the positions in sham-bles, as the Syrians had pillaged the sensitive monitering position, to offer their Soviet advisers a first-hand grab at the secret intelligence-gathering devices. Syrian resistance in the position had been crushed. A FN MAG gunner in HABOK'IM HARISHONIM, Benni Masass, had 'personally' taken care of a fair portion of the Syrian defenders, firing his machine-gun wildly in a mad dash to clear the area of Syrian paratroopers.

At 11.00 hours, the Israeli and GOLANI flags were hoisted from the listening-post's main antenna. Minutes later, GOLANI communications officers announced an historic 'Calling all stations.... Mount Hermon is in our hands'. The nine-hour battle had turned the once peaceful mountain into a hill of blood and mangled flesh. Fifty-five GOLANI fighters were killed on that October morning, and 79 wounded. It was the brigade's finest and most bloody hour.

During the war's eighteen days of combat, GOLANI lost 130 dead, and 310 wounded. In keeping with IDF élite unit ethic of 'Follow Me!', it was among the senior officers that the greatest casualties were endured. The brigade lost its deputy commander, Lieutenant-Colonel Reuven 'Ruvka' Eliaz, BARAK Battalion commander, Lieutenant-Colonel Yankele Shahar, ARAYOT HAGOLAN Commander, Lieutenant-Colonel Dubi Dror, and SAYERET GOLANI Commander, Major Shmaryahu Vinnik, and dozens of other company, platoon and squad leaders.

THE SINAI EARTHQUAKE: OPERATIONS ALONG THE SOUTHERN FRONT

UNLIKE the fighting on the Golan Heights, the IDF enjoyed the luxury of time and defensive depth against the massive Egyptian Blitz from across the Suez Canal. There were no Israeli population concentrations in the vast emptiness of the Sinai peninsula, and the IDF was afforded the opportunity to concentrate her efforts against the more dire threat posed by the Syrian invasion, before dealing a decisive blow against Egypt. The Egyptians, however, posed a potent military threat of their own; the invasion and almost successful recapture of the disputed Sinai wilderness with more than *nine* divisions. Although, like that of the Golan, the fighting in Sinai was characterized by armour, the campaign afforded the IDF a greater use of her élite units' capabilities.

When Egyptian forces launched their attack over the Suez Canal at 13.50 hours on 6 October 1973, they encountered only sporadic opposition from the inadequately defended Bar-Lev Line MAOZIM (strongpoints), and overran many of them with impunity. While UGDAT ALBERT, the conscript armoured and infantry division defending the Egyptian front, commanded by Major-General Avraham 'Albert' Mendler, tried its best to stem the Egyptian advance, UGDAT ARIK (a reserve armoured division commanded by Major-General (Res.) 'Arik' Sharon), and UGDAT BREN (a reserve armoured division commanded by OC Armoured Corps, Major-General Avraham 'Bren' Adan) mobilized, and raced towards the fighting; little use was made of Southern Command's paratroop and élite force potential. Two battalions from Colonel Uzi Yairi's conscripted Paratroop Brigade were on eager standby, as was SAYERET SHAKED, and a strong KOMMANDO YAMI contingent.

The 247th Reserve Paratroop Brigade (formerly designated as the 55th Brigade) under Colonel Danni Matt's capable leadership was held in Central Command, awaiting an assignment to either front. Delay in sending the brigade into immediate combat produced anxious and hostile emotions among the ranks, as the men felt a dire need to contribute to the defence of their country. During the first stage of the fighting, only GDUD YOSSI, a battalion commanded by Lieutenant-Colonel Yossi Yaffe, was flown to Sinai to relieve pressure on the northernmost Bar-Lev Line MAOZ of 'BUDAPEST', one of the few remaining positions yet to surrender. Attempts by other infantry formations to relieve 'BUDAPEST' met with failure and harsh losses. With little recourse available, Southern Command requested the talents of the 'red berets'. 'BUDAPEST' was surrounded by a strong force of Egyptian commandos, and the recently mobilized paratroopers, who only days before were enjoying the wondrous joys of civilian life, had to fight a fierce battle to reach their beleaguered comrades. IDF studies have often shown that reservist formations, made up of experienced and more cautious fighters, often outperform their conscript counterparts. Such was true of the battle for 'BUDAPEST', where the Egyptian siege was decisively crushed. Although only suffering one slightly wounded FN MAG gunner, GDUD YOSSI killed 45 Egyptians.

OC Southern Command, Major-General Shmuel 'Gorodish' Gonen (7th Armoured Brigade commander in 1967), had reservations about dispatching the conscript paratroopers into the Sinai fray, especially since it was a young force with little combat experience. The severity of the the IDF predicament during the war's first days offered Gonen little alternative, and on 8 October he ordered the paratroopers to counter the ever-audacious Egyptian commando heliborne landings deep behind Israeli lines in southern Sinai. With the IAF fighting for its life against the deadly Egyptian SAM umbrella, Egyptian MI-8 helicopters ferrying commando formations operated unhindered. They attacked convoys and destroyed fuel installations and ammunition dumps. Their elimination was given obvious top priority, and what developed was a pursuit campaign similar to that in the Jordan Valley during the War of Attrition. This time, however, the inexperienced paratroopers were facing the élite of the Egyptian Army.

Mobility and fire-power were the secret weapons for victory in southern Sinai's often brutal pursuit campaign. The conscripts' courage and abilities aside, credit for the eventual victory truly belongs to the IAF Bell-205 helicopter pilots who flew low-level sorties in pursuit of the Egyptians; and then, under murderous anti-aircraft and small arms fire, rescued wounded soldiers from the battlefield.

The other 'unsung' heroes of the pursuit campaign were the junior paratroop officers, themselves little older than the men they led into battle. Aware of the significance of the campaign and the inexperience of their command, they installed confidence and fearlessness into the ranks, always charging at the helm. Typical of these officers was young Lieutenant Manno, a company commander who, compared to his men, was a veteran of combat expertise. Manno's company was made up entirely of 18-year-olds who only days before had completed their basic training and parachute qualification jumps. Unripe , and still unaware of the responsibility their red beret and silver metal jump wings represented, the young soldiers were thrust into one of the greatest challenges to the survial of the state of Israel ever posed by the Arabs. In the field, however, these 'green' soldiers were to prove themselves as deadly and highly capable combatants.

Dozens of pursuits were conducted against reported sightings of commando landings. The Egyptians foolishly planned to link up with their armoured spearheads to push through the sands of Sinai in a matter of hours; and therefore landed with minimum supplies of food and water. When friendly forces failed to materialize, and the Bell-205s soon appeared over the horizon, the commandos' precarious situation became all too evident. Some opted to surrender, but many of the hard-core chose to make a stand. Fierce close-quarter fighting resulted in casualties on both sides. The Egyptians enjoyed the advantage of Drugenov 7.62mm high-power sniper rifles as well as artillery support, while the paratroopers maximized their speed and cohesion. Pragmatists to the end the Egyptians after an honourable showing on the field of battle, opted to surrender rather than fight to the last man.

The largest 'pursuit' was on 12 October in Wadi A'rndal. The Egyptian commandos expected an immediate paratroop response and had prepared a defensive ring complete with machine-guns and RPGs. When the paratroop company entered the wadi, accurate fire rained down from all sides. The first and only paratroop casualty was Lieutenant Manno, who exposed himself to enemy fire in order to tend to a wounded soldier. His death was a bitter loss for the young conscripts, depriving them of a strict though compassionate commander who had brought them through a fierce initiation in the battlefield. As formidable formations of IDF reservists appeared and the Egyptian front stabilized, the threat of Egyptian commando infiltration diminished. The conscript paratroop battalions were then attached to tank formations to reinforce the IDF's ability decisively to beat the Egyptians.

And then there was SAYERET SHAKED. At the outbreak of the war, SAYERET SHAKED was spread out along the entire length of the Suez Canal, divided along the northern, central and southern sectors. Their main task was joining the conscript paratroopers in countering heliborne Egyptian commando forces which landed between Ras as-Sudr and Abu Rodus in southern Sinai. Drawing on their vast experience against infiltrators, the SHAKED companies quickly secured ten square kilometre zones called boxes, and then closed in from all sides for the kill. Their technique was masterful, and not a stone was left unturned. Commanded by Lieutenant-Colonel Moshe Spector, a tough and experienced SAYERET GOLANI officer, and led by the unit's Bedouin scouts (who sometimes even reached an engagement before the helicopter observation teams!), SAYERET SHAKED was merciless in its task and few prisoners were taken. Following the first week of fighting, and with an impressive tally chalked up, SAYERET SHAKED was 'volunteered' to Major-General Sharon's UGDAT ARIK.

Like SAYERET SHAKED, Colonel Matt's 247th Reserve Paratroop Brigade was also volunteered into UGDAT ARIK. As one of the architects of the IDF's élite forces, 'Arik' chose to provide his armour brigades with as lethal and unconventional an edge as possible. Happy to receive a combat assignment at last, Colonel Matt reached his former 'battalion' commander only to learn that 'Arik' was already planning to cross the Suez Canal, and counterattack into Egyptian Africa. 'Arik' was not known for

▲ Jeep-mounted squads from Colonel Uzi Yairi's Paratroop Brigade's SAYERET TZANHANIM patrol southern Sinai in search of Egyptian commandos on 8 October 1973. (IDF Archives)

'lying about' in defensive holding actions; he wanted to attack, and win the war decisively. But first, there was a small matter of almost 1,000 Egyptian tanks to be dealt with.

On 14 October, the Egyptians mounted the major attempt to crush the Israeli secondary line of defence and break out deep across Sinai. The Egyptian Chief of Staff, General Sa'ad es-Dinn Shazli (the architect of Egypt's special forces), opposed the offensive as it brought the pride of the Egyptian armoured forces beyond the protection of the SAM umbrella. The Egyptians had been under intense pressure from the Syrians to relieve pressure from the fighting on the Golan Heights, and President Sadat bowing to this, ordering the bold offensive. By 14 October, however, the IDF had regained its strength, as reservist formations were organized, equipped and sent into battle. These included thousands of senior IDF officers who returned from their studies abroad, including Lieutenant-Colonel Ehud Barak, commander of a 'special operations armoured force' of returnees from abroad in UGDAT BREN.

On the morning of the 14th, the Egyptians made their move. Unprotected, over-extended, and heading straight for a killing-ground prepared by waiting IDF tank brigades, the Egyptian armour entered the fateful trap. To diminish the effectiveness of the Soviet-made infantry-fired SAGGER and RPG anti-tank weapons, paratroop formations engaged the Egyptian infantry anti-tank units, allowing tank to fight tank in classic fashion. In the day's bloodletting and the largest tank battle since Kursk, 264 Egyptian T-62s, and T-55/54s were destroyed, and more than 1,000 soldiers killed or wounded. The Israelis, back to their old ways, suffered a mere six tanks destroyed. It was the war's turning-point, and allowed the IDF to switch to the offensive!

Operation 'ABIREY LEV' ('stout heart') was the IDF's

pre-war plan for crossing the Canal, devised by 'Arik' Sharon during his tenure as OC Southern Command. It called for a two-division crossing, the establishment of a bridgehead on the Canal's west bank, and the destruction of Egyptian forces along the Isma'iliya-Suez corridor. The crossing would take place at the 'yard', a preconstructed hard brick surface area at Deversoir near the Bar-Lev Line MAOZ of MATZMED, on the northern shore of the Great Bitter Lake. With the tank battle victory of 14 October still fresh in the relieved minds of Southern Command's generals, 'Arik' Sharon formally presented Operation 'ABIREY LEV' to his comrades. Leading UGDAT ARIK's Canal crossing into Africa were elements of Colonel Matt's 247th Paratroop Brigade; which would seize a west bank bridge-head, and secure it for UGDAT ARIK's armoured brigades (Colonel Amnon Reshef's 14th, Colonel Tuvia Raviv's 600th and Colonel Haim Erez's HATIVAT HAIM) to cross on pre-constructed pontoon bridges which would be ferried to the 'yard'.

To ensure that the initial crossing party would not be detected, 'Arik' Sharon called upon SAYERET SHAKED, the only 'commando' force under his direct command, to mount a heliborne assault on the Egyptian electronic monitoring stations on Jebel A'taka, responsible for recording all IDF radio transmissions. It was suspected that the advanced, Russian-built facilities were responsible for the death of Major-General Mendler (killed by artillery fire which homed on his radio transmission), and greatly feared that Jebel A'taka would present a serious threat to the paratroops' initial bridgehead. SAYERET SHAKED made at least three visits to Jebel A'taka on 10,11 and 14 October, although it was the last raid, made in daylight, which seems to have been the most effective. On 14 October, a heliborne force from SAYERET SHAKED landed below the base's outer perimeter (the successful electronic counter-measures employed to ward off SAM attacks and detections remain highly classified to this day), and following a fierce fire-fight, the monitoring station was destroyed. It is rumoured that elements of the SHAKED raiding force remained behind on the west bank, performing highly classified intelligence operations in preparations for the intended IDF breakout on the west bank.

On the night of 15 October, a small force of paratroopers from the élite Amphibious Sapper Unit laid their grey Zodiac craft in the still waters of the Canal, and crossed into Egyptian Africa. They were followed by a small contingent of SAYERET SHAKED officers, and a command element from the 247th Brigade. They secured a stronghold on the west bank's thick underbrush shore and at 01.25 hours on 16 October, Colonel Matt radioed Arik's HQ with the anticipated message 'Acapulco...Acapulco!', the coded signal indicating that the paratroopers had safely reached the west bank. Although only 36 paratroopers made the initial crossing, by dawn the bulk of the 247th Brigade, the 416th, 564th and 565th Battalions, equipped with a rich assortment of infantry anti-tank weapons had consolidated an area 1,000 yards long by 225 yards deep. At 06.43 hours, the first tanks of HATIVAT HAIM crossed the Canal on rafts. While the tank force broke out of the bridgehead to attack Egyptian armour and SAM bases nearby, the paratroopers dug in, preparing for the worst.

The success of ABIREY LEV depended entirely on the opening of the vital Sinai roads (AKAVISH, TIRTUR and LEXICON), which were fundamental in bringing the bulk of the Canal crossing force from UGDAT BREN, as well as its pre-constructed 'Gilowa' bridges to the yard. Already on the night of 15 October, elements of Colonel Amnon Reshef's 14th Armoured Brigade had fought one of the war's fiercest engagements attempting to capture the AKAVISH-TIRTUR crossroads. The brigade's reconnaissance company mistakenly entered through the rear door of the Egyptian 16th Infantry Divison's staging area, and a hellish fight broke out. During the battle, the 14th Armoured Brigade lost sixty tanks, and suffered 121 dead, including 43 officers. The reconnaissance battalion from HATIVAT HAIM, together with a small force from the 247th Brigade, was ordered in to assist the 14th Brigade's efforts, although their tanks came under murderous anti-tank fire from the 'Chinese Farm', an Egyptain agricultural settle-ment set up by Japanese agronomists on four large dunes overlooking the AKAVISH, TIRTUR and LEXICON roads. Time being of the essence in reinforcing the bridgehead, Major-General 'Bren' Adan ordered Colonel Uzi Yairi's Para-troop Brigade into the fray.

On 15 October, the Yairi's Paratroop Brigade was order-ed to take a battalion, commanded by Lieutenant-Colonel Yitzhak Mordechai (a veteran HA'AN TZANHANIM officer, divison commander along the coastal sector during the 1982 'Peace for Galilee' invasion, and at present OC Southern Command), to clear the area. All through the night of the 16th, the armoured columns heading towards the crossing-point were passed by mechanized elements of Mordechai's battalion racing towards the 'Chinese Farm', hoping to clear the area of an enemy presence before too high a toll was exacted from the beleaguered tankers.

Since the true Egyptian disposition of forces at 'Chinese Farm' was unclear, Lieutenant-Colonel Mordechai sent in elements of his 4th Company, commanded by Captain Eitan, to scout the area. Upon entering the 'Chinese Farm' compound, the 4th Company found itself under a murder-ous barrage of small arms, mortar, RPG, and SAGGER missile fire. Initial casualties were stiff, and elements of the 3rd and 5th Companies were immediately dispatched to their aid. Thus began one of the fiercest battles of the Sinai front, which eventually encompassed the entire brigade. The battalion aid station, which was set up along a nearby sand dune, was soon filled with more casualties than it could handle. It became known as 'Wounded Hill', and numerous accounts have been recorded of paratroopers, either on foot, or on M113 APCs, who raced under murderous fire to retrieve wounded comrades.

The initial battle for the 'Chinese Farm' lasted fourteen hours. Both sides had dug-in defensive positions within a

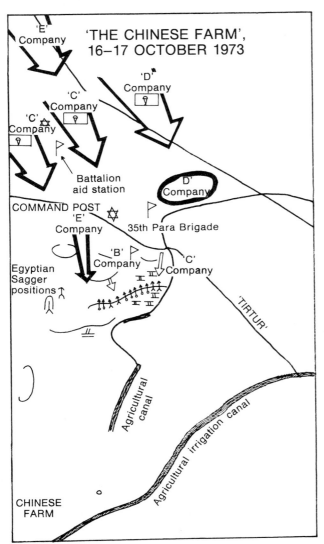

'THE CHINESE FARM',
16–17 OCTOBER 1973

'E'
Company

'D'
Company

'C'
Company

'C'
Company

Battalion
aid station

D'
Company

COMMAND POST
'E'
Company

35th Para Brigade

'B'
Company

'C'
Company

Egyptian
Sagger
positions

'TIRTUR'

Agricultural
canal

Agricultural irrigation canal

CHINESE
FARM

stone's throw of each other, both pinned down under murderous hails of fire. The ferocity of the battle can best be characterized by the fact that SAGGERs were used to snipe at lone Israeli gunners! When the forces ran out of conventional ammunition, they resorted to rocks and fists. The paratroopers were impressed by the Egyptians' tenacious defence, while the Egyptians were in awe of the paratroopers' self-sacrifice for wounded comrades. Throughout 17 October, the battle raged without respite. By nightfall, Egyptian resistance had begun to crumble, although it would take two more days before the Egyptian guns were silenced. The battle did occupy the Egyptians long enough to remove pressure from the crossing operation, although the bloodletting cost the IDF more than 100 killed and 200 wounded. The paratroopers lost more than fifty killed and 120 wounded. For his cool and decisive leadership under fire, Lieutenant-Colonel Mordechai was awarded the I'TUR HA'OZ.

The neutralization of the 'Chinese Farm' and the open-

ing of the TIRTUR, LEXICON, AKAVISH axes heralded the beginning of the end of the October war. With an expanded bridgehead, the IDF's breakout on the west bank of the Canal proceeded meticulously. In brilliant fashion, the IDF successfully cut a wedge between the Egyptian 2nd and 3rd Armies, cutting off the 3rd Army Group completely. With a decisive and final Israeli victory to hand, only to be followed by super-power threats of intervention and a United Nations imposed ceasefire, the IDF pushed itself to gain as much territory on both sides of the Canal. On the last day of the fighting, the town of Suez, a bargaining chip and a tightened noose around the 3rd Army's neck, became a bloodbath.

The crumbling of the Egyptian defence brought feeling of false security in the IDF camp. Unaware of the Egyptians' determination to turn Suez into a Middle Eastern 'Stalingrad', units from the 247th Reserve Paratroop Brigade, and the Yairi's NA'HA'L Paratroop Battalion (flown in early in the war to rejoin the conscript paratroopers) were ordered into the city. The town, destroyed by shelling, had been transformed into a fortress, which soon became a deathtrap for the paratroops.

Although the battle of Suez has come to signify a major 'paratroop' battle, Suez also marked the end for SAYERET HARUV, sent to Sinai only days earlier. When the Syrians and Egyptians attacked on 6 October, the intentions of Jordan's King Hussein remained unclear. SAYERET HARUV, which due to the success of its campaign two years earlier, had been on the verge of disbandment when the order was given to guard the Jordan Valley against Jordanian invasion. When it became clear that Jordan was sending only a token force to the Golan front in a show of 'Arab solidarity', SAYERET HARUV was ordered to Sinai to relieve the battered 50th NA'HA'L Battalion for the final push against Suez.

Commanded by Lieutenant-Colonel Haim Oren, SAYERET HARUV was ferried to battle on ex-Egyptian, Soviet-built BTR APCs. On the first day of fighting in the city, the battalion (attached to UGDAT BREN's 217th Armoured Brigade as a special operations force), succeeded in clearing 10 square kilometres of trenches and Egyptian commandos in fierce fighting. Attacking the city itself from the north-east, the battalion soon found itself surrounded, and in the middle of an Egyptian anti-tank trap. With only an IAF pilot's obsolete map of the city, the HARUV units fought a one-sided, house-to-house battle for survival, managing to extricate itself only at nightfall. In three days of fighting, the small SAYERET HARUV force lost 21 killed, and more than sixty wounded. Battered beyond repair SAYERET HARUV was sent to Gaza for an ant-terrorist tour.

Oddly enough, it had been the small though potent IDF/Navy that was the only battle-ready IDF combat arm at the outbreak of the 1973 War. Equipped with the French-built 'Cherbourg' boats, as well as the indigenous RESHEF 'SAAR 4' class fast attack craft, armed with the lethal GABRIEL sea-to-sea missiles, the HEYL HAYAM

IDF/Navy) ruled the waves. In a series of historic missile battles at sea, the IDF/Navy missile boat fleet destroyed a total of thirteen Syrian and Egyptian Russian-built Osa and Komar fast attack craft without suffering a single loss. The Arab fleets were forced back to home port, where they soon became the targets of the elusive and deadly KOMMANDO YAMI.

The KOMMANDO YAMI had shown marked expansion since their dismal showing in the last 'conventional' war of 1967. With victories at Ras al-Adabia, Green Island, Tripoli, Beirut, and elsewhere, the KOMMANDO YAMI was now a highly experienced attack force of professionals eager to see action. Although the rules of security prohibit the majority of the KOMMANDO YAMI's operations against Syrian (of which raids against Latakia, and Tartus are rumoured to be numerous) and Egyptian targets from being publicized, several spectacularly successful operations warrant examination.

On the night of 16/17 October, a force of naval commandos attacked the Egyptian naval base at Port Said. The Egyptians had expected enemy frogman activity, and prepared a wide assortment of defences, including detonating underwater explosive devices. Undaunted, the KOMMANDO YAMI force (consisting of three 2-man teams) broke through Port Said's defensive underwater net, and mined a KOMAR FAC, and several smaller torpedo-boats and patrol vessels. Two divers, Lieutenant Oded Amir, and First Sergeant Eli Kimchi failed to return. Although the operation was an overall success, it was the naval commando operation against the Egyptian Red Sea base at A'rdaka which was the most famous, and historically significant.

The Egyptian naval base at the port of A'rdaka, situated at the southern mouth of the Suez Canal, approximately 100 kilometres south-west of Sharm es-Sheikh, was one of the major centres of Egyptian naval activity against the IDF during the opening stages of the 1973 War. On 6 October, Egyptian Navy KOMAR FAC fired STYX missiles at Israeli shoreline installations at Sharm es-Sheikh and Ras-Muhamed, severely hindering shoreline movements and operations. Although OC Southern Command, Major-General Gonen, ordered the base destroyed by the IAF, A'rdaka's dense anti-aircraft missile and gun defences made that a difficult undertaking. A'rdaka was then 'given' to OC IDF/Navy, Major-General Binyamin 'Bini' Telem, and IDF/Navy Red Sea Commander, Colonel Zeev Almog, who ordered the KOMMANDO YAMI to remove the Egyptian nuisance.

On 9 October, a KOMMANDO YAMI contingent was ordered to enter A'rdaka at night, and sabotage the harbour installations, destroying as many naval craft as possible. The mission was aborted at the last moment, when a strong fleet of Egyptian torpedo-craft suddenly appeared. Forty-eight hours later, the KOMMANDO YAMI returned to A'rdaka, this time slipping through without being detected. They succeeded in destroying a KOMAR missile boat, as well as inflicting severe damage to the harbour facilities. The Egyptians put up a determined pursuit of the Israeli underwater raiders, but all divers returned to base safely. Yet another raid was carried out on the night of 19/20 October, with severe damage inflicted on A'rdaka, again with no Israeli losses. Cocky and confident, the KOMMANDO YAMI vowed to return once again to A'rdaka.

In the early morning of 21 October, Colonel Almog's headquarters received a shipment of twenty American-made LAW 66mm anti-tank rockets. The LAWs had been one of the first items to reach Israel, courtesy of a generous American arms airlift, and they were rushed to paratroop and infantry units to counter the success of the Russian-

▼ Combined forces of conscript and reservist paratroops race towards the 'Chinese Farm', 16 October 1973. (IDF Archives)

made RPGs and SAGGERs. The LAWs proved to be highly effective against Egyptian armour. Their arrival at Colonel Almog's HQ caused the old naval commando veteran to consider 'special' uses for these new weapons. Hours later, a fourth raid on A'rdaka was ordered.

Throughout 21 October, the small force of naval commandos trained at a frantic pace, perfecting assault tactics and familiarizing themselves with the LAWs. The arrival of the LAWs provided the naval commandos with offensive flexibility, as the Egyptians were expecting an underwater sabotage attempt, not a frontal attack with anti-tank weapons from a distance of 100 metres. Colonel Almog earmarked ten of the LAWs for the operation; the remainder to be used for training purposes. The attack force would make their way towards the target in three Zodiac craft (two for the assault, and one held in reserve, for exfiltration, and covering fire). The past two attacks on A'rdaka had been from a southern approach, and to ensure surprise, a northern attack route was chosen. Strict ordered were issued to aim the LAWs at the OSAs and KOMARs, and not their STYX missile-launchers, as it was justifiably feared that hitting the STYXs' 400 kilogram high-explosive warhead would create an inferno which could very well envelop the KOMMANDO YAMI raiders.

At 17.00 hours, Colonel Almog gave his men their final briefing, and two hours later, the heavily laden Zodiacs set sail for A'rdaka. The men had been 'up' for attack, even though the latest intelligence reports indicated that a 20-kilometre zone surrounding the base was defended by new Soviet sensory devices. At 03.50 hours on 22 October, the three Zodiacs reached the northern mouth of A'rdaka harbour, only to find it empty. The worse was feared, and Colonel Almog ordered his raiders to prepare for an

▲ Naval Commandos prepare their gear before preliminary moves against the Egyptian Red Sea port of A'rdaka, 22 October 1973. (IDF Archives)

Egyptian ambush. As the Zodiacs entered further into the labyrinth of waterways, a lone KOMAR was spotted. At first it was thought that it was the remnants of the craft destroyed on 9 October, but on closer scrutiny, they discovered it manned, and fully equipped.

The KOMMANDO YAMI force succeeded in closing in to 120 yards of the KOMAR, when they were discovered at 04.05 hours. Egyptian shore batteries began to chase the raiders, as did hundreds of Egyptian sailors firing automatic weapons. With the motors pushed to full speed, the Zodiacs closed in to eighty and then forty yards, before firing their LAWs. Heavy enemy fire, choppy water, and the LAWs' own limited capabilities caused difficulties and the first eight shots missed the mark. Frustrated, Almog ordered the gunner to pass a LAW to him, although the young First Sergeant refused, vowing to hit the KOMAR. Practice makes perfect, and the LAW's post-firing blast was followed by a huge explosion, and a fire-ball. The last LAW hit its target for good measure, and with haste the KOMMANDO YAMI returned to Sharm es-Sheikh only to learn of the first ceasefire imposed on the Sinai front.

The A'rdaka raid of 21/22 October had great historic significance. It was learned that the KOMAR destroyed was the same vessel responsible for sinking the IDF Navy's flagship, the INS *Eilat* on 21 October 1967. In addition, the KOMMANDO YAMI covering force was commanded by Major-General (Res.) Yochai Ben-Nun, the PAL'YAM, and IDF/Navy 'sabotage craft unit' commander responsible for the sinking the Egyptian Navy's flagship, the *Emir Farouk* on 21 October 1948. The circle of action and revenge against Egypt had been completed, to be followed by a true and enduring peace lasting to this day and it is to be hoped, lasting forever.

▼ Heavily laden recon paratroopers prepare to deploy against Egyptian commando positions on the West Bank of the Suez Canal following the IDF crossing, 20 October 1973. (IDF Archives)

8

THE AGONY AND THE ECSTASY
Operations against terrorism, 1974–82

TERROR ATTACKS FROM LEBANON AND ISRAELI RESPONSES

'I cannot promise that the terrorists will let us live in peace. But I can, and do, promise that every government of Israel will chop off the hands of those who want to cut short the lives of our children.'

Prime Minister Golda Meir, 1974

THE IDF had been traumatized by the events of October 1973. The once mighty IDF had been truly humbled by improved Arab conventional capabilities on the battlefield, and the era of over-confidence and lightning victories had ended. An Israeli government panel, the Agranat Commission, painfully searched for the facts leading to the 'October Earthquake'. Their findings were meant to relieve a perplexed public, although they resulted in numerous political and military resignations, and a restructuring of military strategies and perceptions. One of the few military bodies left unscathed by the Agranat Commission was the élite forces, whose performance during the war was seen as noble, and of whom a greater role in the next war was demanded. Yet while the élite forces' commanders rested on their laurels, a new threat awoke on Israel's northern frontier.

The 1973 War did not bring peace to Israel. As has been the case in each Arab-Israeli war fought, won and lost, the 1973 War's cessation spawned a new form of warfare on Israel's borders. On the first anniversary of Operation 'AVIV NEORIM', 11 April 1974, three terrorists of Ahmed Jibril's Popular Front for the Liberation of Palestine-General Command (PFLP-GC) crossed the Lebanese border into Israel, and attacked an apartment block in the border town of Kiryat Shmoneh. After killing eighteen people (including a family sitting at the breakfast table) the terrorists were accidentally killed by the explosives they were carrying. The Lebanese border had been neglected following the disbanding of SAYERET EGOZ after the 1973

war, and the fierce war of attrition still waging on the Golan Heights which pitted infantry (GOLANI and para-troop) forces against fresh Syrian and Cuban forces led to a benign military presence along the Lebanese border. Unable to release additional forces to the frontier towns and the border, Northern Command prayed for peace.

Sincere prayers for peace were answered by explosions and bloodshed. On 15 May 1974, a 3-man suicide terror squad of Nayif Hawatmeh's Popular Democratic Front (PDF) crossed the Lebanese border into the frontier town of Ma'alot. The three terrorists had been born in Israel, and their command of Hebrew enabled them to remain undetected. At 04.00 hours, the terrorists attacked the Netiv-Meir Nature Preserve School on a hilltop just outside the city, and seized 103 teenage students as hostages. Recalling the IDF's hostage rescue capabilities in Operation 'Isotope 1', the terrorists wired the entrances, classrooms and hallways with explosive boody-traps. A female IDF officer and one of the hostages, Lieutenant Narkis Mordechai, were released at 08.00 hours, to carry the terrorist's demand to Defence Minister Moshe Dayan, and Chief of Staff Lieutenant-General Mordechai 'Motta' Gur.* Twenty-six Palestinian prisoners, one for each year of Israeli independence, were to be released by 18.00 hours. If not, all the hostages would be slaughtered.

The youth of the hostages placed the Israeli government

---

*Lieutenant-General Elazar had resigned in light of the Agranat Commission findings.

in an impossible moral dilemma. Although the standard of Israeli policy against terrorism had been never to succumb to terrorist demands, a failed military assault with the inevitable carnage among such young people was a price too dear to pay. Negotiations commenced, while a military solution was sought.

The first IDF unit on the scene was a small GOLANI force patrolling the area, and they quickly secured a defensive perimeter surrounding the school. This force was soon reinforced by SAYERET GOLANI and SAYERET MAT'KAL units. As Defence Minister Dayan, who had been ferrying between Ma'alot and Jerusalem by helicopter, concluded the false negotiations, the rescue forces closed in for the kill. Many of the GOLANI soldiers were from northern frontier towns, and many had friends and relations held hostage inside the schoolhouse.

At 17.25 hours the attack commenced. A sniper's bullet killed one of the terrorists, but timing between the first shot and the GOLANI and SAYERET assault resulted in a 60-second gap, during which the terrorists succeeded in turning their weapons on the hapless hostages before they themselves were killed by the rescue force. Moshe Dayan writes that the assault on Ma'alot was not the most successful ordered in his career. Indeed several mistakes ensured disaster; yet. Perhaps the greatest error was waiting for the last moment before ordering in the commandos. The Agranat Commission and Israel's soul-searching following the 1973 War led to a dangerous loss of confidence in the IDF's once mighty capacity for innovation.

The carnage at Ma'alot had been total, and abhorrent. Twenty-two teenagers had been brutally murdered, and seventy were wounded in classrooms covered in blood and fragments of flesh. Still unable to carry out a decisive military response against the Palestinian military infra-structure in its mini-state inside Lebanon, similar to Operations 'KALAHAT', 'BARDAS', and 'AVIV NEORIM', Israel was forced to rely on air-strikes to dissuade the terrorists from further action. The terrorists' victory at Ma'alot, like that of Munich, had dire implications for Israel and the world. The disaster at Ma'alot resulted in a greater vigilance along the northern border, and led to a marked increase in hostage-rescue and anti-terrorist training for paratroop, GOLANI and élite Border Guard units. In fact, Ma'alot was a turning point, and a government memo-randum called for the Israeli Police and Border Guard to maintain internal security. As a result, an élite Border Guard ant-terrorist unit was formed, called the YA'MA'M. Their services would be needed only too soon.

SAYERET EGOZ's absence from the Lebanese border had been painfully felt, and its reconnaissance/ambush role was transferred to the GOLANI Brigade and the élite Druze Muslim reconnaissance unit, SAYERET HADRUZIM, which by late 1974 had been ordered to stop Palestinian infiltration from across the Lebanese border; a task which they carried out in brilliant fashion. Nevertheless, Palestinian terrorists sought new venues of attack against Israel, and on the

▲ The first tragedy: SAYERET GOLANI forces rescue teen-aged hostages from the terrorist-held schoolhouse in Ma'alot, 15 May 1974. (IDF Archives)

night of 25 June 1974 a new front was officially opened.

On that night, an *el-Fatah* 'FORCE 17' amphibious terror squad landed by Zodiac craft along the beach at Nahariyah, a northern sea-front town approximately 12 kilometres from the Lebanese border. Landing three hundreds metres from a housing complex, they quickly seized an apartment block in Balfour Street and took the residents hostage. A HAMISHMAR HAEZRACHI (civilian guard) force, ill-equipped to deal with the terrorist attack, valiantly intervened with antiquated M-1 carbines, but in the ensuing crossfire, three civilians, including a 3-year-old girl, were killed. Their's was not a selective mission, but one intended to kill as many civilians as possible. Their discovery, now compounded by the fact that they were surrounded by police units, armed civilians, and off-duty soldiers, left only one option. SAYERET GOLANI was called in immediately.

Only hours after the terrorist landing, a strong GOLANI presence was in place, and ready for the assault. The veteran EGOZ leader, Colonel Uri Simchoni, had replaced the wounded Colonel Drori as GOLANI Brigade Commander, and his record of special operations ensured a unique approach to the brigade's pressing military responsi-bilities. Determined not to allow the Nahariyah situation to reach a one-way option, as had occurred at Ma'alot; and with supreme confidence in his men, Colonel Simchoni ordered SAYERET GOLANI to storm the building immedi-ately. Satisfied, SAYERET GOLANI Commander Captain Modi, went over the building's blue-prints, gathered his forces, supervised one last weapons check, and proceeded to avenge Kiryat Shmoneh, and Ma'alot.

At 01.50 hours on the 26th, Captain Modi led his heavily laden men into the building. Creeping swiftly along a dimly lit staircase, Modi knocked on the door of a ground-floor apartment to question the frightened tenants as to the location of the terrorists. On learning that the three Palestinians were upstairs, the men with the help of a 'burglar's key', broke into the apartment firing. The long hours of training had paid off, and in a matter of seconds, the three terrorists were dead. In the mêlée, one GOLANI sergeant was killed, and four wounded.

Incensed by the lax security along Israel's northern border, OC Northern Command, Major-General 'Raful' Eitan, ordered GOLANI to respond in the only effective manner he knew, and frequent incursions into Lebanon's 'FATAHLAND' were ordered. From July 1974 to January 1975, dozens of raids into the Lebanese heartland were carried out with the SAYERET and BARAK Battalions in the vanguard. The IDF/Navy also responded to the new Palestinian naval threat, and shelled the Lebanese ports of Tyre and Sidon.

On Wednesday 5 March 1975, Palestinian terrorists mounted one of their most audacious attacks. At 23.15 hours, two Zodiac rubber dinghies carrying eight *el-Fatah* 'FORCE 17' terrorists from 'Abu Yusef Commando' (in memory of the terrorist leader killed during Operation 'AVIV NEORIM'), landed at a southern Tel Aviv beach. After breaking into the nearby 'Cinema 1' theatre and opening fire into the crowd, they seized the small seafront Savoy Hotel, taking twenty of the guests hostage. The police were summoned, although the sound of gunfire in this rough neighbourhood was at first ignored, it being thought that an 'underworld score was being settled'. When it was learned that terrorists had indeed landed, the General Staff, summoned to a late-night session at the Hakirya, only miles away, ordered an immediate military response.

While 'Civilian Guard' and off-duty soldiers helped to clear the area, trading shots with the terrorists in the process, Border Guard anti-terrorist policemen, and paratroop squads were rushed to the scene. Tel Aviv's Hadasah and Ichilov Hospitals were on emergency standby; as were the IAF, IDF/Navy, and numerous élite infantry, paratroop, and reconnaissance formations. The once tranquil seafront was now crowded with scores of generals (including the Prime Minister's special adviser on terrorism, Major-General Rechavam Zeevi), as hundreds of soldiers lined the placid streets and alleys for the assault. Defence Minister Shimon Peres had learned that the Zodiacs had been sent to Tel Aviv by a 'mother ship', and a thorough naval and air search was ordered; his main objective nevertheless remained the rescue of the hostages.

Although the exact designation of the rescue force remains classified to this day, it is widely thought to have consisted of SAYERET MAT'KAL commandos commanded by Colonel Uzi Yairi, former commander of the conscript Paratroop Brigade and deputy Chief Paratroop and Infantry Officer, serving in a senior post in A'MAN.

Peres ordered Yairi not to lead the rescue attempt personally, but Yairi was not an armchair general, and prepared his gear for assault. At 05.12 on the morning of 6

March, Colonel Yairi led his force into the hotel. Gunfire was intense, and just as it appeared as if the rescue would be successful, a thunderous explosion and the collapse of the hotel's south-western corner signalled tragedy. The terrorists had detonated their dynamite charges at the sight of the IDF rescue attempt. Eleven people died in the rubble, including Colonel Yairi, who had survived the 'Chinese Farm' bloodbath, and who was ironically clutching the AK-47 assault rifle given to him as a gift following the February 1973 raid on the terrorist naval unit bases in Tripoli.

The 1970s appear to have been a decade of defeat for Israel. The onset of fanatical Palestinian terrorist outrages at home coupled with a bitterly hard-fought and nationally traumatic victory in the 1973 War, followed by a collapse of the northern frontier to terrorist infiltration and carnage, pointed to future conflicts and defeats. Yet just when it seemed as if the resolve of the nation would slip to all-time depths, the terrorists, cocky and over-confident, brought their war back to an international forum. A seemingly routine hijacking would soon bring the terrorists their most humiliating defeat and prompt a resurgence of the IDF's élite units as Israel's cutting edge.

▼ The second tragedy: combined recon paratroop and Border Guard YA'MA'M anti-terrorist policemen inch their way toward the 'FORCE 17'-held Savoy Hotel in Tel Aviv, 5 March 1975. In the ensuing assault, eleven died, including former paratroop commander Colonel Uzi Yairi, the rescue attempt's commander. (IGPO)

OPERATION 'YONATAN': THE LEGEND OF ENTEBBE

'There are times when the fate of an entire people rests upon a handful of fighters and volunteers. They must secure the uprightness of our world in one short hour.'

Defence Minister, Shimon Peres, 4 July 1976

FOR years, the African continent had been a bastion of pro-Israeli sentiment. Israel capitalized on the Africans' lack of agricultural and military knowledge by successfully conducting a 'hearts and minds campaign', providing generous agricultural and military assistance. The good will created was however shattered immediately following the 1973 War, when the African states sided with wealth and new-found economic leverage of the oil-producing Arab states. On 25 January 1976, Kenyan security police arrested a band of Popular Front for the Liberation of Palestine terrorists belonging to the 'Wadi Haddad' faction, who were attempting to blow an EL AL airliner out of the sky with SAM-7 STRELLAs given to them by Ugandan President Idi Amin.*

At 08.59 hours on 27 June 1976, Air France flight 139 took off on a routine flight from Tel Aviv to Athens and Paris, loaded with holiday travellers. At 11.30 hours, the A-300B Airbus touched down at Athens Airport to disembark 38 passengers, and take on 58 newcomers. Inconspicuous among the passengers boarding at Athens were two fair-skinned Germans travelling on forged South American papers, and two Middle Eastern males carrying Bahraini and Kuwaiti passports (their appearance striking raw nerves among the Israeli passengers anxious at not having flown EL AL). Athens airport had long been known as 'international terrorism's transit lounge', and the criminally lax security arrangements on 27 June justified that reputation. No security officer bothered to man the metal detector, and a Greek policeman paid little heed to the X-ray device searching hand baggage. At 12.20 hours, the flight was airborne, climbing to 31,000 feet. Eight minutes later, flight 139 was hijacked by the 'Che Guevara Cell of the Haifa Unit of the PFLP'.

The two 'South Americans' were Wilfrid Bose and Brigitta Kuhlmann, Baader-Meinhoff terrorists who were working for the PFLP's renegade operations mastermind, Dr Wadi Haddad. As an overtly sadistic Kuhlmann and the two Arabs secured the flight's 256 travellers (including twelve crewmen), Bose ordered the pilot, Captain Michel Bacos, to fly the aircraft (renamed 'Arafat') to Benghazi where it was received with open arms by scores of Libyan officials and Palestinian representatives. After taking on 42 tons of fuel, flight 139 was once again airborne, and at 03.15 hours on 28 June, landed at Uganda's Entebbe airport. Here the terrorists were joined by an additional force of PFLP gunmen flown from Mogadishu** in President Amin's private jet, and hours later, the 256 hostages were hoarded into the airport's 'old' terminal building to await their uncertain fate.

Although the hijacking was clearly a 'French' responsibility, Israel was quick to respond to the crisis. Once radio contact with flight 139 was lost, emergency contingency plans were immediately implemented. Prime Minister Yitzhak Rabin, Defence Minister Shimon Peres, Minister of Transport Ya'akobi, Chief of Staff, Lieutenant-General Gur, Chief Paratroop and Infantry Officer, Brigadier-General Dan Shomron and A'MAN's chief, Major-General Shlomoh Gazit, were all briefed, as a repeat of the 1972 Sabena hijacking was generally expected. With Ben-Gurion airport a likely target, Central Command was placed on full alert. Battle-equipped Border Guard units sealed off the airport, while YA'MA'M, and SAYERET units were mobilized, briefed and placed into firing positions.

Although political efforts were undertaken to resolve the hijacking, most senior IDF commander realized that the only solution available was military action. At first, it was feared that a rescue operation would have to be carried out against Benghazi, although the thought of landing a commando force so far away in such a fanatically hostile Arab country seemed impossible. Nevertheless, long-range rescues were not new to military thinking. The US Special Forces' well-executed, rescue attempt of her POWs at the Son Tay camp in North Vietnam in 1970 had been preceded by seven months of intensive intelligence and logistical planning, coupled with more than 1,000 hours of flying practice given to the mission's helicopter pilots. If any similar action were considered against Benghazi, only a few days of preparation and training would be available to the IDF rescue force. Although such innovative and 'mission impossible' type operations were seen as an Israeli speciality, a post-Yom Kippur War malaise had overtaken the IDF, stifling its imaginative and unique approach to military problems. In addition, its élite forces had suffered two unsuccessful rescue attempts at Ma'alot and the Savoy Hotel, and confidence in their abilities were at an all time low.

Poor morale aside, the IDF had to do something! From day one of the hijacking, a special crisis group had been set

---

*President Idi Amin had once been a staunch ally of the Jewish state, and had even undergone parachutist training at Tel Nof. Israel's refusal to sell him F-4E Phantoms in order to bomb Tanzania, however, caused the dictator to embrace the Arab cause.

**Ironically enough, the scene of West Germany's élite GSG-9 successful rescue operation of a Lufthansa jet in 1977.

up by the Operations Branch at General Staff HQ to coordinate a rescue operation. The planners included Operation Chief Major-General Yekutiel 'Kuti' Adam; deputy A'MAN Commander, Colonel Ehud Barak; and SAYERET MAT'KAL's deputy commander, Major Muki Botzer. Intelligence files were pulled on the African nation, and reports were compiled, as all available contingencies were considered. At first, little was known of Ugandan complicity in the hijacking, and a plan was conceived to parachute a small force of approximately 10-15 commandos into Entebbe, and after killing the terrorists, to return the hostages to Israel with Ugandan assistance. When it became clear that Ugandan soldiers were in full collusion with the terrorists, a different plan had to be conceived.

The crisis group's first operational plan was to parachute a force of naval and MAT'KAL commandos into Lake Victoria. After inflating Zodiac assault crafts and reaching the shores of Entebbe, the rescue force would kill the terrorists and seize the airfield, for a subsequent IAF landing. Ambitious, and inventive, the plan was shelved

▲ Responding to the audacious PFLP hijacking of Air France Flight 139 to Entebbe on 27 June 1976, reconnaissance paratroopers practise disembarkation techniques from a C-130 Hercules transport at an unidentified base in central Israel, 1 July 1976. (IDF Spokesman)

when it was learned that there were alligators in Lake Victoria! Undaunted, the group reviewed even more audacious plans, including a mini-invasion of Uganda by a large-scale force complete with infantry and armour elements which would not only seize Entebbe, but surround Kampala and Idi Amin's Presidential Palace.

To the IAF, an operation at Entebbe was clearly feasible. IAF's Commander, Major-General Binyamin Peled, had convened a crisis group to examine logistics, and it was clear that the IAF's C-130 Hercules aircraft had sufficient range and cargo space for such a mission. Prior to the Ugandan expulsion of all Israelis in 1972, the IAF had flown regular supply flights to Entebbe, and IAF pilots knew the route. All those who had flown to Uganda, including the reservists, were summoned to Major-

General Peled's office for a late-night briefing. After 36 hours of incessant research and calculation, Peled was able to inform Major-General Adam that the IAF could fly as many as 1,200 commandos and their equipment in a non-stop flight to Entebbe. The planes would have to be refuelled at Entebbe, but that and numerous other details remained inconclusive.

Possible terrorist responses were crucial in determining assault procedures, ensuring that a repeat of the Ma'alot tragedy would not transpire. During those 'dark' first days, luck was on Israel's side. It was discovered that the old terminal, and numerous other facilities at Entebbe had been built by an Israeli firm. Their blue-prints, and reports were confiscated, and sent to Major-General Adam's crisis group for immediate evaluation, as was an 8mm 'home' movie taken by an IDF representative in Entebbe in late 1971.

On Tuesday 29 June, the terrorists announced their demands: the release of the hostages in exchange for forty Palestinian and European terrorist held in Israel, six in West Germany, five in Kenya, one in Switzerland, and one in France, as well as a $5,000,000 ransom to be paid by the French. That day, Wilfrid Bose read a list of names, in which the Jewish and Israeli hostages were separated from the gentiles (the Air France crew gallantly chose to remain behind), who were to be freed. The 103 Jews and Israelis and the crew were made to crawl into a small room inside the 'old' terminal, while the remainder of the passengers were returned to Paris. This *Selektion* by a German terrorist (reminiscent of Dr Mengele at Auschwitz) had ominous and historical significance, and turned the hijacking into an Israeli responsibility. At Orly Airport in Paris, the released hostages were pumped for as much information as possible. They provided a wealth of intelligence, and for the first time since the atrocity had begun, an accurate picture was constructed. The information was rushed to the crisis group, who in turn summoned Chief Paratroop and Infantry Officer Brigadier-General Shomron, and SAYERET MAT'KAL Commander, Lieutenant-Colonel Yonatan 'Yoni' Netanyahu.

Ironically, the release of the non-Jewish hostages made a rescue at Entebbe much easier. Not only were there fewer people to be rescued (fewer aircraft would be needed), but Israel could now act unilaterally without concern for other nations. At 18.30 hours on Thursday 1 July, Defence Minister Peres met the Chief of Staff, and Generals Peled, Adam, and Shomron. Peres was presented with an operational plan for the rescue of the hostages, given a fair (50-50) probability of success. Shomron informed Peres that if the first C-130 could land undetected, it appeared as if the operation had an almost 100 percent success probability. With little time to waste before the terrorists' 3 July deadline, Peres ordered the generals to commence training, while he sought the government's approval for the military response.

Lieutenant-General Gur, one of the IDF's foremost élite force and special operation veterans, understood only too well the requirements of command for such an operation. With full confidence in his Chief Paratroop and Infantry Officer, he named Brigadier-General Shomron the operation's overall commander, and gave him a free hand to conscript the units he felt were capable of successfully carrying out the undertaking. Late that night, Shomron was busy on the telephone, contacting old friends now commanding the cutting edge of the IDF élite units. Only the best would be going to Entebbe.

After an all-night crisis group session, it was decided to make the rescue operation as simple and uncomplicated as possible. The rescue force was divided into five groups:

'Force A', commanded by Lieutenant-Colonel 'Yoni' and Major Botzer consisted of the MAT'KAL commandos, and were to seize the 'old' terminal building, kill the terrorists and prepare the rescued hostages for evacuation.

'Force B', commanded by HATIVAT HATZANHANIM Commander, Colonel Matan Vilnai (the current OC, Manpower Branch), consisted of the best NCOs and officers from SAYERET TZANHANIM, personally chosen for the operation by the brigade commander. Their first task was to place beacons alongside the main runway lights (responsibility given to men commanded by Lieutenant-Colonel Shmuel Arad, the current Chief Paratroop and Infantry Officer), after which they would seize the 'new' terminal complex and 'inhibit' the Ugandan Army's ability to intervene.

'Force C', commanded by GOLANI Brigade Commander, Colonel Uri Saguy (the current Ground Forces Commander), consisted of the best NCOs and officers from the SAYERET and BARAK Battalions, and was to provide covering fire, and assist in the evacuation of the rescued hostages.

'Force D', commanded by Major Shaul Mopaz (from 'Yoni's unit), was to isolate the 'old' terminal with a protective ring of M113 and BTR APCs, and the GOLANI force, in evacuating the hostages.

'Force E', consisted of Brigadier-General Shomron's command group, and was to coordinate all activities on the ground at Entebbe. (It was rumoured that the German GSG-9's Colonel Ulrich Wegener was invited to, and did participate in the raid, tagging close to Brigadier-General Shomron.)

All five forces, as well as the communications, medical, and refuelling elements were to be flown to Entebbe in four C-130 Hercules transports. Two IAF Boeing 707s were also requisitioned, one to serve as a flying hospital, while the other was transformed into an airborne command, control, and and communications centre which carried Major-General Peled and Major-General Adam. In addition, each force was complemented by superbly trained medical teams, including the IDF's best combat physicians. Nothing was being left to chance.

As Chief of Staff Gur sought government approval for the operation, training had already commenced at a base in southern Israel. By the night of 1 July, a full-scale model of Entebbe's 'old' terminal had been constructed, and 'Yoni's officers were hard at work perfecting assault tactics on the building, while the remaining 200 fighters of the rescue forces assembled, and were briefed. To ensure that word of the training was not inadvertently leaked, security was given top priority. Most General Staff members were not even informed as to the preparations, and the training base was sealed tight with all movement both in and out forbidden. To make sure that girlfriends were not impressed by news of the 'heroic' feat by boyfriends eager to score some points, all telephone lines were silenced.

At 09.00 hours on 2 July, 'Yoni' sat down with his men, and briefed them as to their initial tasks and responsibilities. Intelligence reports estimated that 8–15 terrorists were guarding the hostages, and the airport was defended by a garrison of approximately three hundred Ugandan soldiers. Following the briefing, the commandos headed towards the field, where they were divided into 'guerrilla squads', and given their assignment. Under a brutal desert sun, the intensive training began. Hours were spent perfecting the assault, including the drill of stopping a Land-Rover, jumping out, and firing at terrorists in a split-second. Oddly enough, 'Yoni' ordered that each commando concentrate *only* on his assigned task. Normally Israeli special operations require that each man familiarize himself with all aspects of a mission and knows what everyone else is doing. 'Yoni' realized that Entebbe was a unique assignment, and for reasons of security and operational success, he wanted to ensure that his men concentrated solely on their tasks.

To achieve maximum surprise, it was decided to disguise the MAT'KAL assault force as President Idi Amin's entourage. A search through the intelligence files produced photographs of Amin's limousine, and a frantic search for a black Mercedes-Benz 220D was initiated. Unfortunately, the only Mercedes 220D available was a white taxi, but Major Botzer and a few buckets of black paint resolved the crisis!* Idi's Mercedes would be followed by ex-Jordanian Army Land-Rovers painted in Ugandan camouflage schemes, and relying on evidence that Amin employed Palestinian bodyguards, the MAT'KAL commandos all wore Palestinian lizard pattern camouflage fatigues. It was only fitting, that the IDF computer came up with a true 'James Bond' code-name for the operation – 'Thunderball'!

The IAF was also busy with last-minute details. It was planned that the first C-130 would taxi to within 100 metres of the 'old' terminal, making 'Yoni's drive as short as possible. The first C-130 would also precede the other three aircraft by seven minutes; ensuring that by the time the last plane landed the operation, either proceeding well or disastrously, would be in progress. OC Medical Corps, Brigadier-General Dan Micheli prepared the Boeing 707 flying hospital for action, while OC Communications Corps, Brigadier-General Yisrael Zamir summoned his finest technicians to turn the second 707 into a viable command, control, and communications link.

Even though training for the operation was under way at full pace, Operation 'Thunderball' (also called by many 'Thunderbolt') was still at its infant stage, even though the terrorist's deadline was but one day away, midnight on 3 July. At midday on 2 July, the force commanders presented their detailed plans to Brigadier-General Shomron, while later in the afternoon the IAF conducted a full-scale rehearsal with four C-130 aircraft at Ophir Air Base in Sinai with Chief of Staff Gur and Major-General Peled in attendance. The twilight conditions provided ample proof to the the Chief of staff that the C-130 pilots were indeed capable of making a 'blind' night landing. Throughout the day, the assault forces had also trained without respite, each time shaving seconds off the stopwatch, and each time developing different modes of assault. Thousands of rounds of ammunition had already been spent in an assault course forged into each commando's mind. At 22.45 hours, the C-130s together with the entire rescue force performed a dress-rehearsal for the Chief of Staff. At 01.00 hours on 3 July, Lieutenant-General Gur telephoned the Defence Minister, and told him two simple though fateful words: 'we're ready!'

Although equipment was loaded on to the C-130s throughout the morning of 3 July, Operation 'Thunderball' had yet to receive government approval. The preparations continued, nevertheless, and in the early afternoon, the operation commander, Brigadier-General Shomron address his men. He emphasized the importance of the mission not only in terms of the war against terrorism, but also its importance to the IDF and the Jewish State. Each soldier was reminded of Wilfrid Bose's *Selektion*, and its Holocaust parallels which could not be ignored. He stressed that during the *Selektions* at Auschwitz not one world power had bothered to intervene; and only the advent of the long arm of the IDF insured that such future crimes against the Jewish people would *never again* occur. Although the commandos were 'up' for the rescue, the Prime Minister's cabinet was still procrastinating over the diplomatic fallout from such an operation. As the latest possible moment the rescue force could depart from Ben-Gurion Airport soon approached, Gur decided to dispatch the force and inform them of the government's final decision on the way to Ophir air base in the southern tip of the Sinal Peninsula, the flight plan's final staging and refuelling point before the long haul to Entebbe.

In order not to arouse any suspicion by flying in formation over central Israel on the Sabbath, the four C-130s took separate and inconspicuous courses, with strict radio silence observed. Over the Negev and Sinai deserts, upcurrents of hot air made the flight quite uncomfortable, and dozens of the 'élite' suffered from extreme airsickness. While one fighter had to be removed from the operation due to extreme nausea, the operation's chief medical officer decided to issue airsickness pills to all the commandos. Even though the pills would make the men drowsy, it was felt that 'constructive relaxation' would be better than

---

*Following the operation, the owner of the 'white' Mercedes' sued the IDF over damages inflicted to his car, and won compensation.

having the commandos exhaust themselves with fear and anxiety during the 8-hour flight. At 15.30 hours, the four C-130s took off from Ophir, and received authorization for the operation thirty minutes later in mid-air. When the 'green light' was received, most of the officers were shocked, as they had little faith that the politicans would take such risk and responsibility upon themselves. In order to ease the terrorists' into a false sense of security, the government informed the International Red Cross that they would agree to the hijacker's demands, and release the 53 prisoners (including Kozo Okamoto, the sole survivor of the Japanese Red Army massacre at Lod Airport in 1972, and the gunrunning Archbishop Cappuci). The stage had been set.

The four C-130s flew over Egypt, and Sudan en route to Entebbe, but their low-level altitude and electronic countermeasures made them invisible to radar. On the approaches to Lake Victoria, the C-130s encountered a fierce electrical storm, but still the timetable was adhered to. At 23.01 hours, and only thirty seconds behind schedule, the first C-130 and its 86 officers and men touched down at Entebbe. It had followed right behind a British cargo jet, and little notice was taken at Entebbe's control tower. As the wheels touched down, the cargo door was already open, and the vehicles' engines were already running. The runway was code-named 'SHOSHANA', and two units from Lieutenant-Colonel Arad's force ('Force' Doron and 'Force Tali) were already jumping off the plane, placing their emergency beacons all along SHOSHANA's path, in case the Ugandans should extinguish the runway lights. Before the C-130 came to a final halt, Idi's Mercedes and the two Land-Rovers had already deplaned.

The 100 metres to the 'old' terminal were covered at high speed. Fifty metres along the path, the entourage encountered two Ugandan sentries at a checkpost. The Ugandans apparently did not 'buy' the Israeli's attempt to impersonate a Presidential motorcade, but the ruse did gain a few valuable seconds. As the alerted soldiers cocked their weapons, 'Yoni' and Giora (both sitting in the Mercedes' front seat) aimed their silenced 9mm M1951S Beretta automatics, and fired, although missing their marks. While one of the Ugandans ran in panic, the other stood fast, only to be cut down by a burst of 7.62mm fire from a FN MAG light machine-gun mounted on one of the Land-Rovers. Things had not gone according to plan, and the tranquil night had been shattered by bursts of gunfire. Knowing that the terrorists had been alerted, the MAT'KAL force dismounted from their vehicles and raced on foot towards the 'old' terminal.

Major Botzer led the rescue assault. Sprinting along the walkway, he quickly disposed of a Ugandan soldier, emptying his AK-47 magazine in the process. Realizing to his horror that he was out of ammunition, Major Botzer changed magazines on the run. Joined by his second in command Amnon, they decided to break into the terminal together. Alerted, the terrorists began to fire, although their shots rang out in vain. In systematic fashion, Major

Botzer, Amnon, and the remainder of the first team eliminated all four principal terrorists in only fifteen seconds. The commandos with bullhorns yelled to the hostages in Hebrew and English: 'This is the IDF! Stay down!', but the shocked hostages were caught off-guard, and several were hit by both enemy and Israeli fire. The commandos fanned out through the room in search for additional terrorists or Ugandan soldiers, but all they found were thankful hostages lying on mattresses. With a thankful heart, Major Botzer informed Brigadier-General Shomron that the hostages were secure. Yet as the situation inside the terminal became clear, 'Yoni', who was just outside supervising the assault was tragically hit in the chest by a lone shot fired from the control tower.

A second team of commandos had entered the building through another entrance to attack an area known to be used by the terrorists as their living-quarters. They found two men in civilian clothing with hands raised, although upon closer examination, one was found to be carrying a Soviet-made grenade. Instinctively they 'kissed the ground' hard, firing their UZIs in the process. After killing both terrorists, the grenade detonated, destroying the two Arabs in a ghastly fashion, as well as wounding the two commandos. The commandos patched their wounds, and continued with 'purifying' the building. The third team of commandos from the Land-Rover, attacked the floors above, where the Ugandan soldiers were, and killed two, and wounded dozens more. The 'old' terminal was silenced in only three minutes after the first plane had landed. The commandos had conditioned their minds for a bitter fight, but they found their tasks completed in record time. Although ordered to prepare the hostages for evacuation, most commandos found themselves enthralled with the beautiful Air France stewardesses, lying frightened on mattresses in their bras and panties. Only a sharp bark from Major Botzer would bring them back to their assignments.

The lightning strike had been carried out in brilliant fashion, and had even exceeded the modest expectations of Brigadier-General Shomron. By 23.08 hours, all four C-130s had landed at Entebbe. Colonel Vilnai's paratroop force had headed out towards the 'new' terminal on M113s and BTRs to engage the Ugandan forces. The Israelis did not want a fight with the Ugandans, but they were also determined not to let them interfere with the rescue operation. Only those Ugandans choosing to resist were eliminated, the others were offered a fair chance to 'escape'. Colonel Saguy's GOLANI contingent had also landed, making its way towards the 'old' terminal, where they secured a perimeter, and assembled the hostages for evacuation, as did the fourth C-130 carrying the medical teams.

The entire rescue operation lasted only 58 minutes. The wounded hostages were attended to, while the remainder were loaded aboard the waiting C-130, which had taxied to within fifty yards of the 'old' terminal. A Peugeot tender van had been requisitioned to carry the wounded and dead, hile the remainder would make the short journey to the ane on foot. The GOLANI force had interlocked hands, eating a human wall to ensure that none of the bewilder- hostages, many carrying their personal belongings, ent astray.

While the hostages were loaded aboard the C-130, the ttle for the airport's control tower, a crucially strategic int in the operation, was under way. Sergeant Hershko run, due to be released from active duty in only twelve urs, was critically wounded in the battle, and evacuated the C-130s ferrying the wounded. While brief fire-fights ged between the Ugandan and Israeli forces, the entire tuation was controlled from the air by the C3 Boeing 707 ving overhead. To insure that no mid-air pursuit would conducted by the Ugandan Air Force against the slow d vulnerable C-130s, GOLANI and paratroop squads med with RPGs and heavy machine-guns raced to the jacent airfield, and proceeded to destroy between eight d eleven MiG-17 and MiG-21 jet fighters.

At 23.52 hours, the first C-130 carrying the hostages ok off from Entebbe. Lieutenant-Colonel Arad's eacons were operating as planned, providing the blacked- t runway with sufficient light for safe take-off. IAF chnicians had worked feverishly to prepare pumps to eal President Amin's precious aviation fuel for the bare -130 tanks, a process which took almost a full hour to mplete. It was, however, a task completed in vain. idway throughout the operation, Major-General Peled as able to inform his chief pilot on the scene, Lieutenant-

Colonel S., that refuelling privileges had been secured at Nairobi.

At 00.40 hours on 4 July, the last C-130 lifted off from Entebbe. The situation was still tense and uncertain, and the commandos were ordered to keep their weapons at the ready, and to leave their web gear on. When the fleet of aircraft joined the Medical Corps C-130 at Nairobi, the scene quickly changed from a mood of anxiety to one of relief. While the wounded and dead were removed to the hospital plane, the hostages and rescuers were fed, and prepared for the flight back to Israel. The feeling of joy was similar to that of the liberation of Jerusalem in 1967. A true national victory had been accomplished.

Early on the morning of 4 July, the lead Hercules carrying the hostages reached the Red Sea port city of Eilat. The exhausted pilots were astonished to find the streets of the resort town filled with thousands of civilians cheering and waving flags. The C-130 continued to an air base in central Israel where the hostages were freshened up, and given a respite from the past week's tragic events, by teams of IDF psychiatrists who offered words of comfort. At the same airfield, the MAT'KAL force deplaned its men and equipment, and returned to a life of anonym-

---

▼ Faces blackened for security reasons, commandos from Lientenant-Colonel 'Yoni' Netanyahu's MAT'KAL force return to Israel on 4 July with 'Idi Amin's Mercedes Benz'. (IDF Spokesman)

▲ Chief Paratroop and Infantry Officer, Brigadier-General Dan Shomron, the ground commander at Entebbe, briefs the world's Press in Israel, following Operation 'Yonatan', 5 July 1976. (IGPO)

mission accomplished. The Entebbe raid has been th unit's last 'overt' appearance, and officially, they still d not exist. Nevertheless, the next time some mysterious an spectacular occurrence changes the Middle East's militar and political balance in Israel's favour, it will be safe t assume that the 'Chief of Staff's Boys' had something to d with it!

The GOLANI and paratroop soldiers, on the other hand had been greeted as true celebrities upon their return t Israel. The paratroopers became known as the 'heroes o Entebbe', and together with the participating GOLAN forces, were treated to hotel suites along the the Tel Avi shore, and numerous other gifts from a grateful nation The raid had probably the greatest significance for th GOLANI Brigade, for whom Operation 'Thunderball' was rite of passage. GOLANI's participation earned the brigad recognition as an élite force equal to their red bere wearing TZANHANIM comrades, As a sign of this new though well-deserved status, GOLANI was authorized t wear its own distinctive brown beret.

The 100 minutes at Entebbe had resulted in the death of thirteen terrorists, and 35 Ugandan soldiers. Thre hostages had been killed in the raid, as were two soldier 'Yoni', and Sergeant Surin, who died days later from hi wounds. Renamed Operation 'Yonatan' in memory of th late Lieutenant-Colonel Yonatan Netanyahu, the raid o Entebbe was a threefold victory for Israel. It proved to th international community the complicated danger of inter national terrorist cooperation as well as the capability o the Western powers to defeat it by applying élite forces i special operation roles. It also gave the PFLP its mos humbling and humiliating defeat ever, severely hinderin the Palestinians' cause by making them a laughing-stock Yet most importantly, Operation 'Yonatan' brought th IDF out of its Yom Kippur War syndrome of self-doubt It was a sorely needed morale boost, which marked an en to the period of self-defeatism prevalent in many Israel political and military circles. The 'old IDF', capable of th most innovative and successful of military operations, ha clearly returned; stronger and more resolute than ever!

ity; their only reward being a truck-load of cakes and sweets brought in from the nearby KIBBUTZIM. A day after 'Yoni's funeral, the MAT'KAL commandos returned to the desert for more training with yet another spectacular

THE SAGA OF KIBBUTZ MISGAV AM: ISRAEL'S NORTHERN BORDER AND THE WRATH OF THE 'RED AND BROWN BERETS', 1978–82

HOWEVER much the raid on Entebbe might have humbled the Palestinian terrorist offensive, it did not silence it. Spurned by the ascent to power of Menachem Begin's ultra right-wing LIKUD party, and the joint Israeli-Egyptian peace process, the Palestinians responded with terror and carnage. On the night of 11 March 1978, seven seaborne 'FORCE 17' el-Fatah terrorists landed on the shores of KIBBUTZ Ma'agan Michael. After murdering an American female nature photographer, the '7' proceeded towards the bustling Tel Aviv-Haifa coastal highway, where after firing at several passing vehicles they commandeered two bus-loads of holiday travellers en route to Tel Aviv. At the Country Club Junction just north of the city, the bus was stopped by police and Border Guard anti-terrorist units, who initiated a tense stand-off. In the confusion, a hostage grabbed one of the terrorist's guns and killed three of the 'FORCE 17' gunmen, before another terrorist threw a grenade, and turned the bus into a fiery hell. With control lost, the Israeli forces opened fire, and attacked. In the mêlée, both terrorists and hostages fled into the smoke-filled night. Thirty-seven people had been killed, and seventy wounded.

For the next eighteen hours, the citizens of Israel remained locked inside their homes under a military imposed curfew, while paratroop and GOLANI units conducted a thorough search of the coastal sector near Herziliya for the escaped 'FORCE 17' terrorists, who were eventually captured. Even though Egyptian President Anwar es-Sadat offered his condemnation of the incident, and called for restraint, severe military retaliation was ordered. On the night of 14/15 March, the IDF invaded southern Lebanon.

In what became known as Operation 'Litani', a direct reference to the geographical limits of the Israeli advance, the IDF mounted its largest military incursion into Lebanon since Operation 'KALAHAT 4' in September 1972. The 15,000-man invasion force consisted of armoured brigades (most notably the 188th BARAK), and conscript paratroop and GOLANI forces. In the effort to diminish

▼ GOLANI infantrymen pass rescue vehicles along Israel's coastal highway following the 11 March 1978 outrage when seaborne 'FORCE 17' terrorists hijacked a bus to Tel Aviv's Country Club Junction, and killed 37 civilians. (IGPO)

▲ GOLANI infantrymen, armed with the newly issued GALIL 5.56mm assault rifles, search a Lebanese village for Palestinian terrorists during Operation 'Litani', March 1978. (IDF Spokesman)

civilian casualties, the Israelis warned of their impending attack, and as a result most of the Palestinian fighters simply escaped across the Litani bridges to sanctuary up north where the Palestinian movements had an extensive infrastructure following the madness of the Lebanese Civil War (1975–). The Israelis also had a tacit agreement with the Syrians, who maintained a 30,000-man 'peace-keeping' force in Lebanon as a result of the Civil War, that the two forces would not engage in combat. In the fighting, 250 terrorists were killed, and thousands of tons of military equipment were captured in a superbly handled mobile guerrilla campaign centred around the efforts of the mechanized forces of the GOLANI Brigade's GIDEON, HABOK'IM HARISHONIM, BARAK and SAYERET Battalions.

The paratroopers had also been quite busy during Operation 'Litani'. Mechanized elements of the conscript Paratroop Brigade commanded by Colonel Yitzhak Mordechai, and heliborne units of SAYERET TZANHANIM accounted for approximately 40 percent of the Palestinian body-count in 'pursuit' actions similar to those in the Jordan Valley. Their heliborne capabilities had been drastically improved following two tragic crashes which killed 74 paratroopers,[*] and the 'airborne' operations inside Lebanon were carried out with care and skill. Following the withdrawal of Israeli forces from Lebanon in June, a combined Naval Commando and SAYERET TZANHANIM force raided the source of the 'Country Club Massacre', the 'FORCE 17' base at Badr-el-Burj, and destroyed the facilities.

The operation, although meeting its objectives, was seen as a failure, a decisive engagment with the Palestinians not being achieved. Nevertheless, the post-1973 combat ethic of SHILUV KOCHOT, or 'combined arms' whereby armour and infantry forces acted as integral elements, was the successful. Three months after the invasion, the IDF force was replaced by the United Nations Interim Force Lebanon (UNIFIL), and a mixed Christian and Shi'ite militia allied to Israel under the command of the renegade Lebanese Major Sa'ad Haddad. Their presence was *intended* to keep Israel's northern frontier secure, and remove the threat of Palestinian guerrilla infiltration from Lebanon, but Major Haddad's army was ill-equipped and inadequately trained to carry out such a task. With Israel's northern border less secure than ever, future terrorist outrages were inevitable.

The non-removable threat along the Lebanese border made GOLANI an extremely busy unit. Together with the Border Guard's élite 'Northern Companies', the border was secured by vigilance. Round the clock day patrols were initiated, as were numerous cross-border ambushes, and contacts with Major Haddad's forces, who were also determined to remove the Palestinian terrorist presence from southern Lebanon. The most intimidating element

[*]The first accident involving a C-130 resulted in the deaths of twenty reservists from the brigade which liberated Jerusalem, and crossed the Suez Canal; the second involved the destruction of an entire SAYERET company when their CH-53 crashed in the Jordan Valley in 1977.

remained the IDF's massive fire-power employed along the frontier, ensuring that any infringement of Israeli territory would be met by immediate and decisive retaliation. Fire-power was a response, not a deterrent, and infiltrations continued.

On 13 January, a band of *el-Fatah* terrorists crossed the border near Ma'alot, but failed to attack any targets, due to the GOLANI Brigade's incessant pursuit. In the end, contact was made near a lodging-house in Ma'alot, where a one-man sensation, Lance-Corporal Yitzhak Revivo, detected and killed the three gunmen. Although a retaliatory raid followed, the Palestinians remained undaunted in their efforts.

On the night of 6/7 April 1980, a 5-man suicide squad from the Iraqi-controlled Arab Liberation Front (ALF) crossed the heavily fortified Lebanese border, by cutting through rows of concertina barbed wire and electrical wire fences. After crawling across, they raced a dozen metres towards KIBBUTZ Misgav-Am where they seized the nursery, and held more than a dozen infants hostage. Units from the GOLANI Brigade, alerted by the cutting of the electrical fence, were first on the scene, and sealed off the nursery. The Brigade OC, Colonel A., OC, Northern Command, Major-General Avigdor 'Yanush' Ben-Gal (the commander of the 7th Armoured Brigade during the 1973 War), Chief of Staff Lieutenant-General 'Raful' Eitan were all summoned, as was SAYERET GOLANI.

'Raful' had little patience with terrorists, and he realized that with such 'young' hostages, a repeat of the Ma'alot tragedy seemed likely. He ordered the SAYERET GOLANI Commander, Captain Giora 'Guni' Harnik, to act immediately. The SAYERET fighters had donned anti-terrorist bullet-proof flak jackets complete with communication devices, and exchanged their 5.56mm GALIL assault rifles for the 9mm UZI, which it was hoped would result in fewer innocent casualties in a close-quarter fire-fight.

The first rescue attempt, however, ended in failure. With only the light of an incendiary flare for guidance, a force commanded by Lieutenant Raz attempted to break into the nursery, only to be met with an unexpected and indiscriminate barrage of machine-gun, grenade, and RPG fire which lasted for more than fifteen minutes. During the mêlée, five SAYERET fighters were wounded, and one killed. Captain Harnik regrouped his men and prepared for another assault.

At daybreak, SAYERET GOLANI was joined by various anti-terrorist squads, including, it is rumoured, SAYERET MAT'KAL and the Border Guard's YA'MA'M. On 7 April at 10.00 hours, the second assault commenced. On the ground floor where the children were being held, Captain Harnik identified a civilian wearing hippie clothing and web gear, and quickly fired a burst from his UZI killing the terrorist before any of the children could be harmed. Already, dozens of SAYERET fighters had thrown themselves upon the hysterical toddlers to insure that no harm came to them. After evacuating the hostages, the SAYERET raced upstairs, where they encountered the remaining terrorists. In a fanatical struggle which lasted three minutes, the remaining four terrorists were killed.

The outrage at Misgav Am resulted in the death of a resident, a 2-year-old girl, and one SAYERET GOLANI fighter. Following the operation, the relieved residents embraced the young GOLANI soldiers in gratitude, although there was little cause for celebration. Although the rescue operation had indeed been a success, the death of one of their children called for revenge.

Following the incident at Misgav Am, 'Raful' ordered a new IDF initiative against terrorism, incorporating air, land and sea attacks. While the IAF flew sorties against training camps, and IDF/Navy missile craft shelled coastal targets and DABUR patrol craft, dozens of commando raids were carried out by Naval Commando, paratroop and GOLANI units. This pre-emptive policy was highy successful, literally eliminating the terrorists' capability to cross the Lebanese border, and forcing them to conventionalize their forces and engage Israel with Katyusha barrages. SAYERET GOLANI, however, remained obsessed by the idea of settling the score with the ALF.

▼ SAYERET GOLANI rescuers re-enact their assault on the Arab Liberation Front-held nursery at KIBBUTZ Misgav Am, 6 April 1980.(IDF Spokesman)

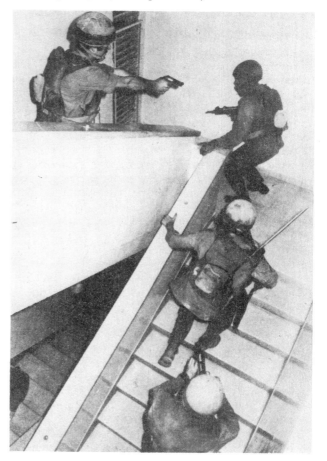

For months following the Misgav Am attack, GOLANI Brigade OC, Colonel A., urged A'MAN to locate the ALF's headquarters in southern Lebanon for a retaliatory raid. In February 1981, Colonel A. received word that the ALF intelligence and operations base was located on the Nabatiyah Heights in the Christian village of El-Kfur; population 1,350. The ALF HQ was a house which held the ALF Battalion command centre, and more than twenty terrorists, complete with advanced communication equipment, and heavy weaponry. The IDF computer code-named the house '183', and its destruction was entrusted to Captain Harnik.

After careful planning, it was decided to assault the village by landing a heliborne force five kilometres from EL-Kfur. The attack force would be divided into three sections:

'Force A', was to be led by SAYERET GOLANI Commander, Captain Harnik, and would consist of the best officers from the unit, whose mission was the destruction of 'House 183'.

'Force B', another force of SAYERET GOLANI fighters which would seal off the village, and ensure that no reinforcements would interfere with the operation, while also providing covering fire for the assault teams.

'Force C', a diversionary and ambush force commanded by GOLANI OC, Colonel A. was to establish an ambush on the Zaharani-Zifta road leading to El-Kfur, and destroy any vehicle heading towards the operation. Colonel A. was also in command of artillery, naval and air units.

The fighters chosen for this operation were the best that SAYERET GOLANI could field (NCOs and officers). Before each mission, there was always stiff competition in the SAYERET's camp to see which fighters would be ultimately picked. For avenging Misgav Am, however, Captain Harnik decided to risk bruising a few egos and take with him to El-Kfur only the best.

At approximately 19.00 hours on 22 February 1981, the three Bell 205 helicopters ferrying the attack force reached the landing zone inside Lebanon. While the ambush force headed for the high ground above the Zaharani-Zifta road, Captain Harnik assembled his men and led them towards the ALF HQ in a forced march. Each fighter carried extra ammunition and sacks of high-explosives, and the mountainous terrain made the march arduous. Approximately half an hour later, 'Force B' was in covering position, while Captain Harnik divided his men into small squads. The men had had more than ten months to train for this raid, and they were determined not to return home empty-handed.

At 22.00 hours the assault commenced. While the covering force provided rifle-grenade and 7.62mm machine-gun fire, Captain Harnik's squad raced towards 'House 183'. The ALF gunmen poured heavy fire on to GOLANI's advance, and a pitched battle developed. Two members of Captain Harnik's team had managed to throw their loads of explosives into '183' and, as they ran for cover, an RPG round smashed a hole through the northern wall. Seconds later the building disintegrated in a cloud of dust and debris. Determined fire was now directed from an adjacent house ('House 182'), and Captain Harnik ordered it destroyed as well. Files were gathered from the rubble and intermittent gunfire continued, as the SAYERET fighters fired at any moving target.

Colonel A.'s ambush force had had an eventless, though anxious night, 'identifying' numerous targets though engaging none. At 01.00 hours they linked up with Captain Harnik's men, and by 01.30 they were already on board their helicopters bound for Israel, although followed by determined Palestinian anti-aircraft fire. The results of Operation 'House 183' were impressive. The ALF had suffered between 6-10 dead, and the destruction of their HQ. SAYERET GOLANI left El-Kfur unscathed, having avenged the loss of their comrade ten months earlier. Although a cause for celebration, the raid would not be SAYERET GOLANI's last foray into Lebanon.

9

'PEACE FOR GALILEE' AND THE QUAGMIRE OF DESTRUCTION:
Operations in Lebanon, 1982 to the present

INTO THE CEDARS OF LEBANON: OPERATIONS DURING THE CONVENTIONAL WAR, JUNE TO SEPTEMBER 1982

'Our objective is Lebanon!'
Defence Minister 'Arik' Sharon, December 1981

FOR years Lebanon had been a sideshow to the Middle East's wars. The emergence of the Palestinians and Syrians as the dominant military powers in Lebanon following the bloody civil war, led Israel to develop a close-knit relationship with the country's Maronite Christian Phalangists. The two found a harmonizing chord in their plight against the 'Muslim' Middle East, and soon impressive amounts of economic and military aid began to flow north of the border. The military power of the Palestinian movements inside Lebanon coupled with the intangible results of Operation 'Litani' persuaded many Israelis that eventually the Palestinian military infrastructure in Lebanon must be eradicated. Numerous MOSSAD reports advocating a further investment in the Phalangists' political/military control of Lebanon, coupled with the naming of 'Arik' Sharon as Israel's Defence Minister in 1981, virtually sealed Lebanon's fate. All that was needed was time to 'train' the army, and a spark!

In 1982 the IDF had the mightiest army Israel had ever fielded. Commanded by two of the most decisive men in Israel's military history, TZAHAL (Acronym for TZAVA HAGANAH L'YISRAEL or Israel Defence Forces) was equipped with the world's best and most modern weaponry, and manned by the world's best and most battle-experienced officer corps. Since the 1973 War, the standing conscript army had expanded by 131 percent to a strength of 172,000, while tripling its armour and me-

chanized elements. The Israeli-Egyptian Peace Treaty of 1982, together with the benign border with Jordan allowed the IDF to concentrate its forces along the northern frontier, deterring any possible Syrian and Palestinian moves. While more dire threats to Israel's security were removed, most notably the IAF's brilliantly executed raid against the Iraqi OSIRAK nuclear reactor on 7 June 1981, the dangers posed by Lebanon were not forgotten. The Syrians' positioning of fourteen SAM-6 batteries in the Beka'a Valley, and the PLO's Katyusha offensive against Galilee in 1981 guaranteed an Israeli military response.

On 3 June 1982, Israel's Ambassador to the court of St James's was seriously wounded in a failed 'Abu-Nidal' assassination plot in London. Although not directly responsible for the attack, the Israelis nevertheless pointed blame at the PLO, and responded with massive aerial retaliatory strikes against PLO Headquarters in Beirut. The PLO countered by determined Katyusha barrages into the northern settlements, to which the Israelis replied with air and artillery strikes. The time for a decisive showdown with the PLO was at hand. On 5 June, the Israeli cabinet met and decided to act militarily. At 11.00 hours on 6 June, a bright summer's day, a 60,000-man Israeli force invaded Lebanon. Operation 'Peace for Galilee', Israel's longest and most controversial war, was under way.

The IDF had originally prepared three pre-war invasion scenarios of Lebanon: a repeat of Operation 'Litani';

Operation 'Little Pines' which sanctioned an IDF thrust forty kilometres into Lebanon to push the Katyushas out of range of Israel's northern frontier, and lastly, Operation 'Big Pines', an all-out invasion of Lebanon, calling for IDF forces to occupy a large chunk of the Lebanon including Beirut and the Syrian-controlled Beka'a Valley. In the end, 'Big Pines' was chosen (although during the first days of the fighting, the Israeli Government promised it would not exceed the 40-kilometre boundary). As always, the success of the operation depended on speed, firepower and the IDF's élite forces in the vanguard.

The GOLANI Brigade, no stranger to Lebanon, was divided into two principal forces for Operation 'Peace for Galilee'. The first, commanded by Brigade OC, Colonel A., consisted of the GIDEON Battalion, together with elements of ARAYOT HAGOLAN, and a small contingent from SAYERET GOLANI. They were attached to UGDAH, a mixed mechanized infantry/paratroop and armoured division commanded by Brigadier-General Yitzhak Mordechai (the HA'AN TZANHANIM veteran), and were entrusted with clearing the coastal sector of Palestinian and Leftist Muslim resistance, assisting an amphibious force of paratroopers from the conscript Paratroop Brigade to seize Sidon, and eventually capture Beirut International Airport. The second half of the GOLANI Brigade was under the command of deputy brigade commander Lieutenant-Colonel Gabi, and attached to Brigadier-General Avigdor Kahalani's mixed armour and infantry division UGDAH. The force consisted of the HABOK'IM HARISHONIM Battalion, HA'AN GOLANI (a sapper company organized along the lines of its paratroop counterpart) and SAYERET GOLANI. They were entrusted with the seizure of the Arnoun Heights, and linking up with Brigadier-General Mordechai's division at Sidon for the push towards Beirut. But first, they had to remove the monster!

Known by its Arabic name of *Kala'at-e-shkif*, the ancient Crusader castle of Beaufort controlled the Arnoun Heights, and much of Israeli Galilee with its 717-metre high perch. PLO artillery spotters had long used the castle as an observation post and artillery fire base in what they considered an impregnable position. The mountain on which it sits is inaccessible except from a northern approach, which was heavily fortified and defended by the PLO's *Kastel* Brigade.* In addition, the PLO had rebuilt parts of the castle, and further fortified them with gun positions, and trenches to complement the existing network of underground passages, tunnels and bunkers. The IAF had paid several visits to the 'monster', but with few results. In the end, Beaufort was given to SAYERET GOLANI.

SAYERET GOLANI were no strangers to Beaufort Castle. For years before the 1982 invasion, Northern Command had planned Beaufort's capture, and they assigned the mission to the best unit under its command. The castle had in fact become something of an obsession to SAYERET chief Captain Harnik, and training for the mission became SAYERET GOLANI's extra-curricular activity. The unit sat through films of the position shot by the RPVs (Remote Piloted Vehicles), in which overviews of the castle's fortifications, communications and trench systems, as well as possible Palestinian escape routes were studied with fervour. Hundreds of hours had been spent in training t assault the 'monster', and Captain Harnik had seasoned hi men to instinctive reactions, with tactics to counter an scenario. The SAYERET fighters expected Beaufort to b hard-fought, but little realized the price they would hav to pay.

Actually, the invasion routes laid down in Operation 'Big Pines' meant that Beaufort would be bypassed. Clearly any push towards Beirut and the Beka'a could hav ignored the token resistance Beaufort would be expected t display. OC, Northern Command, Major-General Ami Drori (the GOLANI OC in 1973, a man quite aware of th dangers of directing battles based purely on *unit pride* and Chief of Staff 'Raful' had in fact issued specific order postponing SAYERET GOLANI's assault until the first day fighting had stabilized. These orders, however, were 'mys teriously lost' in communications channels, and the attac was on.

The original plan called for the SAYERET to be ferried t the castle by M113 APCs supported by a platoon o Centurion MBTs following an extensive IAF and artiller softening-up barrage. While the SAYERET's assault com menced, a 65-man force from HA'AN GOLANI was to captur the ammunition dump complex on the mountain's sout side. H-Hour was set for 11.00 hours, the time of the initia invasion, although a massive traffic-jam of APCs and tank along the narrow Nabatiyah road prevented the SAYERE from reaching the Beaufort vicinity until 16.00 hours Although this would force the attack to take place unde cover of darkness, the prospect caused little concern SAYERET GOLANI fighters were expert night-fighters, an had trained for such a scenario.

The assault was led by Lieutenant Motti Goldman an Captain Harnik. Captain Harnik had been until one wee before the war the SAYERET's commander, and was i 'limbo', awaiting his discharge from active serivce. He ha served the brigade admirably for years in a wide assort ment of posts within the brigade, including squad an platoon commander, brigade operations officer, and finall leader of the SAYERET. So when Captain Harnik learned tha his unit was going into action, he donned his uniform fetched his gear and headed across the border. Learn ing that his replacement, Captain Kaplinski, had bee wounded, Captain Harnik persuasively commandeere an M113 to his unit's column after receiving a 'forma invitation to the war by the brigade OC. After crossin the River Litani by the Akiye Bridge together wit Lieutenant-Colonel Gabi's command group, he appro ached the column of twenty APCs, and came on the unit' radio frequency to announce to the nervous fighters som

*Knowing that the IDF intended to invade Lebanon, PLO Chairman Yas Arafat was able to organize three conventional brigades in 1981 from th various PLO factions: the *Yarmouk, Karameh* and *Yarmouk*. Each con sisted of approximately 2,500 fighters.

very familiar words of comfort: 'KUDKUD NOKEM', 'Vengeance Calling', Captain Harnik's old radio call sign.

On the move, Captain Harnik assembled his fighters, and separated them into squads according to the 'old' training methods he had designed and perfected. The original plan called for a mechanized assault, but twilight made that a very risky undertaking, so he opted instead for a charge on foot. The columns proceeded to within 200 metres of the positions. After making sure that his men were ready, Captain Harnik ordered the M113s to turn on their headlights, and ordered his men to charge!

The SAYERET fighters leapt from the safety of their M113s and proceeded to attack along a stretch of tarmac road towards the first line of defences along the northern ridge; with war cries, and incessant bursts from their GLILON (short-barrelled version of the 5.56mm GALIL rifle) and AK-47 assault rifles. Many of the *Kastel* Brigade defenders had already realized their dire situation and fled, but those who remained fought with suicidal determination. A vicious fire-fight broke out as the GOLANI soldiers were forced to 'purify' each bunker and trench with grenades and automatic fire. Due to the ferocity of the battle, most of the attackers ran out of ammunition early on, even though they had carried extra supplies against such a possibility. As a result, Palestinian and GOLANI dead were stripped of their weapons and packs. Conventional weapons proved of little use, however, as grenades failed to even scratch the thick stone and cement walls, so satchel charges were used.

The battle raged for hours. The fighting in the labyrinth of caves and passageways showed the SAYERET fighters only too well how little use their training films had been. The extent to which the Palestinians had reinforced and fortified their defences became painfully clear. The Palestinians were capable defenders, maximizing their well-concealed RPG and RPK machine-gun nests. They had taken their toll of the attacking GOLANI fighters, inflicting heavy casualties on the small force. After six hours of non-stop fighting, only one surviving machine-gun post remained. Captain Harnik and Lieutenant Goldman closed in on the position. While one threw a grenade, the other would race for cover firing bursts from his automatic. More than twenty fragmentation grenades were thrown at the gun position, but with little effect. Suddenly, a Palestinian gunner emerged from a hidden passageway and fired a burst at 'Guni', hitting him in the chest. Infuriated though undaunted, Goldman charged wildly, firing his GLILON while simultaneously hurling a satchel charge at the position, destroying it in a fiery burst. This action brought Goldman a bravery citation from the Chief of Staff, and ended the life of one of SAYERET GOLANI's most beloved commanders, a man who had known the joys of civilian life for only one short week.

After dealing with escaping *Kastel* Brigade fighters, Goldman was finally able to report Beaufort Castle secure at 06.30 hours on 7 June. The battle, a side-show to the larger situation developing, had been extremely costly

▲ Major-General Ze'ev Almog, the ex-Naval Commando chief, and OC IDF/Navy during the 1982 Lebanon War. (IGPO)

for SAYERET GOLANI. Seven of the unit's best, including Captain Harnik, had been killed, and fifteen seriously wounded. In retrospect, it can be seen as the tragic culmination of Captain Harnik's personal war against Beaufort, in which man fought mountain, and mountain won. Bitter, and numbed, the seasoned veterans of SAYERET GOLANI rejoined the brigade for points beyond. While the SAYERET headed towards Jezzine, the BARAK Battalion continued its advance into the Beka'a Valley, baiting the Syrian presence. The day after the 'monster' had fallen, with great pomp and ceremony Prime Minister Begin and Defence Minister Sharon handed over the castle to Major Haddad's ragtag militia. Chief of Staff 'Raful' was also in attendance, but he looked on in silence, outraged by the cost of its capture. To the small family of SAYERET GOLANI, the death of one of their own could never constitute a victory, only a loss!

Brigadier-General Kahalani's division continued its advance through the Nabatiyah highlands, then swung north-west in a classic pincer movement towards Sidon, where the division was to link up with elements of Chief

Paratroop and Infantry Officer, Brigadier-General Amos Yaron's (of Jerusalem, and AVIV NEORIM fame) mixed force of paratroopers and tanks from Brigadier-General Yaron's force as well as Brigadier-General Mordechai's division. It had fought a lightning campaign along the coastal sector, destroying most pockets of Palestinian resistance, while at the same time bypassing the major refugee camps in and around the port city of Tyre which were to be mopped up by the paratroops and GOLANI.

For years, the KOMMANDO YAMI had conducted their own unique covert intelligence and 'elimination' campaign against Palestinian targets along the Lebanese shore. On the morning of 7 June, a KOMMANDO YAMI task force* landed at a point due north of the mouth of the River Awali. After clearing Palestinian forces from the area, they signalled to an IDF/Navy Missile Boat to send the next wave of fighters, amphibious elements from SAYERET TZAN- HANIM, which was to expand the bridgehead, and deploy in ambush position to cover the mission's main protagonists, the vanguard of Brigadier-General Yaron's division, the conscript Paratroop Brigade commanded by Colonel Yoram 'Ya-Ya' Yair. It would be the largest amphibious operation in IDF/Navy history, and would bring the paratroops to their first, and hardest fought battle in Lebanon.

Since late on the night of 6 June, the depleted conscript Paratroop Brigade, centred around the NA'HA'L Battalion, had been en route to Sidon on the IDF/Navy's obsolete though still seaworthy fleet of landing craft. The 'calm' seas had taken their toll of many of the paratroopers, and while they vomited into buckets, the seasoned sailors looked on curiously. Wearing life-jackets, the paratroopers and their M113s were the first to land, followed by supporting tank units. The landings on the whole were uneventful. The IAF and IDF/Navy had kept the pressure up with strafing runs and shellings, and except for token Katyusha fire, the Palestinians failed to respond to the ominous Israeli move. Lulled into self-confidence by the ease of the landings, the IDF forces continued on to Sidon and the adjacent Ein el-Hilweh refugee camp, where the Palestinians had a surprise in store.

The Sidon/Ein el-Hilweh salient would not be an easy victory. Seven years earlier, when intervening on behalf of Lebanon's endangered Christian forces, it had taken the élite of the Syrian Army more than a month to clear Ein el-Hilweh of an armed Palestinian presence. The vicious street-to-street, and house-to-house fighting resulted in hundreds of dead and wounded, and ended only when

ZSU-34 anti-aircraft guns were brought into root out sniper positions. Unlike Beaufort Castle, and Mount Hermon, and the 'Chinese Farm' in the previous war, the Ein el-Hilweh camp was not a battlefield, but a neighbourhood filled with innocent civilians. 'Raful' had issued strict orders that civilian casualties be kept to a minimum. Although this adhered to the TOHAR HANESHEK 'purity of arms' ethic, and indeed many Israeli soldiers risked their lives to save Lebanese and Palestinian non-combatants, it eliminated the use of heavy fire-power in the built-up areas, and ensured increased Israeli casualties. As always, the difficult tasks fell to the élite forces, but nothing in their training had prepared them for Ein el-Hilweh.

Together with the NA'HA'L Paratroop Battalion, SAYERET TZANHANIM and various reservist paratroop form- ations, the attack on Sidon-Ein el-Hilweh was led by GOLANI's 'first' force, commanded by the Brigade's OC. The assault into the camp was led by the GIDEON Battalion, flanked by half of the SAYERET, and supporting armour. The capture of the salient was entrusted to Brigadier- General Kahalani who, recalling the grievous loss of life endured by his famous OZ 77th Battalion on the Golan Heights in 1973, urged Colonel A. to minimize casualties at all costs. As a result, Colonel A. ordered that Ein el- Hilweh be 'eaten slowly', block by block, house by house, room by room, without any time limitation. It would be a task not easily fulfilled. Even though the IDF Training Branch had implemented urban combat and street- fighting training to all infantry and paratroop units, no- thing could have prepared them for the battle to come. As many GOLANI soldiers would comment after the battle: 'if a soldier ever wants to know the meaning of fear, let him visit Ein el-Hilweh!'

The GOLANI effort began with a concentrated infantry assault through the southern entrance to the camp, hoping to clear a route for Kahalani's armour. As the lead units from the GIDEON Battalion entered the concentrated squalor, they soon realized why it had taken the Syrians so long to accomplish the same. The camp was defended by the fanatic fringe from numerous Palestinian terror fac- tions, who were quite willing to martyr themselves against the loathed Israelis. The close proximity of the stone and concrete houses, coupled with a series of heavily fortified bunkers and machine-gun posts turned every block into a major fortress. The battle, fought at close range, and often with fists and rocks, lasted well into the night, without any significant GOLANI breakthrough. The young GOLANI con- scripts were horrified by the Palestinians' use of their own civilians as hostages, and by their shooting of the faint- hearted wishing to surrender. Tanks and five battalions of self-propelled artillery were called in to root out sniper nests at point-blank range, although the process was tedious, and costly. Numerous vehicles were hit by 14- year-old *Ashbal* (lion cub) terrorists firing RPG-7s.

◄▲ Paratroopers from the 35th Brigade take a quick snooze aboard an IDF/Navy landing craft on 7 June 1982, hours before the landing near Sidon. (IDF Spokesman)

◄ Recon paratroop units assault a terrorist stronghold during the battle for the Ein el-Hilweh refugee camp, 8 June 1982. (IMoD)

*In 1982, the IDF/Navy was commanded by the KOMMANDO YAMI veteran, Major-General Zeev Almog.

The assault was renewed at 08.00 hours on 8 June. The IAF began an aerial offensive against the salient, but this gave little result. The GOLANI fighters soon discovered the extent of the defensive arrangements protecting Ein el-Hilweh, as the Palestinians were fighting from well-concealed and camouflaged positions connected by an underground network of passages and embrasures. Realizing that massive doses of fire-power were needed, the IDF offered the civilians a chance to escape towards the sea. Many of the camp's defenders shed their lizard pattern camouflage uniforms, only to slip back into their defensive positions at twilight. GOLANI's sputtering advance was halted in the heart of the camp by a well-organized anti-tank position, and once again the attackers were forced to retreat and start afresh the following morning. Colonel A. did not want to fight such a determined resistance at night, and on unfamiliar territory.

On 9 June, although Ein el-Hilweh was far from secure, the main Israeli emphasis centred around the paratroops' efforts for Sidon. Brigadier-General Kahalani's division had been ordered to speed north, and responsibility for the salient was transferred to Brigadier-General Yitzhak Mordechai, a veteran of the close-quarter fighting at 'Chinese Farm'. Mordechai's division were veterans of the battle for Tyre, and its surrounding refugee camps, and a fresh approach was applied to Ein el-Hilweh and Sidon. The camp was divided into grids, and each grid was to be purified in systematic order, which enabled the GOLANIs to concentrate fire-power. To reinforce the GOLANI infantrymen, units from Colonel 'Ya-Ya' Yair's 35th Paratroop Brigade were heli-lifted from the advance on Damour back south to help end the fighting in Ein el-Hilweh and Sidon.

Brigadier-General Mordechai's tactics worked. While the beleaguered GOLANI forces opened the main road into the camp, and inched their way towards victory, Yair's Paratroop Brigade was busy clearing out Sidon in the same fashion. Paratroopers were sent into the *casbah*, although they were ordered to steer clear of protracted fire-fights, and always to follow closely behind bulldozers which had been called in to clear the narrow streets for tank movement. Three days later Sidon was declared secure; best indicated by the fact that EL AL opened an office in the city, issuing airline tickets to anyone with the cash to escape the fighting. Fighting continued however in Ein el-Hilweh.

Although the GOLANI attackers were ordered to follow their tanks and APCs into battle, most opted to advance on foot, preferring not to become easy prey for RPGs and anti-tank missiles. When heavy resistance was encountered, tank, artillery and IAF support was called in. As the battle developed, it became clear that the Ein el-Hilweh's defence was not led by PLO officers, but by a Shi'ite Muslim cleric named Haj Ibrahim, who incited the defenders into zealous and suicidal determination. The IDF even brought in psychologists to reason with the remaining defenders, but they were greeted by the battle cry 'Victory or death.' As the fighting drew to a end, napalm attacks were ordered against areas cleared of civilians. Slowly the GOLANI noose tightened, and on 12 June, Colonel A. ordered the final assault. After fierce fighting, the camp's central bunker fell, followed by Haj Ibrahim's mosque HQ. On 14 June, the camp was finally cleansed of armed resistance. The Palestinians had indeed fought to the death, and in the week's bloodletting, the GOLANI Brigade suffered heavy casualties. The continued IDF advance north towards Beirut, however, signalled an expansion of the hostilities.

The IDF's efforts in central and eastern Lebanon made war with Syria inevitable. While a mixed mechanized and armoured division commanded by Brigadier Menachem Einan thrust into the Shouf Mountains to cut off the Beirut-Damascus Highway, two other divisions pushed into 'FATAHLAND', to cut off any possible Palestinian or 'Syrian' retreat. Yet in the vanguard of this effort was 'KOACH PELED' ('Force Peled'), a mixed armour, infantry, paratroop and helicopter force commanded by Brigadier-General Yossi Peled and coordinated into an anti-tank spearhead. Centred around the Paratroop Brigade's anti-tank force.* KOACH PELED also consisted of two *ad hoc* armour reconnaissance forces, and two squadrons of Bell-209 Cobras, and Hughes Defender 500 helicopters. KOACH

▼◄ Heavily laden paratroopers from Colonel Yoram 'Ya Ya' Yair's Paratroop Brigade board a CH-53 north of Sidon, for the quick flight to the close-quarters battle at Ein el-Hilweh. (IDF Spokesman)

▼ Carrying his kitbag and DRAGON ATGW, paratrooper David Cohen prepares to be heli-lifted to Ein el-Hilweh. (IDF Spokesman)

PELED's main task was the destruction of Syrian armour in the Beka'a Valley, a task it was well equipped to accomplish. This anti-tank force was armed with a wide array of weaponry, including the soldier's personal RPG-7s, LAWs, and DRAGON ATGW and the squad and platoon jeeps and M113s fitted with the venerable TOW anti-tank missile. It is important to note that as the Syrian-IDF clashes grew into open warfare, both the Syrian and Israeli tankers fought courageously and effectively. Although the Israeli tank gunners destroyed scores of Syrian tanks, most were destroyed by the élite paratroopers' missiles. A fact underscored by the heavy toll Syrian commandos equipped with similar weaponry exacted from IDF armour.

Wednesday 9 June was a momentous day for the fighting in the eastern sector. On 8/9 June the 188th BARAK Armoured Brigade was engulfed in a well-executed Syrian ambush in the village of Ein Zehalta. A fierce battle raged, while SAYERET OREV units raced along the mountain roads to outflank and defeat the Syrian noose. Although they succeeded in destroying numerous T-62s, air support was urgently needed to extricate the BARAK Brigade. The presence of nineteen SAM sites in the Beka'a Valley made such an undertaking quite risky. Defense Minister Sharon, who had taken personal control of the conflict, ordered the destruction of the missiles.

The IAF's air raid on the missile sites, and the ensuing dog-fights in which more than eighty Syrian MiGs were blown out of the sky, have entered folklore, owing to the IAF's skill, technical mastery, and supreme human courage. Yet the IAF was not the only force conducting spectacular operations. On 9 June, GOLANI's HABOK'IM HARISHONIM Battalion and a force from SAYERET GOLANI captured the Syrian/Soviet ELINT station high on Jebel Barouk, the highest peak in the area, controlling the entire Beka'a Valley. In an attack reminiscent of the legendary battle for Mount Hermon in 1973, the HABOK'IM HARISHONIM and SAYERET fighters climbed the steep cliffs, and after engaging a well-entrenched Syrian defence, seized the position. Fierce tank and infantry battles raged all along the Beka'a front, most notably at Sultan Yakoub, and the Beirut-Damascus Highway at Ain Dara.

▲◄ Paratroopers on the road to Damour pause to receive instructions from battalion command, June 1982. The 'unconventional' nature of much of the Lebanese fighting suited the élite forces' capabilities perfectly. (IMoD).

▲ SAYERET GOLANI makes its cautious way through the graveyard of airliner skeletons at Beirut International Airport, 1 August 1982. (IDF Spokesman-Ligad Rotlevi)

Also making an appearance was SAYERET SHAKED, which by 1982 had converted to a mechanized strike battalion. It had not seen combat since 1973, and its last operation was the removal of fanatical orthodox Jewish settlers from the Sinai settlement on Yamit, before it was returned to Egypt in April 1982. Nevertheless, the SAYERET fought impressively, protecting IDF armour from Syrian armour and commando attack in Hasibiyah, Kfar as-Zait, Kfar Kuk, and Ein Hilweh (not to be confused with the refugee camp), as well as conducting numerous pursuit operations against Syrian commandos. The small unit suffered heavy losses, including the deputy battalion commander, Major Udi Vinter, killed while leading a rescue attempt of a wounded tanker. After the war, SAYERET SHAKED returned to Southern Command, where it would develop into the nucleus of the reborn GIVA'ATI Infantry Brigade.

With the IDF's success in beating the Syrians into submission, the emphasis of the war soon shifted in dramatic fashion towards the Lebanese capital; the IDF's first ever offensive against an Arab capital city. Yet while the IDF advance on Beirut, the 'Mecca' of Palestinian terrorist movements, proceeded beyond anyone's wildest projections, Syrian and Palestinian forces in and around the capital began to resist with a vengeance. The IDF had got almost to the gates of Beirut, even though the promised Christian military participation never materialized. Clearly the fighting was going be the IDF's sole responsibility, and the advance continued.

---

*Although anti-tank operations were the responsibility of the Armoured Corps, SAYERET SHIRION, lessons learned in the 1973 fighting proved the importance of élite *infantry* forces equipped with portable anti-tank weapons.

One of the main obstacles along the road to Beirut was the exclusive suburb of Kfar Sil, just east of the airport. Lined with villas, complete with swimming-pools, foreign servants and Mercedes in the driveway, Kfar Sil was not only home to Beirut's upper crust, but also to most of the influential Palestinian and Syrian commanders in Lebanon. It was defended by a strong force of 'crack' *el-Fatah* regulars from 'FORCE 17', a company of Syrian-sponsored *as-Saiqa* Palestinian fighters, as well as a combined force of twenty-eight Syrian T-54s, and a company of commandos for good measure, armed with a wide variety of anti-tank missiles. Kfar Sil was a wall of resistance blocking any the IDF armour advance into south-west Beirut. The threat had to be removed – a task assigned to GOLANI, and a battalion of paratroopers.

The battle for Kfar Sil, described by Chief of Staff 'Raful' as the most brutal of the war, began on Thursday 10 June in the ultra-exclusive playground neighbourhood of Dokha whence the Syrians hit a column of advancing IDF armour with deadly accuracy. Massive aerial and artillery bombardments were called in, and the attack resumed on Saturday with the GIDEON Battalion, SAYERET GOLANI and paratrooper attack force. While the paratroops were entrusted with silencing a small ridge known as 'Radar Hill', the GOLANI and armour force was sent into Kfar Sil's built-up area. Their initial advance was greeted by a murderous hail of small arms and anti-tank fire. At ranges of less than four metres, GOLANI and Syrian soldiers attempted to throw grenades into each other's tank turrets. The fighting was fought in such close proximity, that Syrian soldiers often ended up in Israeli positions, and vice versa.

To terminate the battle quickly before casualties mounted, the GIDEON Battalion was ordered to clear the right-hand section of the main thoroughfare, and the SAYERET the left-hand side. The battle for the main street, a stretch of road barely a kilometre long, took the two battalions more than nineteen hours of incessant fighting to complete. For many, these were the longest nineteen hours of their lives; for many others, they were their last hours. As always, the officers were the first casualties, effective leadership being transferred to junior officers and NCOs. They led their subordinates first against the commandos and Palestinian regulars, and then against the T-54s. Their most effective weapon was the LAW rocket which turned the Syrian T-54s into flaming hunks of steel. On the morning of 13 June, the battle died down, as the village, its junction, and command of Beirut International Airport were under GOLANI control, although dozens of GOLANI fighters lay dead and maimed. The road to Beirut was now open!

The victory at Kfar Sil signalled the end of the first stage of Operation 'Peace for Galilee', and marked the beginning of the next bloody campaign: the siege of Beirut. The success of the siege, sealed by an IDF/Navy blockade, and a link-up of IDF and Phalangist forces in Christian East Beirut, now depended on the cutting off of the strategic Beirut-Damascus Highway where GOLANI and paratroop forces were fighting fiercely; the most intensive fighting taking place at Ba'abda, Behamdoun and Aley. The ambiguity of the Israeli Government's statement of objectives, led many, mainly among the élite GOLANI and paratroop forces, to question orders and tactics. Already the war was morally questionable, and it was felt by many that the IDF was being used for reasons not directly connected with Israel's immediate national security. This uneasiness was best expressed on 24 June when Defence Minister Sharon intended to visit a reservist paratroop battalion which had seized a section of the highway after suffering extremely heavy losses. The visit was prevented by a division commander, Brigadier-General Menachem Einan, who knew of his men's hostile sentiments. Sharon visited GOLANI instead!

The final élite force operation during the siege of Beirut was GOLANI's capture of Beirut International Airport on 1 August 1982. The neighbourhood surrounding the airport was a maze of tightly packed slum dwellings where the Palestinians made use of the built-up area for defence. Initial GOLANI attempts to advance were answered by murderous barrages of anti-tank fire. Rather than risk heavy casualties in a protracted fight, as had been suffered in Ein el-Hilweh, SAYERET GOLANI was ordered in. Treating each enemy position as if it were a building where hostages were being held, SAYERET GOLANI systematically assaulted each apartment block, house, and room from where fire was directed. The tiresome strategy paid off, and the brigade proceeded to seize the airport.

On 19 August, the PLO and Syrians agreed to evacuate Beirut. Under the supervision of a multi-national force from the United States, France, and Italy, 14,398 Palestinian fighters and Syrian soldiers were evacuated by sea and land (through the Beirut-Damascus Highway). On 23 August, elections were held in Lebanon, and as expected, Bashir Gemayel was elected President by an overwhelming majority. Events indicated that Israel's June invasion had been a striking military and political success. On 2 September, the GOLANI Brigade marked its withdrawal from the southern sector of the city with an impressive military ceremony on the International Airport's apron. Colonel A. paid homage to the brigade's sacrifices and achievements, and informed his brigade of their pending positioning elsewhere in Lebanon as a preamble to their return to Israel. As the Israeli and GOLANI flags were lowered from the airport, many of the assembled fighters sighed with relief to be leaving such a dreadful place. Their joy was to be premature.

On 14 September, a bomb placed by the Syrian Socialist Nationalist Party (SSNP) at Phalangist HQ killed President-elect Gemayel. The vengeance-crazed Phalangists blamed the Palestinians, and attacked the refugee camps of Sabra and Shatilla, murdering hundreds of the inhabitants. With the two weeks' of Lebanese law and order shattered, the IDF moved into West Beirut. The second Lebanon War had begun!

THE IRON FIST: OPERATIONS DURING THE UNCONVENTIONAL WAR, OCTOBER 1982 TO THE PRESENT

'I am protecting Galilee.'
A GOLANI Company Commander, Lebanon 1985

BY October 1982, Israel's four-month war in Lebanon had cost the IDF 368 dead. As at the present, the IDF has suffered well over 700 dead, and Israel's continued presence has had little effect on Lebanon's continuing internal strife. Palestinian fought Palestinian, and ruling Lebanese Christians fought leftist Muslims, Shi'ite fundamentalists and scorned Druze in an all-out civil war which rivalled the 1975–76 conflict in its carnage. Lebanon's continued nonentity status guaranteed Israel a non-secure northern frontier, and resulted in the IDF's subsequent occupation of Lebanon. Israel's segmented occupation of Lebanon, which continues to this day, by the establishment of an 11-mile-wide security belt north of the Israeli border, is characterized by a savage guerrilla war waged by Shi'ite Muslims, who in June 1982 ironically embraced the IDF as saviours and heroes. The Khomeini disciples were joined by their traditional nemesis, though 'brothers in arms' against the hated Israelis; Palestinian terrorists who returned to their strongholds in southern Lebanon in the wake of IDF withdrawals. In such an unconventional war, where the rules of engagement are ambiguous, armour and artillery forces proved of little value. It was an infantryman's war, one where GOLANI, paratroop, and the IDF's other élite forces fought an incessant campaign to survive.

Israel's initial involvement in Lebanon produced a dire problem few IDF commanders could have envisaged, which also provided a glimpse into the unique operational style of a hitherto unsung 'Israeli' élite force. During the IDF invasion, thousands of Palestinian and leftist Muslim terrorists shed their uniforms to blend into the civilian and refugee populace. The 60,000-man IDF force in Lebanon soon found itself engulfed in pursuit and investigative duties it was neither trained nor equipped to execute. As a result, IDF division commanders turned to the only 'Israeli' force capable of meeting such a challenge, the National Police's 'infantry' – the Border Guard.

Formed in 1950, the Border Guard (MISHMAR HAGVUL) is a professional, paramilitary police force entrusted with securing Israel's frontiers as well as its ports of entries, public venues, and areas of sensitive security. Although a police force, service in the Border Guard is considered as fulfillment of the national service requirement. Its ranks, however, remain highly professional, with 87 per cent of its men signing on for years of service. It is also Israel's only truly integrated 'security' service, made up of Jews, Druze,

▼ A GOLANI FN MAG light machine-gunner passing a smiling Lebanese family in South Beirut's suburbs, September 1982 (IGPO)

▲ A 'Northern Company' Border Guard Policeman stands by the treasure of weaponry captured at the hideout of Tyre's *el-Fatah* commander Azmi Zerayer, 26 August 1982. (Courtesy Yoel Barnas)

▼ Members of the Druze minority élite SAYERET HADRUZIM reconnaissance company man positions opposite Syrian lines in the Beka'a Valley, November 1982. (IGPO)

Circassians, Bedouins, and other 'Arab citizen' volunteers. Men are usually assigned to bases close to their community, and an extremely loyal and efficient execution of duties is characteristic of this force. It was the Border Guard that opened the chapter of the 'pursuit', taught to the paratroopers years later, with such chilling effects. Although the Border Guard on the whole can not be considered a combat élite, the National Police High Command dispatched its best units to Lebanon: the élite Northern Companies (20 and 21), and the YA'MA'M anti-terrorist unit; on 15 June they crossed into Lebanon.

What made the Lebanese situation so ideal for the Border Guard was that they were the only Israeli force sufficiently trained in dealing with a civilian populace. Armed with intelligence files and a 'policeman's intuition', the Border Guard companies, distinctive in their green berets, set out through the villages and large towns of southern Lebanon in search of Palestinian terrorists who had escaped the IDF's June onslaught. With an effective 'harsh' reputation preceding them, the Border Guard NCOs were able to 'coerce' information from local civilians, while their knowledge of Arabic gained the trust and admiration of many others. Their results were phenomenal. The approximately two hundred men of the Border Guards were credited with 3,867 of the more than 8,000 Palestinian and Lebanese terrorists captured and sent to detention at the Ansar camp. They also seized 1,169 assault rifles, 187 pistols, seven tons of high-explosives, and hundreds of other items from the terrorist arsenal, ranging from Czechoslovak hunting-rifles to Katyusha rockets.

While many of the Border Guard pursuits yielded small fish, more determined efforts netted senior PLO commanders. Perhaps the most famous 'catch' was that of Tyre's *el-Fatah* battalion commander, Azmi Zerayer who had been high on the Israelis' wanted list for quite some time; his brutal methods having bought him immunity hitherto. 'Northern Company' and YA'MA'M units, however, were hot on the trail, and finally cornered him on 26 August 1982. After seizing a member of Zerayer's entourage and *persuading* him to talk, Border Guard sniper and assault units surrounded Zerayer's hide-out, a deserted villa in a citrus grove. In a lightning assault, Zerayer was literally caught 'with his pants down with a local maiden'; and subsequently killed in the ensuing fire-fight.

The Border Guard's successful campaign also had its price. Dozens became casualties in a determined Palestinian resistance, which included car bombs, and sniping attacks in the *casbahs* of Tyre, Sidon, and the refugee camps. To counter the 'booby trap' threat, the Border Guard called in the services of the National Police bomb-disposal experts, an élite group of professionals who are probably the busiest men in Israel. Responding to more than 3,000 calls a year to examine suspicious objects or complicated Eastern bloc explosive devices, their courage makes the streets of Israel safe from carnage. In Lebanon, they were pushed beyond human limits, defuzing undreds of bombs and explosive devices, saving not only the lives of Israeli forces, but of countless Lebanese civilians as well. Many were awarded citations of valour; some, posthumously. The Border Guard campaign was also marked by two distinctive tragedies. On 11 November, a mysterious explosion destroyed the Border Guard's HQ in Tyre, resulting in more than 34 deaths and scores of wounded. On 1 November 1983 a Shi'ite suicide-bomber, driving a grey Peugot 504 filled with hundreds of kilograms of TNT, crashed through the Border Guard HQ in Tyre. Unlike the attack on the US Marine compound in Beirut days earlier, in which 241 US servicemen were tragically killed, the Israelis had fortified the HQ, and casualties were 'limited' to seventeen dead, and dozens of wounded.

The severe loss in manpower to the Border Guards (55 dead, and 36 wounded) resulted in their eventual withdrawal from Lebanon. Their responsibilities were transferred to GOLANI and paratroop forces (both conscript and reservists), who were also to suffer heavy casualties at the hands of the determined and entrenched Palestinian, leftist, and Shi'ite guerrillas. These élite 'assault' soldiers, reduced to 'patrolling policemen' amid a hostile population became known as the 'Tyre Generation'. Unlike the conventional military campaign fought in Lebanon from June to October 1982, this 'occupation' was not only politically unclear but militarily harsh. Although the IDF remains an apolitical body, the political nature of the IDF presence led to erosion of support at home, and increased feelings of isolation among the forces serving inside Lebanon. Lesser units would have been unable to deal with the strain, but the 'Tyre Generation' remained resolute.

A routine GOLANI or paratroop patrol consisted of a squad of heavily armed and armoured soldiers, supported by mechanized vehicles. They were under strict orders to keep the peace, eliminate guerrilla activity and, most importantly, secure the lines of communications. The latter proved a most difficult task, as well-concealed explosive devices placed on the sides of roads took almost as heavy a toll as had been endured during the invasion of Lebanon itself. The troops responded with ambushes reminiscent of the SAYERET EGOZ era along the northern frontier in the 1970s, where small units interdicted the terrorists' ability to reach Israel.

The occupation of Lebanon provided these élite units with an opportunity to train in all too realistic surroundings. It created for the first time in the IDF's history a situation where junior officers were educated in the 'art of guerrilla warfare' in actual 'hot' zones of operation. Soldiers were taught not to allow civilian cars to pass while a patrol was nearby, and 'to shoot first, and examine evidence later'. It created a whole new breed of élite unit officer and NCO cadre, whose sole objective was to execute a mission while securing their men's safety to the best of their abilities. Although many have criticized this process as a brutalization of the once 'holy' élite force commander,

it minimized casualties amid the suicide-bombers, martyrs, and a local population where the enemy camouflaged itself well. From the initial occupation near Beirut to the withdrawal to the River Litani, and then to the 11-mile-wide security belt, more than 300 GOLANI and paratroop riflemen were killed in this frustrating war!

The last stage of Israel's occupation of southern Lebanon, in which valiant attempts were made to uproot the Shi'ite and Palestinian terror campaign, became known as the 'Iron Fist' policy. It was the continuance of the IDF's long-standing policy of striking against terrorist strongholds in order to ensure the safety of Israeli forces from terrorist attack. It was a throwback to the Jordan Valley 'pursuit' campaign, where small groups of élite infantry forces secured large territories from enemy activity. Israel's 'Iron Fist' in Lebanon continues to this day.

One of the IDF's premier and traditional responses to terrorism in southern Lebanon was the use of aerial bombing and strafing runs using combat aircraft and attack helicopters. Guarding the safety of the invaluable pilots amid the barrages of portable SAM-7 and anti-aircraft guns is the IAF's élite Aeromedical Evacuation Unit (AEU), one of the IDF's finest combat units. This highly secretive unit of airborne rescuers is entrusted with a wide assortment of tasks, ranging from rescuing someone from a deep ravine, to assisting a pregnant Bedouin woman in a remote desert village.* Their main task however remains the rescuing of downed pilots deep behind enemy lines. The unit is a volunteer force of conscripts who usually extend their three years of mandatory service to become career unit members. Besides their extensive medical training, the AEU members undergo a concentrated 'paratroop' infantry basic training, followed by intense specialization courses in amphibious operations, mountain climbing, and survival training in climates and terrains as diverse as the the snowy peaks of Mount Hermon to the blazing sun of the barren desert. Other instruction includes skiing, scuba, cycling, and high-speed 'aggressive' driving techniques.

Although most of the AEU's flight surgeons are reservists, their exposure to civilian medical innovations increases their ability to deal with severe battlefield casualties. Flight medics permitted to volunteer into the AEU are all candidates who have received exemplary grades in advanced medical specialization courses given by the IAF. Yet it is the combat rescuer who has the most arduous task of retrieving the wounded soldier or downed pilot, and securing an evacuation zone from which the AEU helicopter can make a hasty exfiltration. The main helicopter deployed is the Bell-212, though they are trained to use larger craft such as the CH-53, and even fixed-wing C-47, and C-130s. Each AEU craft is equipped

*The AEU's reputation made them favourites among the Bedouin of Sinai, before the peninsula's return to Egypt in 1982. Many in fact waited until their wives were in labour before summoning the authorities for medical assistance, ensuring that their children would be brought into the world by the smiling doctors of the AEU!

with the Air Mobile Life Support Unit (AMLSU) which transforms each aircraft into an airborne intensive coronary care unit. During Operation 'Peace for Galilee', the AEU evacuated 2,518 casualties by air to hospitals in Israel, and numerous combat rescuers and flight surgeons were cited for bravery.

On 16 October 1986, a routine IAF bombing run on Tyre turned into one of the most 'public' and dramatic rescue operations ever conducted by the AEU. During the raid, Palestinian gunners managed to hit a F-4E Phantom, causing one of the bombs on the undercarriage to detonate. In the fiery blast, the navigator was killed, but the pilot baled out to safety. While a joint force of Palestinian and Shi'ite guerrillas fanned out in search for the downed pilot, AEU helicopters and a supporting flight of Bell-209 Cobra gunships were summoned to the rescue. The rescue force zeroed in on the pilot through signals given off by an electronic homing device he carried. As the rescue armada closed in the supporting gunships fired at truckloads of guerrillas also racing towards the scene. AEU combat rescuers sealed off a narrow defensive perimeter, and engaged the guerrillas, while a Cobra pilot threw down straps to the pilot who hooked himself to the underside of the helicopter, and was flown back to Israel dangling from the aircraft.

An interesting, and most important offshoot of Israel's experience in Lebanon was the rebirth of the GIVA'ATI Infantry Brigade in 1983–84. Born of the small remnants of SAYERET SHAKED, the GIVA'ATI Brigade was re-activated as the IDF's version of the US Marine Corps, in the wake of the successful amphibious landings off the cost of Sidon on 7 June 1982. Originally little was expected of the new force entrusted to Southern Command, while officers and NCOs showing extreme promise were being gathered to form a cohesive unit. At first, only the best soldiers were awarded the honour of undergoing parachutist training, but soon entire companies and battalions were following suit. Like the GOLANI Brigade before it, GIVA'ATI was forced to prove its capabilities, and worthiness to be considered a true élite. As a result, GIVA'ATI commanders worked their conscripts twice as hard as their brown and red beret counterparts.

Emphasis was placed on battlefield performance, discipline and, most of all, weapons proficiency. Unit pride became the incentive to achieve superhuman results in mock exercises, and amphibious training with the IDF/Navy, to receive naval and armour (including captured T-55 and T-62 tanks upgunned and re-armoured to meet IDF specifications) instruction, diversified the military approach which in turn bred innovation. In fact, the combined infantry and naval proficiency made the GIVA'ATI fighters the most versatile soldiers in the IDF Tradition was also of major importance, and the 'old GIVA'ATI Brigade's reconnaissance battalion SHU'ALE SHIMSHON was resurrected; manned by the brigade's finest officers and NCOs. Soon, many paratroop and other élite unit conscripts began to take notice of the new and unique unit, and transferred into GIVA'ATI's ranks.

During seasonal military exercises, the young 'upstart' brigade made a striking impression. In mock combat, they not only outperformed GOLANI units, but the paratroops as well. Slowly, GIVA'ATI was transformed into the IDF's premier infantry force, beating the TZANHANIM's and GOLANI's once irreversible élite reputation into submission. Although the brigade's excellence was soon rewarded with the privilege of wearing a distinctive 'purple' beret, one ultimate test remained – Lebanon.

The introduction of GIVA'ATI units in security operations inside the Lebanon security belt and along Israel's heavily fortified northern frontier provided an effective, though costly baptism under fire. Although the GIVA'ATI conscripts were not yet infected with the harshness of the 'Tyre Generation', they were brought through their adolescence with Lebanon madness looming not far from their horizons. Yet GIVA'ATI has proven itself in Lebanon. From night-long ambushes, to patrols along the security fence on the Lebanon-Israel border, to fire-fights with Shi'ite and Palestinian terrorists, the 'purple berets' have shown themselves able combatants in the field. The brigade's rite of passage has been purchased at a high price however. As has always been the case among the IDF élite forces, it has been the officers, men in command barely older than those they lead, that have fallen first in battle, casualties in the tradition of 'Follow me!', one very dear to the GIVA'ATI commanders.

Lebanon today remains the centre of IDF élite force operations. Be it from land, sea, or air, the élite forces continue to act on pre-emptive vigilance to ensure that the nation's northern borders remain secure; a task not easily accomplished. Since the Israeli pullout from Lebanon in June 1985, there have been hundreds of attempts by Shi'ite and Palestinian terrorists not only to kill IDF forces in the security zone, but to infiltrate across the northern border into Israel proper. Yet in their way stands the trilogy of determination, three symbols of tradition and military zeal: the paratroops, GOLANI, and GIVA'ATI.

10
POSTSCRIPT

CONCLUSION

'The paratroopers and the élite units are the 'incubator' which nurtures fighters and officers.'

Moshe Dayan, 1955

To understand the importance to Israel of élite units and the élite unit commander, one does not need to look farther than the make-up of the IDF's senior command structure. In April 1987, Lieutenant-General Dan Shomron became the Israel Defence Force's thirteenth Chief of Staff. A SAYERT TZANHANIM officer, Shomron succeeded Lieutenant-General Moshe Levy, another paratroop veteran who in turn had succeeded Lieutenant-General 'Raful' Eitan, a PAL'MACH veteran and one of the paratrooper's most famous warriors. Today in fact, the IDF General Staff is a forum of ex-élite unit officers; men who have risen through the ranks of special operations to command the army defending the country they have fought so hard to preserve. They include the famous and courageous commando genius Deputy Chief of Staff, Major-General Ehud Barak; Manpower Branch Chief and former SAYERET TZANHANIM Commander, Major-General Matan Vilnai; and the Ground Forces OC and former GOLANI Brigade Chief, Major-General Uri Saguy. They represent not only the past in Israel's forty-plus years of struggle for survival, but its future.

The sheer number of ex-élite unit officers serving in top posts within the IDF indicates the importance these élite units have had in modern Israel's brief, but hard-fought history. While many nations shun their special forces as 'covert loners', and threats to the traditional norms of military behaviour, Israel has accepted them as the striking response to its dire geo-political and military situation. Yet as special forces go, the apolitical nature of the IDF élite units remain commendable and noteworthy. It is a mark of Israel's nature, and a mark of its most shielding strength.

The importance of élite units to Israel's defence remains significant. Great effort is invested in conjuring new methods of training to increase effectiveness in the light of all possible military scenarios. To free more men for combat assignments, uniquely motivated female NCOs have for years been serving the TZANHANIM as parachutist

---

▼ The IDF's most decorated soldier, ex-SAYERET chief, and current Deputy Chief of Staff, Major-General Ehud Barak, seen here during his tenure as IDF Military Intelligence Chief. (IDF Spokesman)

▲ Recon infantrymen from the GIVA'ATI Infantry
Brigade's SHU'ALEI SHIMSHON reconnaissance battalion assault a sand-hill during recent manoeuvres in the Negev
Desert. (IDF Spokesman)

instructors. Recently, however, women have even been commissioned as combat infantry and weapons instructors, offering new generations of paratroopers, infantrymen, and Naval Commandos their first indoctrination into the art of special operations. The role of women, as seen years before in the PAL'MACH, is a reflection of the egalitarianistic ideals which have come to characterize Israel's élite units.

Yet what makes these units élite is not the training they receive, nor the moral fibre of the young men who volunteer into them, although Israel boasts thousands of such souls. It is the determination of a nation and a government to utilize such forces against any target, anywhere in the world where Israeli national security or Israeli lives are endangered. From Beirut to Entebbe, the IDF élite have proven their skills, capabilities and resolve. With such legendary exploits to emulate, today's élite soldiers face great challenges, whether seizing enemy fortifications or rescuing hostages.

Today, Israel boasts one of the best armies in world. The IDF is commanded by some of the best military minds modern warfare has yet produced, and can field a modern, mobilized fighting force of almost half a million. Yet it must offer Israel great comfort that in an age of technically saturated battlefields and laser-guided weapons, new generations of 'Rafuls', 'Shomrons' and 'Baraks' continue to do the impossible under the harshest circumstances, to be rewarded only with the knowledge and conviction of having done their duty!

On 7 March 1988, three Palestinian terrorists belonging to Yasir Arafat's *el-Fatah* crossed the supposedly peaceful Egyptian border into Israel. It was the height of the Palestinian *intifadah* or uprising, and their mission, to seize hostages in a southern Israeli settlement, was intended to show the world that it was indeed the PLO who pulled the strings in the West Bank and Gaza Strip. Armed with explosives, automatic rifles and enough ammunition to hold off a battalion, the terrorists had the capabilities to inflict horrendous carnage. They were detected, however, pursued at high speed by the Israeli Police, and just as it appeared they would be cornered and caught, they stopped and held hostage a crowded civilian inter-city bus carrying workers from Beersheba towards their jobs in the Dimona nuclear facility. The rest is a split second of history. As senior IDF officers were flown in by helicopter, the National Police Border Guard anti-terror unit squad the YA'MA'M prepared a perimeter, a CP and assault plans. Negotiations with the terrorists ended when they began killing hostages (three in total would die), and the YA'MA'M reacted decisively. In little under half a minute, the three *el-Fatah* lay in a pool of blood. But for Khalil al-Wazir, the PLO's military commander and Yasir Arafat's right-hand man (better known as 'Abu-Jihad' or 'Father Holy-War') the murder of three Israelis sparked a great victory for Palestine.

With world attention glued to the Israeli handling of the Palestinian uprising; few expected that the Israelis would retaliate with anything more than a token IAF strike against a Palestinian base or two in southern Lebanon. Yet, when revenge came, it struck in a brilliant and historically fitting fashion. It would be almost fifteen years to the date of Israel's brilliant Operation 'AVIV NEORIM', the assassination of three of the top Black September Organization commanders in Beirut when, according to the *Washington Post*, the mighty sword of the IDF élite would cut down 'Abu-Jihad' in his playboy terrorist lair in the exclusive Tunis neighborhood of Sidi Bu-Said. The operation, whose code-name has yet to be disclosed, was almost identical to AVIV NEORIM. MOSSAD agents posing as 'Arab' tourists arrived in Tunis on Thursday 14 April and proceeded to hire two minibuses and an estate car. On late Friday night, 15 April, a group of approximately thirty naval commandos (and, it is believed, SAYERET MAT'KAL commandos) landed on the Rouad beach by means of rubber dinghies launched from IDF/Navy missile boats in international waters. They were met by the hired vehicles and driven towards the target. It was almost identical to Operation 'AVIV NEORIM', were it not for the technological superiority the Israelis possessed in 1988, utilizing an IAF Boeing 707 ECM and electronic command post aircraft disguised as a civilian airliner to suppress a good portion of the Tunis telephone and radio traffic during the operation. Yet, just like AVIV NEORIM, the two men pulling the strings for the mission were Major-General Ehud Barak, the deputy Chief of Staff, and Major-General Amnon Shahak, head of A'MAN, both commanding the Tunis raid in the 707.

At 01.30 hours on 16 April, 'Abu-Jihad' sat in his modest study to watch videotapes of the Palestinian uprising in Gaza, when he heard a suspicious noise outside. The 'hit squad' had split into two forces, and while one headed and killed a PLO bodyguard in a car outside, and another PLO gunman in the basement, the second squad (including, it is rumoured, a blonde woman in white overalls videotaping the entire raid) broke through the villa's front gate in search of 'Father Holy-War'. They found him on the landing and pumped over 70 bullets into his body from silenced pistols and submachine-guns to insure a 'job well done'. Minutes later the squad had departed, taking with them a mine of intelligence, through files found in 'Abu-Jihad's' possession. By the time Tunisian authorities reached the scene, the Israelis had long since departed.

Although the killing of 'Abu-Jihad' was most certainly the work of Israel, the Israeli government never officially took credit for the raid. Clearly the high veil of secrecy surrounding the operation had its 'field security' justification, but it had another meaning as well – the long arm of Israel's élite, in all its anonymity, firepower, and innovativeness, could and would strike anywhere it saw fit.

SELECT BIBLIOGRAPHY

Adan, Avraham ('Bren'). *On the Banks of Suez*. Arms & Armour Press, London, 1980

Allon, Yigal. *The Making of Israel's Army*. Vallentine Mitchell & Co. Ltd., New York, 1970

— *Shield of David*. Wiedenfeld & Nicolson, London and Jerusalem, 1970

Amir, Aharon. *Lebanon, Country, People, War*. Hadar Editors, Israel, 1979

Arad, Yitzhak. *1000 Days: June 12 1967–August 8 1970*. Ministry of Defence, Israel, 1971

Asher Jerry, and Hammel, Eric. *Duel for the Golan*. William Morrow & Co. Inc., New York, 1987

Avneri, Arieh. *HAMAHALUMA*. Revivim Publishing House, Israel, 1983

Banks, Lynne Reid. *Torn Country*. Franklin Watts, New York, 1980

Bar On, Mordechai. *Six Days: Israel Defence Forces*. Ministry of Defence, Israel, 1968

Bar Zohar, Michael, and Haber, Eitan. *The Quest for the Red Prince*. William Morrow & Co. Inc., New York, 1983

Ben Amnon, Shlomoh. *Following the Arab Terrorist*. Madim Books, Tel Aviv, 1978

Ben David, Ofer. *Hama' aracha Belevanon*. Israel, 1985

Benziman, Uzi. *Sharon: An Israeli Caesar*. Adama Books, New York, 1985

Bercuson, David J. *The Secret Army*. Stein & Day Publishers, New York, 1984

Bethell, Nicholas. *The Palestine Triangle*. Andre Deutsch Ltd., London, 1979

Dayan, Moshe. *Diary of the Sinai Compaign 1956*. Weidenfeld & Nicolson, London, 1966

— *Story of My Life*. Weidenfeld & Nicolson, London, 1976

Dobson, Christopher, and Payne, Ronald. *Counterattack*. Facts on File Inc., New York, 1982

Dror, Zvika. *The Arabists of the PAL'MACH, HAKIBBUTZ HAMEUHAD*. Publishing House Ltd., Israel, 1986

Dupuy, Trevor N. *Elusive Victory: The Arab-Israeli Wars, 1947–74*. Harper & Row, New York, 1978.

Eitan, Rafael. *Raful: A Soldier's Story*. Ma'ariv, Tel Aviv, 1985

Evron, Yosef. *Israel's Defence Industry*. Ma'ariv, Tel Aviv, 1980

Gabriel, Richard A. *Operation 'Peace for Galilee'*. Jill Wang, USA, 1984

Gal, Reuven. *A Portrait of the Israeli Soldier*. Greenwood Press, New York, 1986

Galber, Yoav. *LAMA PIRKU HAPAL'MACH*. Schocken Publishing House Ltd., Tel Aviv, 1986

Golan, Aviezer. *The Independence War*. Ministry of Defence, Israel, 1985

Gur, Mordechai. *The Battle for Jerusalem*. Popular War, New York, 1974

— *'D' Company: A Story of a Paratroop Company MA'ARACHOT*. Ministry of Defence Publications, Israel, 1977

Harel, Yehuda. *Growing Achievement*. Citation Madim Books, Israel, 1970

Herzog, Chaim. *The Arab-Israeli Wars*, Arms & Armour Press – Lionel Leventhal Ltd., London, 1982

— *The War of Atonement*. Weidenfeld & Nicolson, London, 1975

Hirst, David. *The Gun and the Olive Branch*. Faber & Faber Ltd., London, 1977

Insight Team of the Sunday Times. *The Yom Kippur War*. Doubleday & Co., New York, 1974

Israeli, Rafael. *The PLO in Lebanon: Selected Documents*. Weidenfeld & Nicolson, London, 1983

Katz, Samuel. *Battleground: Fact and Fantasy in Palestine*. Bantam Books, New York, 1973

— *Days of Fire*. Karni Publishing Ltd., Israel, 1966

Lacouture, Jean and Simonne, and Rouleau, Eric. *The Third Battle and Arab Countries*. AM HASEFER Books, Tel Aviv, 1968

Laquer, Walter. *The Road to Jerusalem*. The Macmillan Co., New York, 1968

Laskov, Haim. *Military Leadership*. Ministry of Defence

Soldiers from the IDF 'Alpine' unit, negotiate high
ows near the summit of Mount Hermon on the Golan
eights. (IDF Spokesman)

Tel Aviv, 1985

evy, Moshe. *The 48th Soul*, MA'ARACHOT. Ministry of
Defence, Tel Aviv, 1981

ossin, Yigal. *Pillar of Fire*. Shikmona Publishing Co.,
Ltd., Jerusalem, 1983

ovich, Netanel. *The War For Independence*. Masada, Tel
Aviv, 1966

arshall, S.L.A. *Sinai Victory*. The Battery Press, Nash-
ville, 1985

ilstein, Uri. *A History of the Paratroopers*. Vols. 1–4,
Schalgi Publishing House Ltd., Tel Aviv, 1985

akdimon, Shlomoh. *Low Probability*. REVIVIM Publishing
House, Israel, 1982

a'or, Mordechai. *The HAGANAH*. Israel Defence Forces,
Israel, 1973

eff, Donald. *Warriors at Suez*. Linden Press, New York,
1981

etanyahu, Benjamin. *Terrorism: How the West Can Win*.
Farrar, Straus & Giroux, New York, 1986

'Ballance, Edgar. *No Victor, No Vanquished: The Yom
Kippur War*. Presidio Press, California, 1978

— *Language of Violence*. Presidio Press, California, 1979

arry, Albert. *Terrorism: From Robespierre to Arafat*.
Vanguard Press, New York, 1976

Rabinovich, Abraham. *The Battle for Jerusalem*. The
Jewish Publication Society, New York, 1972

Rivlin, Gershon. *The Tenth Anniversary of the Israel
Defence Forces*. Ministry of Defence, Israel, 1958

Schiff, Zeev. *A History of the Israeli Army, 1870–1974*.
Straight Arrow Books, San Fransisco, 1974

— *October Earthquake: Yom Kippur 1973*. University
Publishing Projects Ltd., Tel Aviv, 1974

Schiff, Zeev, and Ya'ari, Ehud. *Israel's Lebanon War*.
Simon & Schuster, New York, 1984

Shavitt, Matti. *On the Wings of Eagles*. Madim Books,
Israel, 1970

Shazly, Sa'ad es-Dinn. *The Crossing of the Suez*. America-
Mideast Research, San Francisco, 1980

Shiffer, Simon. *Snow Ball*, YEDIOT ACHARONOT. Books,
Edanim Publishers, Israel, 1984

Shimshi, Elyashiv. *Storm in October*, MA'ARACHOT. Ministry of Defence, 1986

Stevenson, William. *90 Minutes at Entebbe*. Bantam Books,
New York, 1976

Various Editors, *TZAHAL BEHEYLO: Encyclopedia for Military and Security – Volumes 1–18*, REVIVIM Publishing
House Ltd., Tel Aviv 1981

Weizmann, Ezer. *On Eagle's Wings*. Macmillan Publishing
Co. Ltd., New York, 1976

JOURNALS

BAMACHANE – IDF weekly magazine

BITON HEYL HAVIR – Israeli Air Force magazine

IDF Journal – bi-monthly English-langauage military
magazine